TIDES IN ENGLISH TASTE

(1619–1800)

A BACKGROUND FOR THE STUDY OF LITERATURE

By

B. SPRAGUE ALLEN

VOLUME II

NEW YORK
ROWMAN AND LITTLEFIELD, INC.
1969

LIBRARY OF CONGRESS CATALOG CARD NO. 58-14144

Printed in U.S.A. by
NOBLE OFFSET PRINTERS, INC.
NEW YORK 3, N. Y.

CONTENTS

ILLUSTRATIONS

TIDES IN ENGLISH TASTE

CHAPTER XIII

THE INFLUENCE OF THE FAR EAST UPON LITERATURE

I. The Indian Contribution

The full significance of Orientalism is not apparent unless we consider one other aspect of its influence. The references to it which I have been quoting and discussing have been concerned with the art of the Far East and were made either in its praise or in its disparagement. I now wish to indicate its effect upon men of letters, who, in a disinterested spirit, made use of current ideas about the Orient and its people because the Far East stimulated their imagination and afforded fresh material with which the creative spirit was free to play. These writers were not in any sense critical of the Orient, but they turned to it as a source for fresh points of view, for its novelty as a background, and for the new human situations and types of personality that it suggested. A survey of the plays, the tales, the essays, and other works of various kinds that were colored by the contact between the East and the West supplements what has been said about Oriental art and illustrates what must always be of great interest: the consequences of the impact of one civilization against another. While I am confident that a more thorough search than I have undertaken would disclose a larger number of works affected by the Far East than I am able to name, those that I shall discuss will reveal, I hope, with sufficient fullness the nature of that influence. For the sake of convenience and clarity I shall consider first the influence of India and then that of China and Japan.

The poetry, the romance, the exoticism of India apparently made no impression upon the seventeenth-century dramatist of contemporary life. If he associated service in the East India Company with innumerable opportunities for strange vivid experiences in an unknown world, his imagination was not stirred by the thought of those experiences. The character that he chose to depict was the Englishman who had been engaged in the Indian trade, but he never dreamed of representing him as one who, having had extraordinary adventures, was in any respect different from thousands of his fellow-Englishmen who had remained at home, bogged in the routine of commercial life. The Indian trader was merely the successful merchant whom conventional drama had long made a familiar figure, and all that the dramatist ever conceived of his bringing back from his sojourn in the East was vast wealth and a too-great pride in his prosperity.

In *Sir Courtly Nice* (1685) Crowne, it must be acknowledged, deserves some credit for not letting slip an opportunity for the introduction of a few picturesque incidents to give his material local color. Prevented by the long-standing hostility between his family and hers, Farewel cannot carry on his love-affair with Leonora, and enlists the quickwitted Crack in his service. Crack first gains access to Leonora in the guise of a tailor who, knowing the liking of English women for foreign fabrics, wishes to dispose of some French silks. Next the resourceful Crack impersonates a feeble-minded gentleman, Sir Thomas Callico, son of Sir Nicholas Callico, President of the East India Company, and in that role outwits Leonora's brother, prevents her marriage with Sir Courtly, and brings about her union with Farewel. As Sir Thomas, Crack is attended by East Indian natives in their fantastic costumes, and as a result is followed in the street by gaping crowds. In the course of his intriguing Crack gives the lovers a supper served by Eastern slaves and entertains them with a dance and a dialogue sung by an Indian man and woman. This song, the stage directions state, was "an imitation of a song sung by some natives of India before the late King." One may well doubt the strict authenticity of such Oriental elements — in these matters the Restoration had no conscience —, yet they suggest a popular curiosity in the East, and they afforded a clue which subsequent dramatists eager for spectacular effects might have followed advantageously.

As Steele has depicted him in *The Conscious Lovers* (1722), Sealand is typical of the rich and powerful class of merchants that the expanding British commerce of the eighteenth century was rapidly developing. Sealand had gone to India as an enterprising young man who wished to improve his fortune, and, having made good, he respects himself and demands respect from others. He is described as "the great India merchant"; and when he challenges the social usefulness of Sir John Bevil, representative of the idle, self-complacent landed gentry, and defends industry as honorable employment, he reveals a laudable class-consciousness and sounds an unmistakable note of democracy in a society in which the man engaged in commerce was to insist more and more upon recognition from those whose birth was their chief claim to distinction.

As the century advances, however, the attitude of the dramatist toward the merchant who has acquired a fortune in the Indian trade undergoes a modification. He is inclined to depict him satirically as a rich, vulgar upstart who loves display and flaunts his wealth to the disgust of all sensible people; indeed, the epithet *nabob*, applied to these men who had gained riches in the East, came to have a discreditable connotation. In Samuel Foote's comedy *The Nabob* (1772) Sir Matthew Mite is insolent with the pride of wealth, and as a would-be patron of archeology presents gifts, nearly all rubbish, to the Antiquarian Society, in recognition of which he secures the coveted election to its membership. Foote's satire stirred the wrath of two Anglo-Indians, who called at his house with the intention of giving him the good beating they thought he deserved. He not only placated them, but so delighted them with his wit that they accepted his invitation to dinner and went away singing his praises![1] A note of contempt is also present in Colman's *The Man of Business* (1774), where Lord Riot describes Golding, the Indian banker, as "full of treasure as a mine, with a certain income as large as a jaghire; sent home whole lacks of rupees by the last Indiaman, and bushels of diamonds as plenty as Scotch pebbles."[2] In *The Belle's Stratagem* (1780) Mrs. Cowley ridicules the taste of the nabob Mr. Ingot, who paid £1000 at an auction for a picture of "the divinest plague at Athens" to embellish his children's nursery; as it matched *Dick Whittington and his Cat*, Ingot thought that the two pictures would "make good companions."[3] The titles of two plays that I have not seen, *Israelites or The Pampered Nabob* (1785) and *The Nabob Outwitted* (1797), indicate that here as in the other comedies the rich Indian trader was the target of laughter.

Obviously the power of sheer wealth to force itself into prominence in a society which was gradually becoming commercialized aroused resentment among people of birth, refinement, and culture. They rightly saw that the advent of the nabob threatened the supremacy of those standards by which they enjoyed social prestige. Even if the dramatists personally had nothing at stake in such a situation, probably both envy and snobbery had their share in causing them to make the grievance of the upper classes their own.

Drama was not alone in reflecting this critical attitude toward the man from India. For the *Lounger* Henry Mackenzie, author of *The Man of Feeling*, wrote in 1785 two amusing and significant papers (nos. 17, 36). They tell of the demoralization in John Homespun's family that followed the return of the son of his neighbor Mushroom from India. Provided with a fortune of £100,000, young Mushroom set up his family in a grand style. His mother and sisters appeared in church bedecked with "flowered muslins and gold muslins, white shawls and red shawls, white feathers and red feathers," and his wife made the neighborhood dizzy with her stories of "nabobs, rajahs, and rajah-pouts, elephants, palanquins, and processions . . . full of gold, diamonds, pearls, and precious stones, with episodes of dancing girls, and *otter* of roses." The farm-house in which the family had always lived became Mushroom Hall, and Mrs. Mushroom's "muslins from Bengal" made Homespun's daughters dissatisfied with their simpler gowns. So far-reaching was the example of their rich neighbors upon the Homespuns that they even made clumsy attempts to serve their own fat barnyard fowls in the form of curries and peelaws. On the other hand, Marjory Mushroom confesses that, in spite of their wealth, the pains which her plain, unfashionable family have endured in their effort to acquire style have destroyed their happiness, and they are not to be envied as much as people think. They are all in subjection to their French butler, Monsieur de Sabot, who instructs the family in the mode. To save the new curtains and chair-covers, the elder Mushroom is driven to seek a quiet smoke in the stable; and to inform himself about the great collection of pictures that he has bought, young Mushroom is compelled to spend hours in his gallery, "getting by heart the names and the stories of all the men and women that are painted there, that he may have his lesson pat for the company that are to walk and admire the paintings till dinner is served up." Nor do these experiences complete the troubles of the Mushrooms. They all live in dread of the friends who knew them in the days of their poverty and who have a bad habit of making painful disclosures in the presence of Lord Squanderfield and Lady Betty Lampoon. Ignorant of the fashions, they are, moreover, at the mercy of their new and more sophisticated acquaintances. Lady Betty induces the family to replace their antiquated damask beds with chintz hangings, and when young Mushroom undertakes to improve his estate, people of taste bewilder him with contradictory suggestions about knolls, canals, and ruins as attractive garden features. So with the humor of satiric exaggeration Mackenzie has represented the family as in a turmoil because of their foolish, vulgar effort to lead a life for which they are unsuited. However, after making due allowance for exaggeration, one can be certain that there is much unpleasant truth in Mackenzie's absurd picture, and that he is speaking from knowledge when he describes the aspirations of the newly rich from India and their bad influence upon their equally silly neighbors.

A much sterner note of criticism is heard in the *Memoirs of a Nabob*, in the *Town and Country Magazine* (1771). There a nabob is defined as "a person who in the East-India company's service has by art, fraud, cruelty, and imposition, obtained the fortune of an Asiatic prince, and returned to England to display his folly, vanity, and ambition." The savage spirit of this description colors the narrative, in which is depicted a fellow of low birth who is in turn a barber, a valet, and a clerk. In India this scamp makes a fortune. "But to his honour be it said, he was never guilty of murder, either by treachery, force, or poison, *a rare instance in a nabob!*" Ultimately he comes back to England to secure an heiress and to set up an establishment in Berkeley Square.[4] Similarly harsh in its judgment of the Anglo-Indian is *The Nabob or Asiatic Plunderers* (1773). This bitterly satiric poem is, in fact, an outburst of moral indignation against the exploitation of the Indians by rapacious English traders whose practices bring Christianity into discredit. Their crimes, the author declares, are the fruit of "Low-thoughted Commerce! heart-corrupting trade." Its materialism, its worship of self-interest, and its passion for gold undermine the character of those who engage in it. In other words, the glamour of a beneficent activity with which sentimental optimists like Thomson enveloped commerce in the earlier half of the century has vanished, and against the nabob is directed the wrath which always follows disillusionment.

It is greatly to the credit of the intellectual honesty of the English that they rarely shirk the disagreeable duty of self-criticism when their sense of justice has been offended even by a fellow-countryman. This admirable quality is revealed not only by the anonymous author of *The Nabob*, but also by John Scott in what he calls an East Indian Eclogue, *Serim, or, The Artificial Famine* (1782). Based on a report that English agents in India were guilty of monopolizing the rice crop so as to force the natives by starvation to be more active in their search for gold and pearls as well as in the payment of money for the necessaries of life, the poem is, for the most part, a Hindu's prayer to the God of the Ganges to succor his suffering people, and as such is a terrible indictment of British rule in India.[5] On two counts, then, the nabob incurred the hostility of Englishmen at home. If in India he was avaricious and cruel in his dealings with the natives, he earned their moral disapprobation. If in England he was vulgar and self-assertive in the display of wealth, he gained their contempt as an intruder who upset and confused social standards based upon birth and breeding. In short, the nabob's sudden acquisition of money, the means by which he acquired it, and the ways in which he spent it raised disturbing ethical and social questions to which contemporary dramatists, essayists, and poets were by no means indifferent. The East brought its problems as well as its art to eighteenth-century England.

A second group of plays presents the man from India in a more favorable light. The writers of these plays have no satiric intention, but they represent the return of the absentee to his English home as precipitating the dramatic situation which constitutes the substance of the action. In Dryden's *Sir Martin Mar-all* (1667) Old Moody has just heard that his natural son

Anthony, who has been brought up in the East Indies secretly and whom he has not seen since he was a child, is about to land in England. In the emergency Sir Martin attempts to impersonate Anthony, but he ignominiously fails in the role of an inhabitant of a region he has never seen, and his chatter about "the Mogul's country," the hurricanes, and "your great Turk of Rome and Persia" is his undoing.[6] Lillo's *Fatal Curiosity* (1736) differs from other plays of this type in that the theme of the absentee is treated tragically. Young Wilmot and Eustace arrive in England still clothed in their "Indian habits," and so tanned is the former by his

> long stay beneath the burning zone
> Where one eternal sultry summer reigns

that he looks

> more like a sun-burnt Indian
> Than a Briton.

It is indeed his altered appearance and foreign garb that prevent his recognition by his parents and are responsible for his murder at their hands. His wealth, accumulated in India, tempts them to crime.[7]

On other grounds, moreover, dramatists were interested in the absentee. They were hard pressed by the need which in every age has afflicted dramatists hampered by an unrealistic technique: in their throng of characters they had to have some one willing person who could function as a *deus ex machina* for the purpose of extricating the other characters from the difficulties in which they were entangled. The playwrights of the seventeenth century, followed by those of the eighteenth, pitched upon the English merchant long absent in India to assist them in this dilemma. In a series of comedies, when unscrupulous persons are attempting to perpetrate some fraud or bring about some unsuitable marriage, and when the rogues are on the very eve of success, the absentee returns, discloses his identity, outwits the schemers, rescues the innocent, rewards the virtuous, and, according to recipe, brings the action to a most happy conclusion. If he has wealth — and generally he is fabulously rich —, so much the better, for in an imperfect world his money is at hand to aid those in distress. In Caryl's *Sir Solomon* (*c.* 1669), Mr. Barter is true to his type. Supposed to have been lost at sea, he has made a fortune in India, and after an absence of years returns in time to claim his daughter from her pretended father, to save her from a hateful marriage, and to bestow her upon her longing lover. Although Sheridan's genius for comedy was great, in the actual construction of the plot of *The School for Scandal* he manipulated merely with masterly skill devices employed by dramatists before him. Sir Oliver Surface represents a fusion of two conventional types: the absentee and the disguised observer. The latter, embodied, for example, in the Duke in *Measure for Measure* and Old Flowerdale in *The London Prodigal* (1605), is the person who conceals his identity for the purpose of observing the conduct of another, of whose character he wishes to have reliable first-hand knowledge. Sir Oliver performs his role to perfection. He gains a thorough understanding of Charles and Joseph as they, unaware of his identity, reveal themselves to his watchful eye. Moreover, at the close of the play, on the strength of the information thus secured, he is able as the uncle who has unexpectedly returned from India in possession of great wealth to set all to rights and to display the *deus ex machina* functioning in the glory of his munificence. In two later comedies the absentee is equally conspicuous for the promptitude of his arrival and for the activity of his benevolence: Colonel Talbot in Pilon's *He Would Be a Soldier* (1786) and Mr. Cleveland in Holman's *The Votary of Wealth* (1799) both reach England in time to expose fraud and to reward the deserving according to their merits. These two merchants, as well as Mr. Barter, young Wilmot, and Sir Oliver Surface, are, like Mr. Sealand in *The Conscious Lovers*, honorable gentlemen, and their delineation offsets the satiric depiction of nabobs who are distinguished by nothing but their wealth and vulgar social climbing. Nevertheless, that the role which the man from India played in eighteenth-century drama was utterly conventional is only too clear, and his stereotyped characterization is only additional evidence of the imaginative sterility of the dramatists of the time.

To suggest, for purposes of comparison, what modern dramatists have done with the role of the absentee, it is necessary merely to recall *Pillars of Society*, *Ghosts*, *Magda*, and Hauptmann's *The Reconciliation*. The authors of these plays have psychologized the situation of the man or woman who returns to the old family home after a long sojourn in a different environment, and they raise questions of absorbing interest. Will the absentee's richer, wider experience prevent his readjustment to the domestic conditions in which he passed his youth? What will be his attitude toward ethical and social standards the validity of which he now finds it difficult to acknowledge? To what extent will his family be antagonized by the liberality of his ideas? Upon the settlement of these problems the destiny of the individual is made to depend. Of course, these spiritual questions were obviously beyond the ken of the eighteenth-century dramatist, but had he possessed any imaginative vision, he could have discovered in the man from India more individuality than is revealed by the representation of him as a successful merchant and beneficent *deus ex machina*.

The Votary of Wealth is one of a small group of plays written in the last quarter of the century which indicate that as the English gained a more intimate knowledge of India, dramatists were awakening to the possibilities of the Oriental material and were venturing to introduce characters and scenes that created something of the atmosphere of the East. In Holman's comedy, Cleveland's daughter is accompanied to England on her long voyage from India by the Hindu girl Gangica. Delineated sympathetically and with some attempt at realism, she is sentimentalized according to current formulas which the age knew by heart; she is copper-skinned and speaks only broken English, but her virtues shine through these handicaps and are all the more enhanced by them. In the perilous situation in which Julia finds herself, Gangica is always faithful to her mistress and proves herself brave, tender-hearted, and devoted to her English friends. Rousseau had taught his generation freedom from race prejudice, and our dear Gangica was the gainer thereby. In Mrs. Inchbald's *The Mogul Tale* (1784) an English doctor and a cobbler and his wife from Wapping are wafted from England in a balloon as far as India and drop into the garden of the seraglio of the Great Mogul. The dramatic promise of this excellent situation, which anticipates that in Archer's *The Green*

Goddess, where an aeroplane inherits the role of the balloon, sputters out in two acts of silly farce. However, the audience probably enjoyed the novelty of the Oriental setting, the picturesque costumes, and the sight of the Mogul seated on his throne surrounded by slaves and eunuchs.

In *Such Things Are* (1787) Mrs. Inchbald again stages the action of her play in India. In handling this material, however, she is distinctly critical of the world she depicts. As her background she has chosen to represent conditions in the principality of an Indian potentate where everyone seeks the favor of the cruel despotic ruler and lives in fear of his resentment. In such an environment, as Mrs. Inchbald's delineation of several characters proves, the position of the Englishman was anomalous. Sir Luke fears that his criticisms of the royal rule will reach the prince's ears. Lord Flint, who came to India as a youth, has spent years in the evil atmosphere of the courts of petty, arbitrary princes until he has become a dangerous intriguer and as cruel as the very princes whose good will he has stooped to gain. His deterioration is probably typical of what happened to many Englishmen who were exposed to the temptations of a long sojourn in the alien world of the Far East, and had Mrs. Inchbald had sufficient insight, she could have made Lord Flint a character of absorbing moral interest. As it is, he is only superficially delineated, and she is to be commended for suggesting the possibilities of such characters rather than for her ability to realize them in the concrete. But what gives *Such Things Are* its real significance and justifies its title is its humanitarian purpose. The social conscience of the time had been stirred by Howard's prison reforms, and Mrs. Inchbald has embodied his ideals in the character of Mr. Haswell. In contrast to Lord Flint — his name stigmatizes him — Haswell is a sentimental philanthropist who visits the Sultan's prison to relieve the distress of the victims of that prince's cruelty and who, in desperate cases of injustice, does not hesitate to intercede for the sufferers. Even the Sultan has to admit to Haswell that "the widow speaks your charities, the orphan lisps your bounties, and the rough Indian melts in tears to bless you." Under these circumstances it is no surprise to anyone who is familiar with eighteenth-century literature to discover that, in the end,

Haswell brings the Sultan to a sense of the wrongs he has committed and gains from him the assurance that he will adopt whatever measures Haswell suggests for the improvement of the prisons of the principality. Haswell's accomplishment, as Mrs. Inchbald depicts it, is, in a sense, prophetic of the civilizing influence which the English were destined to exert in India. All in all, in spite of its sentimentalism and frequent conventionality, *Such Things Are* has an importance that is not shared by the great majority of plays that were affected by England's contact with the Far East.

Mrs. Inchbald was not the only dramatist who was familiarizing London audiences, in the last years of the century, with characters and incidents drawn from Indian life. James Cobb, a diligent manufacturer of light operas, also discloses an interest in India that was probably due to his position on the staff of the East India Company. In *Love in the East* (1788) Martin Mushroom — the name may have been suggested by the two satiric papers in the *Lounger* — represents a nabob in the making — a man who glories in the fact that he who began life without a "half crown in his pocket" is now "one of the richest men in Bengal." His wife typifies, as does Lady Tremor in *Such Things Are*, the vulgar, aggressive woman who had gone out to India in hopes of finding a husband in a country where the English men outnumbered the women. As Mushroom brutally puts it, "she brought out a face as badly patched up as her reputation for a venture in Bengal; besides which she hadn't stock in trade enough to fill one of her own bandboxes." Such a couple returning to England and on the strength of their money setting up as people of fashion would bring the very name of nabob into dispute and deserve the ridicule which the type occasioned. The opening scene of *Love in the East* disclosed a view of Calcutta with Anglo-Indians, natives, and sailors on the shore, but otherwise the setting of the opera was in no way unusual.

But in Cobb's later opera, *Ramah Droog* (1798), his plot gave him ample opportunity to exploit the unfamiliar, exotic phases of Indian civilization. A troop of English soldiers have been captured by the forces of an Indian Rajah and are imprisoned in the great fort of Ramah Droog. The romantic kernel of the action is the love of the Rajah's daughter for the gallant captain of this troop — a love which he cannot return because his heart is already given to Eliza. Then there is the comic Irishman Liffey, who, in return for having cured the Rajah of illness, is made head physician, commander-in-chief of the army, grand judge in the civil and criminal courts, chief of the elephants, purveyor of buffaloes, principal hunter of tigers, admiral of the fleet, and grand vizier with a dozen wives. Liffey is, indeed, an eighteenth-century forerunner of Pooh-Bah. But it is the scenes of the opera that abound in romantic atmosphere:

Act I, i.	A courtyard adjoining to the Rajah's Palace.
Act I, ii.	A plain, with a distant view of the Rajah's Hill Fort.
Act II, iii.	An apartment in the Palace. The Rajah discovered seated on his throne, smoking his hookah; the women of the Zenana are around him, some dancing, others playing on musical instruments and singing.
Close of Act II.	Entrance of the Palace. Enter the Rajah on an elephant, returning from hunting the tiger, preceded by his hircarrahs or military messengers and his state palanquin. The Vizier on another elephant. The Princess in a gaurie, drawn by buffaloes. The Rajah is attended by his Fakeer or soothsayer, his officers of state, and by an ambassador from Tippoo Sultaun in a palanquin; also by Nairs or soldiers from the south of India — Poligars, or inhabitants of the hilly districts, with their hunting dogs, — other Indians carrying a dead tiger, and young tigers in a cage — a number of sepoys — musicians on camels and on foot — dancing girls, etc., etc.

I leave it to some historian of stage production to determine to what extent one should give credit to this amazing stage direction. But even if only a fraction of these spectacular effects were realized, we can understand why the opera was "performed with universal applause at the Theatre Royal, Covent Garden." With all the pageantry of the Orient, India was invading the very heart of London.

The last quarter of the century is distinguished from its predecessors, as the plays and operas I have been discussing plainly show, by a more vivid imaginative realization of Indian life and the personality of its inhabitants, both native and English-born. On other and very different grounds, however, it may be said that the period marked a turning-point in the history of India's cultural relations with the Western world. At this time her strange, unfamiliar civilization excited the intellectual curiosity of men of scholarly gifts who lived in India and were the first to undertake to master Sanskrit. Under the leadership of the great Orientalist Sir William Jones, who sat as judge in the Indian courts, men of kindred tastes in the service of the East India Company were encouraged to translate Indian literature and to interpret its significance to Western readers. *The Asiatick Miscellany*, published in Calcutta in 1785, was a valuable collection of various tracts, poems, and accounts of native manners and customs, reprinted, as the editor said, to preserve a record of Indian civilization before it was modified by contact with Europeans.

In the same year Charles Wilkins published his prose translation of the *Bhagavad-gītā* under the patronage of the East India Company. This work had been recommended to the attention of the Company by no less a person than Warren Hastings himself, in a eulogistic letter that provides ample evidence that his interest in Indian literature was neither perfunctory nor superficial. Having wisely urged that the poem be not judged by standards of European criticism deduced from the practice of ancient and modern writers, he declared the *Bhagavad-gītā* "a performance of great originality, of a sublimity of conception, reasoning, and diction, almost unequalled." [8]

Encouraged by this achievement, Wilkins two years later, upon his return to England, translated the *Hitopadesa*, the famous book of fables embodying the ethical idealism of the Indians, and at Warren Hastings' instigation Halhed translated from the Persian a digest of Sanskrit law-books. Sir William Jones made English versions of numerous hymns, elucidated with valuable notes on Indian mythology, and translated Kalidasa's great drama *Sakúntala* and excerpts from the *Vedas*. He was also instrumental in the foundation of the Bengal Asiatic Society "for inquiring into the history and antiquities, the arts, sciences, and literature of Asia." Under the title *Asiatic Researches*, the Society issued in 1788–92 the first three volumes of its studies. About the same time the East India Company subsidized the publication, under the editorship of Alexander Dalrymple, of a collection of tracts called *Oriental Repertory*, with the avowed purpose of promoting a more accurate knowledge of the East. As even such a brief summary makes clear, the last decades of the century witnessed an extraordinary advance in Oriental scholarship by which the English-speaking world was given an opportunity to acquaint itself with the masterpieces of Indian literature.

This enthusiasm for Oriental studies was widespread. In 1790, in an address to the clergy of the archdeaconry of Ely, Richard Watson, Regius Professor of Divinity at Cambridge, exhorted those who had a bent for languages not to devote their talents to the translation and exegesis of the Greek and Roman classics, a field of knowledge to which only meager additions could be made, but to turn to the Oriental literatures, which were "unknown or unexplored." He urged that competent scholars should be sent abroad to collect manuscripts in Persia, India, and China and that the universities of Europe should undertake the translation of manuscripts already in their possession. Such an investigation of "the ancient and modern state of the manners, arts, and literature of the Eastern nations" would, he argued, throw light on the early history of mankind and constitute a valuable commentary on the Scriptural narrative.

Obviously Orientalism, in no uncertain fashion, was entering into competition with classical antiquity as worthy of serious and even profound investigation, and was challenging the right of the latter to monopolize the attention of the learned as it had done for centuries without dispute. As a matter of fact, this rivalry between the two types of intellectual interest was but another phase of that opposition between Orientalism and classicism which had been developing ever since the second half of the seventeenth century, when the two cultures had been brought face to face. Scholarship was now to reveal the soul of the distant country from which the English had been importing chintz for nearly two hundred years, and by the accumulation of stores of information make it possible to reconstruct India's historic past and to comprehend her present civilization in the light of that past. Out of this more accurate knowledge of India was to emerge a new literature which aimed to give an authentic picture of the East and a sense of its atmosphere by what to-day often strikes us as a too thick impasto of local color.

With this development of the nineteenth century we are not concerned, but in passing one may point out that of this deliberate, studied Orientalism Southey's *The Curse of Kehama* (1810) and Moore's *Lalla Rookh* (1817) are the fruit. In preparation for his long narrative poem Moore, as Rossetti irritably remarks, "wrote, talked, and perhaps thought saracenically." It was, in fact, to be no longer possible for a writer to place the scene of his work in India without feeling that his choice imposed upon him an unescapable obligation to conjure up as far as lay in his power the sumptuously varied world he was describing. This imaginative realization of the East by the sheer force of his genius Shelley achieved in his *Indian Serenade* to a degree never dreamt of by either Southey or Tom Moore.

II. The Chinese Contribution

British relations with China, established by commerce and cemented by the importation of Chinese manufactures, reacted in due time, as did the contact with India, upon English literature. With some degree of truth it may, indeed, be said that in so far as English men of letters turned to China as a source for material, they did so because they really knew little about the country and its people. Of the Chinaman as he was, Europeans were almost completely ignorant, since their opportunities for getting acquainted with his appearance and personality at first hand were so rare as to be almost negligible. Lecomte gives the history of a poor and enterprising Frenchwoman who succeeded in palming herself off as a member of "one of the best Families in *China*." In this role she secured all manner of assistance from well disposed persons who were impressed by her sad story of seizure by a pirate, transportation to France, and abandonment in Paris. When Lecomte, to test her account of herself, engaged in an interview with her, he immediately recognized that her story was an ingenious hoax. As he very pertinently remarks, greater familiarity with the Chinese physiognomy would at the outset have exposed the woman as an impostor and made the perpetration of her fraud beyond the range of possibility.[9]

Even in the second half of the eighteenth century a Chinaman was an object of curiosity in England. Loum Kiqua, who came to England from Portugal in 1756, excited so much interest that he was received by members of the royal family and "was much caressed" by the nobility. When Joseph Ames the scholar had an opportunity to see him, he hastened to inform a friend of his good fortune and to betray incidentally some odd ideas about the race and language of the Chinese:

> I . . . saw the Chinese Mandarine, who behaved very complaisant, yet could not speak English — only, as I am informed, Portuguese, of all the European languages. Their great antiquity makes them the proper subject of an universal antiquary. What I have read of them shews that they are the descendants of Noah and his wife, after they came out of the Ark; and that they are the likeliest persons in the known world to read the hierographical signatures of Thebes and Egypt, not being used to read by an alphabetical character, as the manner was in more enlightened later ages.[10]

Loum finally returned to Canton on a vessel of the East India Company on which accommodations were courteously arranged for him.[11] Chitqua, another Chinaman, who undertook to visit England in 1769, had a much more unpleasant experience. For a time he supported himself by modeling busts in clay, exhibiting them in Pall Mall, and selling them for ten guineas, or full-length figures for fifteen guineas. His troubles began when he embarked to return to his own country. His strange garb and speech aroused the suspicions of the sailors, and when he fell overboard at Gravesend and was fished out of the water half dead, their superstitious fears increased, and they cursed him as a "Chinese dog." Terrified by their hostility, Chitqua begged the ship's carpenter to make him a coffin in which he might be taken ashore, as Chinese custom would not permit burial at sea. The more friendly captain finally succeeded in getting him off the ship safely at Deal and in putting him on his way to London. Arrived there, Chitqua could not make clear his former address; a mob gathered, and when the poor Chinaman began to experience English hospitality in one of its more robust forms, he was rescued by a passing gentleman who fortunately recognized him. So as to make him less conspicuous and less liable to molestation, Chitqua was persuaded to wear English garb in the future. When Richard Gough, the antiquary, met him in 1770, he was so elated at his opportunity to see a Chinaman with his own eyes that in a letter to a friend he was moved to describe Chitqua with the greatest detail.[12]

It followed that at a time when the sight of a Chinaman was so exceptional as to occasion extraordinary remark, writers were obliged to depend for their knowledge of the Chinese upon such facts as they might glean from books of travel and from such impressions of their dress and personal appearance as they might secure from the observation of Oriental art. If they peered at the screens, the wallpaper, and the porcelain, they were amused by exotic birds and vegetation, by conventionalized rocky landscapes, and by quaint little people who sat in patches of garden, sauntered across frail, arched bridges, walked with dignity under bell-shaped umbrellas, or sipped tea in the open porches of diminutive houses with odd upturned eaves. It was this bizarre, romanticized China which impressed itself upon the European imagination — a land sufficiently remote and unreal to encourage the free play of the fancy. The result was the creation of an imaginative world in which strange and unaccountable incidents occurred. Such a world had much in common with the spirit of the court masques, and as might be anticipated, it was in the congenial atmosphere of those spectacular entertainments of the Jacobean period that the Chinese first made their appearance on the English stage. The Oriental, to be sure, had been a frequent figure in Elizabethan dramas, but in no one of them was the scene laid in China or a Chinaman a character.[13]

The evidence that the Chinese participated in the masques is unfortunately too meager to permit much comment. Reyher records that on January 1st, 1604, there was a performance of a *Ballet des Chevaliers des Indes et de la Chine*.[14] From the description of another early Jacobean masque, which has not survived, we learn that the maskers were introduced to the audience by a Chinese magician.[15] Finally, in the recently published *Designs of Inigo Jones* there is mentioned a drawing of a Chinese dwarf, a character in some unidentifiable masque and described as "a heavy stunted figure with peaked beard and moustache, bald head and pigtail." The very make-up of the figure suggests that it had been devised with one eye on a piece of porcelain or on a lacquer screen.

As the masque is akin to the opera, it was natural for the latter to take over from the former the fantastic Chinaman of the court entertainment. In 1692 in *The Fairy Queen*, an operatic version of *A Midsummer Night's Dream* and one of those distortions of Shakespeare which disgraced the seventeenth-century stage, four of the acts closed with a spectacular transformation scene that had no relation whatsoever to the plot. The last of these represented, according to the stage direction, incredible to relate, "a transparent prospect of a Chinese garden; the architecture, the trees, the plants, the fruit, the birds, the beasts quite different from what we have in this part of the world." After a Chinese man and woman have sung and six monkeys, advancing from among the trees, have danced, another marvel is unfolded: "Six pedestals of China-work rise from under the stage; they support six large vases of porcelain, in which are six China-orange trees. . . . The pedestals move toward the front of the stage, and the grand dance begins of twenty-four persons." This dance of "twenty-four Chineses" is followed by the appearance of Hymen.[16] Praised by Downes and Gildon for its costumes and spectacular features and delighting the court and the town, this strange concoction of Shakespeare and Oriental extravaganza was probably all the more bizarre because the scenic designer could have had only the vaguest notion of Chinese architecture and Chinese gardening.

The tradition of the fantastic associated in this fashion with the representation of China and the Chinese upon the stage was perpetuated in the eighteenth century by the harlequinade. Probably no one of those mentioned below has survived, even if it was ever printed, but to judge by the titles, culled from Nicoll's play-lists, it is evident that the ingenious devisers of the harlequinades recognized the value of Orientalism for their whimsical and hilarious entertainments: *Arlequin Docteur chinois* (1720); *Harlequin Invisible, or, The Emperor of China's Court* (1724); *The Chinese Triumph* (1747); *Proteus, or Harle-*

quin in China (1755) by Henry Woodward; *The Mandarin, or, Harlequin Widower* (1789). As William Chetwood's *The Emperor of China Grand Volgi, or, The Constant Couple and Virtue Rewarded* (1731) is described as a "dramatic opera," it is a fair guess that the performance capitalized the fanciful and the grotesque in its depiction of the Chinese. In the same tradition was Noverre's famous ballet *Les Fêtes Chinoises*. One of its startling exotic features was a spectacular march in which the participants were a mandarin borne in a palanquin by six white slaves, a Chinese lady drawn in a car by two negroes, and a great troop of Chinese playing upon native musical instruments. At the close, the amphitheatre in which the dancers had taken their places was transformed into a porcelain shop, and before each of the thirty-two Chinese performers rose a porcelain vase which concealed him from the spectators. The ballet having been presented with splendor and immense success at Lyons, Marseilles, and Strasburg, Garrick finally in 1755 induced Noverre to come to England for the purpose of producing it at Drury Lane. Although, fearing an anti-Gallican demonstration, Garrick had taken the precaution to announce in the newspapers that Noverre himself was a Swiss and his wife a German, and that only a few of the dancers were French, such disgraceful outbreaks occurred on each of the six nights on which the ballet was performed that in the end it had to be withdrawn in the interests of public safety.[17]

The Travellers, an opera by A. Cherry which was performed at Drury Lane in the first decade of the nineteenth century, constitutes an instructive commentary upon the gay inconsequence of these earlier representations of the Chinese in masque, ballet, and harlequinade. Whereas in the seventeenth and eighteenth centuries the dramatist and scenic designer had given the leash to their fancy, producers, as the knowledge of the Orient became in time more accurate and extensive, felt obliged to represent a country even as remote as China with some degree of archeological truth. In *The Travellers* the exterior of the Emperor of China's palace was copied, we are told, "from a correct drawing of the palace of Pekin," and the imperial throne which appeared in the scene in the Hall of Presence was, we are assured, "a correct fac-simile of that which appertains to the court of Pekin." Such oppressive artistic sincerity may smack of the pedant, but in any case it is far removed from the irresponsible mood in which porcelain vases, lacquer screens, and crude pictures in travel-books provided the designer with his conception of Chinese architecture and costume. The conscientious attempt to reproduce on the stage authentic details of an Oriental world is parallel to the premeditated local color of *The Curse of Kehama* and *Lalla Rookh.*[18]

In addition to the light-hearted operatic versions of the Far East there are a number of tragedies in which the scene is laid in that part of the world. But Elkanah Settle's *The Conquest of China* (1675), Aaron Hill's *The Fatal Vision or The Fall of Siam* (1716), and Michael Clancy's *Hermon, Prince of Choraea* (1746) have little to recommend them. To what extent Settle's play is Chinese may be judged from the names of the characters: Orunda, Alcinda, Amavanga, Quitazo, and Lycungus. Like all the heroic plays, whether Roman, Egyptian, Spanish, or Mexican in setting, *The Conquest of China* suffers from a total lack of either the historic or the geographical sense. In defiance of their national psychology, the characters all talk the swelling language of love and honor. Hill's tragedy, which is no whit superior, reveals the vagueness of current impressions of China. As he complacently explains in his dedication, "our distance from, and dark ideas of, the Chinese nation and her borders, tempted me to fix my scene in so remote a situation." The play substantiates his confession of ignorance. Bogged in the tradition of heroic tragedy, a conquered Oriental general complains of "those killing tears" of his princess, and an emperor in his megalomania defies death and dreams of world-empire as many a strutting Restoration monarch had done before him. The ballets and the operas gave, one may venture to think, a more accurate picture of the Chinese than did these fourth-rate tragedies, for the producers of the former at least recognized that the Chinese had an individuality of their own, even though it was made up, as they represented it, of little but picturesque whimsicality.

More interesting and certainly more important than these pseudo-Chinese tragedies in the grand manner are the plays inspired by Prémare's translation of *Tchao Chi Cou Ell, ou Le*

Petit Orphelin de la Maison de Tchao (*Chau Shi Ku Eul, or, The Little Orphan of the Family of Chau*). This drama, incorporated in the third volume of Du Halde's *Description de la Chine* (1735) and in the second volume of the English translation (1741), excited among men of letters great interest as a specimen of Chinese tragedy at a time when, even in the face of ridicule, *chinoiserie* was enjoying widespread favor throughout Europe. The play was essentially a story of crime and its ultimate, although long-delayed, punishment. In the satisfaction of a terrible hatred Tu ngan ku, the chief war minister of China, succeeds in exterminating all the members of the family of Chau except a recently born male child. By her resourcefulness the mother saves the infant, and then hangs herself lest under torture she might betray its whereabouts. Duped into believing that the child has been slain, the minister, Tu ngan ku, adopts and brings up as his own the very orphan of the house of Chau who has been saved from death. Twenty years pass. The old physician of the Chau family discloses to the orphan, now a gallant youth, his real parentage so that he may proceed forthwith to avenge the slaughter of his relations by Tu ngan ku. The youth then exposes the crimes of the minister to the King, sees to it that Tu ngan ku suffers a horrible death by torture, and is rewarded with the elevation of his ancestors to a higher rank.

Aside from the childlike simplicity with which its story was told, the tragedy was in the opinion of classicists open to one serious outstanding objection: it flagrantly violated the unity of time. As a conservative the Marquis d'Argens in his *Lettres Chinoises*, translated from the French in 1741, condemns the play on this score, and also deplores the shocking violence of the mother's death upon the stage. With the classicist's confidence in his critical formulas he suggests that the defects of the Chinese technique could be corrected by the mere narration of the orphan's early life and his mother's suicide and by the limitation of the play as a whole to the exposure and punishment of Tu ngan ku.[19] In his *Discourse on Poetical Imitation* (1751) Richard Hurd expresses a more favorable opinion, venturing, perhaps with the classical "die-hards" in mind, to point out that the plot was similar to that of the *Electra* of Sophocles and that the Oriental dramatist had unconsciously obeyed Aristotle's principles. He believes the tragedy would have been improved by beginning nearer the catastrophe, that is, at the moment when the orphan, having arrived at maturity and having learned the injuries of his family, undertakes his revenge; none the less Hurd feels that this qualification does not invalidate his main contention. That the Chinese playwright, guided by his innate sense of what would render his material dramatically effective, arrived at results not essentially different from those of Greek tragedy establishes, in Hurd's judgment, the universality of the principles of dramatic composition. Hurd's method of proving the merits of the Chinese play is identical with that of Addison, who, when he wished to vindicate his admiration for *Chevy Chase* (*Spectator*, no. 70), pointed out similarities between the ballad and the "heroick" poems of Homer and Virgil. It must be admitted that both Addison and Hurd had to labor hard to reconcile to the canons of classicism a work that was, in each case, the product of entirely different literary conditions. Haunted, perhaps, in his dreams by the reproaches of Aristotle and Castelvetro, Hurd may have repented his rashness; at all events, he subsequently omitted from his *Discourse* his commendation of *The Little Orphan of the Family of Chau.*

When eighteenth-century dramatists seized on the plot of the Chinese tragedy for their own purposes, they handled it, of course, with all due deference to classical prejudice. Of the three English plays on this theme the first, *The Chinese Orphan* (1741), was by William Hatchett.[20] Describing it as "altered from a specimen of the Chinese tragedy in Du Halde's History of China," he maintains the unity of time by the confinement of his plot, for the most part, to the first half of the Chinese drama. His play, as a result, is concerned primarily with the birth and concealment of the orphan, and represents the disclosure of the prime minister's crimes and his ruin as following not long after the child's birth and while he is still "the little sufferer" and the "dear babe." In the interests of unity Hatchett has sacrificed the fine ironic circumstances of the original, the minister's bringing up as his adopted son the boy who is destined to be the instrument of his destruction. For the same reason Hatchett has rejected the vitally human and emotional situation in which the son, having reached maturity, learns of his duty to avenge the extermination of his family. Hatchett manages to retain, however, some of the simplicity of the original, and that he "interspersed" his action with "songs after the Chinese manner" indicates his conscious effort to keep near to the spirit of his text.

Arthur Murphy's version (1759), a free adaptation of Voltaire's *L'Orphelin de la Chine* (1755), scrupulously observes the classical proprieties. Unlike Hatchett's tragedy, it focuses the dramatic attention upon the second half of the orphan's life, beginning at the moment when, as d'Argens had suggested, he hears that he is the heir to the throne of China and must take vengeance upon Timurkan, the pitiless Tartar usurper. It follows, according to formula, that in due time the orphan slays Timurkan off-stage, and that Zamti, the great mandarin, who brought up the royal boy in secret, is broken on the wheel behind the scenes. The play was a pronounced success; it provided Garrick with one of his best roles, that of Zamti, and enjoyed frequent revivals in the course of the next forty years. What is especially significant, however, is the prologue by William Whitehead, in which, perhaps with his tongue in his cheek, he pleads for the appreciation of the novel Orientalism of the plot:

> Enough of Greece and Rome. The exhausted store
> Of either nation now can charm no more;
> Ev'n adventitious helps in vain we try,
> Our triumphs languish in the public eye;
> . . . .
> On eagle wings the poet of to-night
> Soars for fresh virtues to the source of light,
> To China's eastern realms: and boldly bears
> Confucius' morals to Britannia's ears.
> Accept th' imported boon; as echoing Greece
> Receiv'd from wand'ring chiefs her golden fleece;
> Nor only richer by the spoils become,
> But praise th' advent'rous youth, who brings them home.

As the reviewer of the play in a contemporary journal, Goldsmith was too much of a classicist to respond to this appeal by an acknowledgment of gratitude for "the imported boon." In the mood of a censor of manners and taste Goldsmith complains that, wearied by all the normal and usual sources of enjoyment, the jaded European "has, of late, had recourse even to China, in order to diversify the amusements of the day." In view of the favor bestowed on *chinoiserie* in gardens and in the decoration of houses, it is not surprising, in Goldsmith's opinion, that this perverted taste should have its effect upon literature. Voltaire, he thought, was fully aware of this craze, and simply capitalized it. He improved upon his source, to be sure, by departing from "the calm insipidity of his Eastern original," a quality which Goldsmith thinks is generally characteristic of Chinese literature. Murphy, in turn, has improved upon Voltaire and has departed still farther from the original, with the result that his "play, if not truly Chinese, [is] at least entirely poetical."[21] Goldsmith is here taking his stand beside such contemporaries as Cooper, Brown, Shebbeare, Jackson of Battersea the paper-stainer, and the periodical essayists who in this decade, 1750–60, were resisting the claims of Chinese culture to the enjoyment of public esteem. They were not inclined to echo the cry "Enough of Greece and Rome," and least of all were they likely to adopt the suggestion that they welcome anything from China as if it were a "golden fleece."

The influence of China upon English literature was not confined to such dramatic types as the masque, the harlequinade, the opera, the heroic play, and the imitations of *The Little Orphan*. A considerable body of English satire also acquired some of its most characteristic qualities from prevailing conceptions of both China and Japan. Of the forms which satire assumed in the eighteenth century, one of the most popular was that amusing epistolary *genre* established by *L'Espion Turc* (1684), a book written in French by an Italian, Giovanni Paolo Marana. According to the device to which the success of Marana's work gave currency, the "spy's" letters purport to be those of an Oriental written to a friend in his native land in comment upon the European country he is visiting. In this disguise the author endeavors to show how the customs, the institutions, the culture, and indeed the whole civilization of a Western people impress an unbiased Easterner who encounters them for the first time and is able to form an objective judgment of them. At first the visitor from afar naively takes everything at its face value, and credits as truth all that he is told, but in the course of his experience he is amazed and amused to discover the difference between principles and practice. On the other hand, while the author of such letters depicts the European as egoistic, complacent, insincere, and even hypocritical, he never fails to idealize the Oriental, who remains to the end the disinterested seeker after truth. The inquirer sees things as they are rather than as they seem to be; yet the sense of humor with which the author has generally endowed him preserves him from the bitterness of disillusionment, and his irony plays not too severely over the contradictions he observes. Moreover, if the author has wit and imagination, he can make these pseudo-letters the more diverting by taking full advantage of the disguise he has assumed, and by his style, diction, allusions, and point of view can create, as far as may be, the impression that the letters are actually the authentic correspondence of a philosophical Oriental.

That the ideal "spy" qualified to be a censor of European manners should frequently be Chinese, and sometimes Hindu, is a manifestation of the tendency of the age to indulge in undiscriminating enthusiasm for remote and virtually unknown races. It is easy to imagine that the people one does not know are superior to those with whom one comes in daily contact. Moreover, the eighteenth century was discovering Confucius and was ready to believe that his fellow-countrymen possessed a share of his sagacity. Even as late as 1770, in a letter from an Englishman in Canton published in the *Gentleman's Magazine* the Chinese are eulogized to the disadvantage of the English. The writer praises the Chinese for their placidity and their refusal to give way to passion and to scold at every irritating circumstance in life. He is not surprised that they look with contempt on the English, since the latter lose their self-control on every trivial occasion; and as an Englishman the writer feels only shame, because his fellow-countrymen should, he thinks, "excel those enlightened heathens." He even ventures to say that should a person who has resided for several years in a Chinese family take his place by an English fireside, "he would seem to have exchanged a civilized society for a confusion of savages." [22] This laudation of the Chinese was so prevalent that Johnson and Wesley, as I have pointed out, felt the necessity of combating it. The point of view had, indeed, almost crystallized into a dogma, and for literary purposes was adopted even by writers who did not, in fact, hold it to be correct. That the writer of "spy" letters should, in a considerable number of instances, be Chinese is not, under the circumstances, as remarkable as might appear at first sight.

The Chinaman did not appear as the critic of English manners in the earliest English imitations of *L'Espion Turc*. A man described as an Indian takes that role in Tom Brown's adaptation of Dufresny's *Amusements sérieux et comiques*, but as Brown's ideas of geography were nebulous, it is impossible to decide whether his Indian is from America or from the Far East. In any case, the device is employed with only incidental effectiveness, as Brown does not sustain the part, speaking too often in his own person rather than in that of the Indian. In one of the papers in the *Spectator* (no. 50) an American Indian plays the censor, in another (no. 557) a Javanese. In both of these essays Addison avails himself to the full of the humorous possibilities of his literary disguise. A Persian is the judge of morals in Lyttelton's *Letters from a Persian in England* (1735), modeled after Montesquieu's *Lettres Persanes* (1721); it is the first full-sized English book in which the point of view of the observant foreigner is maintained with consistency throughout. Lyttelton's work was followed the next year by *Letters from a Moor at London to his Friend at Tunis*, the dullness of which fully justified the author's refuge in anonymity.

It was apparently in a French work, the *Lettres Chinoises* of the Marquis d'Argens, translated into English in 1741, that a Chinaman acted as the satirist for the first time.[23] In the middle of the century, when the taste for *chinoiserie* was keenest, Walpole adopted the idea in two essays written for the *World*, but unpublished. His Chinese sage is amazed at the wilderness of books which Europe produces, and the futility of pedants who continue to increase their number. As the "Inquisitor of the World of Books" Walpole mockingly arrogates to himself the right to destroy any work that displeases him. To give an air of legality to his proceedings, he asserts that he is descended in a direct line from Chi Hoang Ti, the Emperor of China, who, according to Du Halde, ordered the destruction of all books in his empire. Closing with a eulogy of his Oriental ancestor, Walpole equals in these two essays the best of the ironic satires which give such zest to the pages of the *World* and make it to-day one of the most readable of eighteenth-century periodicals. But his deft handling of a "spy" might have remained unknown had Walpole not published *A Letter from Xo Ho, a Chinese Philosopher at London, to his Friend Lien Chi at Peking.* Written on May 12, 1757, sent to the press the next day, and passing through five editions in a fortnight, it delighted readers by its exposure of the irrationality of the Englishman's political psychology. Even if he did live in what purported to be a Gothic castle, Walpole himself was attached to his Chinese goldfish and evidently relished an occasional literary holiday in the Orient.

With these forerunners, Continental and English, to guide him, Goldsmith produced *The Citizen of the World* (1760–62), a masterpiece of the *genre*. With far more skill than most writers who have adopted this epistolary form as the vehicle of their criticism, Goldsmith by means of quaint, amusing detail and quirks of style maintains through the long series of letters the illusion that the writer is Chinese, a newcomer in a strange world who is frequently bewildered and ill at ease in his effort to understand it. Moreover, Goldsmith does not arrange the letters in a mere mechanical sequence, checking off like the compiler of a guide-book each topic as he has done with it, but he imparts to the correspondence an artistic integrity by suffusing it with the personality of the imaginary writer, the humorous, kindly, shrewd Chinese philosopher. He has created a character, whereas others have been too often content with an automaton as the mouthpiece of their ideas.

It is a Chinese humanist, it should be noted, and not a man nourished by Greek and Roman culture, that Goldsmith has represented as achieving the cosmopolitanism that justifies his description as a "citizen of the world." In his judgments Lien Chi Altangi is capable of a most admirable detachment. When he visits a lady of distinction, he offends her by his contempt for the Chinese decorations of her house — rooms crowded with jars, mandarins, and pagods which were useless, and on that account in the worst of taste, because their owner did not know for what purpose they had been made and employed in China. Nor is Lien any more impressed by what is pointed out to him as a

Chinese temple in the garden. It might as well be called, he honestly declares, an Egyptian pyramid. His correspondent Fum Hoam, shocked by the moral anomalies of western nations, doubts the superiority of Europe and rejoices that he is "a native of that kingdom which derives its original from the sun." Chinese history exhibits "an antient extended empire, established by laws which nature and reason seem to have dictated," and Europe is "the theatre of intrigue, avarice, and ambition."[24] This is Goldsmith's statement of the paradox that lies at the core of all "spy" literature. Its edge is sharpened or blunted according to the mood of various satirists.

The Citizen of the World was followed in 1765 by *The Chinese Spy, or, Emissary from the Court of Peking, commissioned to examine into the Present State of Europe*, a pedestrian piece of work without freshness or insight. A few letters, however, successfully burlesque conventional types of stage characters, the absurdity of the acting, and the number and variety of scenic devices. The ridicule of contemporary tragedy and its ranting heroes is a minor supplement to *Tom Thumb.*[25] A few years later in a paper in the *Sentimental Magazine* a mandarin is depicted as sitting in judgment upon the English passion for card-playing.[26] At the same time, in *The Spiritual Quixote* Richard Graves made a passing thrust at this literary habit of setting up foreigners of outlandish antecedents as qualified critics of England. In the course of his wanderings, Wildgoose, the fanatic Methodist, falls in with one Graham, grotesque philosopher, who is the author of an unpublished manuscript. Its title satirizes the progeny of *The Turkish Spy*: *Literae Hottentoticae, or, Letters from a beautiful young Hottentot to her Friends at the Cape.* This work, Graham explains, is "an account of the many barbarous customs and preposterous opinions which she had observed in our metropolis, during her three years' abode amongst us."[27] But the *genre* of the "spy" was not to be put out of court by a casual jest. Several years later Charles Johnstone attempted to enter into competition with Goldsmith in *The Pilgrim, or, A Picture of Life, in a Series of Letters written by a Chinese Philosopher to his Friend at Quang-Tong* (1775). Literary expediency and not respect for the intellectual power of the Chinese inspired Johnstone to mask himself as an Oriental sage.

What he really thought of them he makes plain in *Chrysal, or, The Adventures of a Guinea*. There he laughs at the antiquary who buys Chinese books although he cannot read them, and who carries off "in triumph" from an auction "the curious, the rare, the inestimable key, into all the mysterious, the profound, the sublime wisdom of that prince of all philosophers, legislators, and hierarchs, the divine Con-fut-see, and all his learned, and judicious disciples and commentators." [28]

One of the few books in which the satiric method of *The Turkish Spy* is employed without a glint of humor is *A Chinese Fragment* (1786). The author, Ely Bates, according to the British Museum catalogue, represents himself as a Chinaman who has been deeply impressed by Christianity and who has gone to England to examine, at first hand, the great religious system in operation. The result, painful to relate, is disillusionment at the gulf between doctrine and practice. The English, he finds, profane the Sabbath, act frivolously in church, neglect family worship at home, reject all simplicity in both their dress and their houses, find amusement in the moral dangers of the masquerade and the gayeties of Ranelagh, read novels and corrupting romances, admire the sentimentality of Sterne, and enlist under the banner of a sophist like Shaftesbury or a scoffer like Voltaire. The cheerless conclusion of his indictment is that if Christianity be true and if any people be in danger of extermination for their sins, the English "have cause to tremble." It was this "odd" book which moved Wesley to assert that as for the Chinese "they are almost as *religious* but nothing near so honest as the Turks. So that I account the contrasting them with the Christians to be a mere pious fraud." [29] Wesley was too clear-headed to be browbeaten into the belief that the Chinese in comparison with other nations deserved to be enthroned on a peak of moral superiority.

At the very close of the century, as her brother Charles, a distinguished Orientalist who had served in the British forces in India, had stirred her interest in that country, Elizabeth Hamilton replaced the popular Chinese "spy" by a no less shrewd Hindu as an observer of contemporary conditions. But in the *Translation of the Letters of a Hindoo Rajah* (1797) what Miss Hamilton unmasks is not the follies of social life but the sophistry of the anarchical doctrines of revolutionary idealism. In particular she makes fun, in a spirit of hilarious gayety, of the ideological theories of William Godwin, whose *Political Justice* was the bible of radical agitators and the devil's own book in the eyes of panic-stricken conservatives. Oddly enough, another book in which an Indian functions as the critic appeared in 1802 in America. Written by Samuel Knapp, *Letters of Shahcoolen, a Hindu Philosopher, residing in Philadelphia, to his friend El Hassan, an Inhabitant of Delhi* also assails the speculations of the extremists, and especially the individualistic ideas of Mary Wollstonecraft, the apostle of woman's rights.

In these various English works which were modeled after *The Turkish Spy* the American Indian, the Persian, the Hindu, and the Chinaman were the foreigners whom the authors employed as the mouthpieces of such wisdom as they possessed.[30] But of these non-Europeans, as this survey has disclosed, it was the Chinaman conceived as the inhabitant of a Utopia and a prodigy of learning and sagacity who served most often as the analyst of contemporary society. In conclusion, it may be remarked that the custom of glorifying the non-European to the detriment of the European became the routine of the followers of Rousseau. Indeed, in his candor, his intellectual honesty, and his disconcerting habit of viewing all things with the cool eye of reason the wise Oriental is akin to the man of nature, who, in the second half of the eighteenth century, with equal clarity of judgment and frankness of expression calmly exposes the shams and inconsistencies in what passes for civilized society. But whereas the perception of these defects only bewilders the Oriental, then amuses him, and at the most makes him a harmless cynic, there are implicit in the criticism by the man of nature a flaming revolt against things as they are and a longing for the rejuvenation of society.[31]

For other works didactic or satiric in purpose China supplied the background and suggested whimsical ideas which men of wit were delighted to develop with zest and playful humor. China made its due share of contributions especially to that arsenal where periodical writers kept stored the devices by which essays might be enlivened in spirit and diversified in treatment. Addison tells the story of the Chinese women tied up in sacks and sold in the marketplace to whoever would run the risk of a purchase,[32] and he locates in China the scene of his antediluvian romance of Hilpa and Shalum.[33] Steele writes the florid letter from the Emperor of China to Pope Clement XI in which it is proposed that the former marry one of the papal nieces, "the Darling of God's Right Eye."[34] With a mock sobriety that proves that he could hold his own in the royal line of eighteenth-century ironists, Chesterfield discusses the tickling of ears, a Chinese pastime, enjoyed by everyone from the Emperor to the coolie, and finds an analogy between this pastime and the English passion for flattery widespread among all classes.[35] In another paper in *Common Sense* (no. 16) he interprets the Chinese allegory of the rat in the venerated image as signifying the unscrupulous minister of state who, to the injury of his country, ingratiates himself in the favor of a prince and maintains himself there against all comers. Chesterfield expresses surprise that the art of rat-catching is in such low estate in China, but he has to admit that it is declining even in old England. Akin in its capricious spirit to these mocking periodical essays is *Mi Li*, the Chinese fairy story which Walpole included in his *Hieroglyphic Tales*. The charming lady for whom the Chinese prince is searching turns out to be, by way of compliment, Miss Caroline Campbell, daughter of one of Walpole's friends. In its wit and the grace of its unexpected climax the tale does not fall short of being a little masterpiece, and like Walpole's sketches in the manner of "spy" literature exemplifies the facility in paradoxical fancy possessed even by minor writers in the eighteenth century. The Chinese gentlemen who live in these periodical essays are the cousins of the Chinese harlequin who disported himself on the contemporary stage. In effect, Addison, Steele, Chesterfield, Walpole translated into narrative the humor and whimsicality of Chinese life as they perceived it in the scenes that animated lacquer screens and blue and white china.

Political writers as well as periodical essayists made excursions into the Orient. For the construction of the framework of his satire *The Consolidator, or, Memoirs of Sundry Transactions from the Moon* (1705) Defoe adopted the popular idea that the Chinese were superior to Western nations. With characteristically misleading gravity he asserts that he has made many voyages to China; impressed by the genius of that "ancient, wise, polite, and most ingenious people," he intends to prepare a description of Chinese technical arts which will enlighten the Western world and expose "the monstrous ignorance and deficiencies of European science." In indicating the scope of his plan, Defoe gives in a spirit of fantastic satire an account of instruments and machines as extraordinary as those devised by the philosophers of Swift's kingdom of Lagado, and proceeds to explain that the supreme competence of the Chinese in the sciences is due entirely to the knowledge which was brought to them from the moon. By means of a machine, called the consolidator, Defoe himself journeys to the lunar world. The account of the conditions he found there constitutes the body of the narrative, and under a thin disguise enables Defoe to satirize the political and religious strife of contemporary England.

But when, in *The Farther Adventures of Robinson Crusoe* (1719), he had an opportunity to express a different opinion of the Chinese, he did not hesitate to do so. As Crusoe, Defoe confesses that "we wonder at the Grandeur, the Riches, the Pomp, the Ceremonies, the Government, the Manufactures, the Commerce, and Conduct of these People" because, having thought that the Chinese were pagan barbarians, one is proportionally surprised to discover that they have a civilization at all, and consequently magnifies its merits. Crusoe scoffs at the trade of China, its architecture, and its undisciplined and inadequately armed military forces. When he returns to England he is oddly impressed by what he hears people saying about the wealth and glory of China, for from personal observation he knew "that they were a contemptible Herd or Crowd of ignorant sordid Slaves, subjected to a Government qualified only to rule such a People." The wisest of the Chinese are superstitious, believing that when the sun is eclipsed a dragon has run away with it, and as for the mass of the people, Crusoe thinks their standard of living is so low that an Englishman could not endure it. On the whole, when the misery and poverty of the Chinese are borne in mind, it appears probable that the American savage is actually happier.[36] That Crusoe should be intolerant in his judgment of the Chinese is thoroughly in keeping with the psychology of a man in his position and of limited education; to hate foreigners was one of the cherished prejudices of a "true-born Englishman" in the eighteenth century, and the lower he was in the social scale, the more outrageous was his hostility. However, as Defoe had too much plain common sense to be hypnotized by the legends about China, he probably put into the mouth of Crusoe something of his personal opinion of the Chinese, smirking at his recollection of his praise of them in *The Consolidator.*

Another pseudo-history, concealing like *The Consolidator* contemporary events under a disguise, is the brief tract *An Account of the Court and Empire of Japan.* The writer, possibly Swift himself, recounting some incidents of party strife that took place at the time of the accession of George II, pretends that he is narrating an episode in Japanese history which occurred in the early years of the Christian era. Under the name of Lelop Aw, Sir Robert Walpole is attacked with violence. In his *The Adventures of an Atom* (1769) Smollett, under a similar veil of Orientalism, depicts English conditions when ostensibly he is describing the political situation in Japan as observed by the atom from its post of vantage in the bodies of the various Japanese officials of which it has chanced to form a part. The pretence of Japanese history has been employed not because the Orient made any appeal to Smollett's imagination, but rather as a wise precaution in the interest of self-defence. The Orientalism is indeed of the most perfunctory sort. George II becomes Got-hama-baba, the Duke of Newcastle Fika-kaka, William Pitt Taycho, and Frederick the Great Brut-an-tiffi. Of these historic personages and their contemporaries Smollett gives satiric portraits of vitriolic bitterness, and as he paints them his venomous irascibility shrinks from no indecency likely to degrade his victims in the eyes of his readers. Got-hama-baba is "rapacious, shallow, hot-headed, and perverse; in point of understanding, just sufficient to appear in public without a slavering bib; imbued with no knowledge, illumed by no sentiment, and warmed with no affection. . . . His heart was meanly selfish, and his disposition altogether unprincely." The people he rules over are equally contemptible. They "are the tamest animals in the world" and "may be compared to an ass, that will crouch under the most unconscionable burden, provided you scratch his long ears, and allow him to bray his belly-full." [37] To call such a nation with such a king Japanese was merely a label and a libel; indeed the world of *The Adventures of an Atom* has the grotesqueness of an Aristophanic dream. The China of *The Consolidator* follows tradition and approximates Utopia, but the Japan of Smollett's political satire envisages a moral topsy-turvydom.

Although it is fortunately forgotten to-day except by eccentric persons who insist on disinterring old books long unread, *The Oeconomy of Human Life*, published in 1750, was blessed in its own time with such an amazing demand that the British Museum has on its shelves no less than twenty-one editions that issued from the press before the end of the century. A writer in the *Athenaeum* states that in all there were nearly fifty English editions of *The Oeconomy* as well as French, German, Italian, Spanish, Portuguese, and Welsh translations.[38] Some of this popularity may have been due to its appearance in an ingenious Oriental disguise thoroughly in accord with the taste of the age for literary masquerading of one sort or another. The author knew what he was doing when he prefixed to his work *An Account of the Manner in which the said Manuscript was discover'd.* According to this cleverly fabricated narrative the Emperor of China, a highly cultivated man, dispatched a very erudite scholar to Thibet to search the ancient library of the Lama for ancient manuscripts. Among others the manuscript of *The Oeconomy of Human Life* was discovered and was translated into Chinese. However, the ultimate origin of the work, whether it was Indian or an Indian translation of a lost Chinese treatise, is still a matter of debate, we are told, even among Chinese scholars. Be that as it may, the wisdom of this ancient philosophical treatise so impressed an Englishman long resident in China that he translated it for the gratification of a friend in England.

Unfortunately the text of the book itself does not justify this elaborate fiction which introduces it. With some ingenuity, but with no imaginative power or force of expression, the author has "faked" an Oriental style, affecting a figurative language and a gnomic brevity in his sentences. The commonplaceness of his thought and the vogue of the book only testify to the insatiable appetite of the eighteenth century for moral platitude. Richardson would have approved of it, and the readers of his novels must have rejoiced in it. In 1784, under the title *Chinese Maxims*, a Miss Susannah Watts solemnly turned it into a volume of heroic verse in seven parts. But from those who did not relish its moralizing it invited and secured ridicule. It was burlesqued in *The Oeconomy of a Winter's Day* (1751) and in *The Oeconomy of Female Life* (1751), a cheerfully cynical collection of aphoristic instructions to women on the conduct of an amour, on the management of husbands, on intrigues, and on widowhood.

As to the question whether Chesterfield or Dodsley was the author of this pseudo-Oriental ethical treatise, authorities are in disagreement. The writer of the article on Dodsley in the *Dictionary of National Biography* favors Chesterfield, while Ralph Straus in his special study of the publisher decides for Dodsley after a careful review of the external evidence. Internal evidence, I think, also substantiates this conclusion. No one familiar with Chesterfield's cynical evaluation of women in his letters to his son could imagine that he was responsible for the softly sentimental description of woman in *The Oeconomy.* The woman described has modesty, fidelity, tender affections — in a word, the undynamic virtues of Milton's Eve:

> She is cloathed with neatness, she is fed with temperance; humility and meekness are as a crown of glory circling her head. . . . Submission and obedience are the lessons of her life, and peace and happiness are her reward.

Could Chesterfield have written this passage without crossing his fingers and putting his tongue in his cheek? I think not. But I am certain his enjoyment of the parody in *The Oeconomy of Female Life* would have been unequivocal. "The man to whom thou speakest, shall say unto himself, thou delightest in him: and what is there for thee to wish but that he think so, altho' thou sayest it not?"[39] The sentiments of *The Oeconomy of Human Life* are not, moreover, those of a sophisticated man of the world, but of one whose moral sympathies were with the code of a Defoe or a Richardson. Yet their Oriental dress relieves the triteness of the ideas and, for a moment, obscures the essential mediocrity of the book.

No doubt, although its author was known to be an Englishman, the Indo-Chinese masquerade of *The Oeconomy* enhanced its reputation among undiscriminating readers who were ready to credit the Chinese with superior moral insight. The legend that the Chinese had their eyes uplifted to the stars died hard. Raynal's deification of the Chinese in his "philosophical history" occurred twenty years after the first edition of *The Oeconomy of Human Life*, and was to continue the habit of bestowing the blue ribbon upon remote non-European races. Scott of Amwell's *Li Po, or The Good Governor* (1782), is inspired by the same optimism. Suggested by Du Halde's account to the effect that "the Chinese government, though arbitrary, is well regulated and mild" and that no ruler can there attain glory unless the welfare of his subjects is his primary concern, the "eclogue" depicts the self-reproach of the viceroy, Li Po, because as an administrator he has not always been guided by justice and pity.

In addition to the plays, letters of Oriental "spies," periodical essays, and political satires which sprang from the contact of the East with the West, there is evidence of a genuine desire to know and understand Chinese literature itself. Of this laudable ambition Thomas Percy is an example. What distinguishes him is that his interest in books was not circumscribed by the ancient classics and the English works that imitated them. In his conception of literature he was essentially a cosmopolitan, and his historic sense made interesting to him remote civilizations and the poetry of peoples who had never heard of either Aristotle or the *Ars Poetica*. As a liberalizing influence he did his share in emancipating the taste of his contemporaries from the tyranny of Greece and Rome. Of his larger plan to translate examples of Runic, Greenland, Lapland, and Peruvian poetry, his Chinese miscellanies were but a part. When, in speaking of his first collection, *Hau Kiou Choaan, or, The Pleasing History* (1761), he says that "the principal merit of these volumes [is] that they afford specimens of Chinese composition," he describes them correctly. Intrinsically as translations the Chinese novel, the collection of Chinese proverbs, and the Chinese verse have little value, and certainly would not whet the appetite for more of their kind; as Percy honestly reminds his readers, the poetry is a translation of a translation, that is, an English version of a French rendering of the original Chinese. Percy's own estimate of Chinese poetry is that it is trivial, and of that brief epigrammatic form which had lost favor in Europe. Like the verse, the proverbs had been gathered by Percy from various authors who had written about China. In view of his lack of any first-hand knowledge of China it would be unreasonable to expect that Percy's results would be any better than they are. In *The Matrons* (1762), a mischievous collection of six stories of faithless wives, Percy included the account of the wife of the Chinese philosopher which he found in Du Halde and which Goldsmith had already exploited in *The Citizen of the World.* More informative than literary in character is Percy's *Miscellaneous Pieces relating to the Chinese* (1762). He gives a new translation of Prémare's version of *The Little Orphan*, accompanied by Hurd's favorable criticism of the tragedy, and *A Description of the Emperor's Gardens and Pleasure-Houses near Peking* and *A Description of the Solemnities observed at Peking on the Emperor's Mother entering on the Sixtieth Year of her Age.*

Percy's aim to popularize a knowledge of the Chinese and their literature was indirectly supplemented by John Brown, author of the famous *Estimate*, in the course of his effort to come to a better understanding of the nature of poetry itself. His *Dissertation on the Rise, Union, and Power, . . . of Poetry and Music* (1763), revised as *The History of the Rise and Progress of Poetry* (1764), a pioneer work of its kind, took as its initial principle that as poetry was an art based on emotions common to mankind, its nature could be determined by a study of man in "his *savage* or *uncultivated* State" before the influences of civilization had obscured the operation of his spontaneous feelings and thought. In illustration of this principle he examines the poetical development in Greece, Peru, India, and China. His deductions are not important, but his method was full of promise because it admitted an evolutionary conception of poetry and, anticipating the procedure of scholars like Gummere in America, sought for poetic origins among primitive or semi-civilized peoples. Brown's point of view, like that of Percy, implied liberality of judgment because it testified to an interest in all poetic activity no matter where or when it might manifest itself.[40]

Such catholicity only offended the exclusive, aristocratic classicist. As the idea of any connection between the poetry of the ancients and that of some barbarous race was as repugnant to him as the thought of the ancestral monkey to the anti-Darwinian, it is not surprising that one of Brown's critics exulted in "the obvious ridicule which arises from the searching for the seeds and principles of all the most refined and transporting poetry of Greece in the dreary wilds of North America . . ."[41] In spite of such a protest, the monopoly of classicism as the sole form of literary expression deserving of respect was nearing its end. Within a few years Warren Hastings was to plead for the independent recognition of the *Bhagavad-gītā* and its exemption from the conventional standards of European criticism. Percy's Chinese publications and Brown's inclusion of China in his discussion of poetry were signs of the development of this more comprehensive definition of literature. That China was associated with that development bears some testimony to the impression which the Orient had made upon the mind of Western Europe.

This survey of the poetry and prose that were influenced by the relations of England with India and China supplements the discussion of the vogue of Oriental art. It reminds us that in the eighteenth century, although the theater-goer who returned home from a performance of *The Harlequin in China* or *The Chinese Orphan* probably lived in a Palladian house, as likely as not he read before he went to bed a letter of *The Citizen of the World* in a room gay with porcelain and Chinese wallpaper and furnished with a Chinese bed canopied with Indian chintz. Although these decorations in the classical environment of the English house were such alien elements that their absence of proportion, perspective, and symmetry excited the disgust of people of orthodox taste, the literature that had been colored by the Orient rarely had such a disturbing effect. The reason is plain. Neither in quantity nor in quality was it of sufficient importance to alarm the classicists. After all, the outstanding works of the period, the books that come to mind most readily, *Hudibras*, *A Tale of a Tub*, *The Rape of the Lock*, *Pamela*, and

A Sentimental Journey, were not affected by Orientalism. *The Citizen of the World* is the only work by a great author decisively dependent upon its Oriental atmosphere.

What Orientalism contributed to English literature did not in any deep or vital sense modify its form and spirit as did, let us say, the renewed interest in the Middle Ages. Its primary service was to enrich the content of literature with some fresh material drawn from new realms of experience. The Oriental world gave a new costume to the harlequin, suggested a picturesque setting for operas, offered the merchant engaged in Eastern trade as a convenient *deus ex machina* or made him as a nabob an object of ridicule, provided amusing ideas for ironic essays and political satires, and presented a philosophical "spy" capable of exposing the follies of contemporary England. But, while on our guard against overrating the intrinsic value of these contributions, we should remember that the volume and depth of a great national literature are proportional to the number and variety of the minor streams that pour into the main channel. As a mere document, any literature is the more fascinating when it reveals vividly the influences that have shaped the life of the people that created it, and records the adventures that have enlarged their experience and awakened their consciousness of worlds beyond their national boundaries. The Chinese harlequin, the nabob, and the spying sage are figures that ultimately owe their existence to English commerce, which established connection between the West and the Far East. The very presence of these figures varies the pattern of eighteenth-century literature and is the outward symbol of human and artistic relationships between the East and the West that have been vitalizing English life ever since their establishment. Even if such Oriental elements do not make the literature greater fundamentally, they increase its historical interest many fold. More important as an influence in the world of ideas was the antithesis between Eastern and Western civilization and the eulogy of the former at the expense of the latter. The currency of this antithesis was due not entirely to its acceptance as a belief, but partly to literary exigency. It provided a point of vantage from which a satirist could attack his fellow-Englishmen more effectively. But it would be an error to assume that this respect for the Chinese was invariably tainted with insincerity. The travel-books praised the Chinese and enveloped them in glamour, many of their readers accepted their estimate, and in consequence the prestige of the Chinese was sufficiently great to stir Johnson and Wesley to denial and resentment. In so far as this favorable opinion was established in the popular mind, it robbed the ancients of a few rays in their halo of glory, prepared the way for a more tolerant consideration of non-European peoples, and undoubtedly in the last decades of the eighteenth century served to stimulate and justify the more serious study of Oriental languages and literature.

CHAPTER XIV

THE CHALLENGE OF THE MIDDLE AGES

I. The Persisting Interest in Gothic Architecture before Walpole

In an article rich with suggestive ideas Professor Lovejoy has said: "The first great revolt against the neo-classical aesthetics was not in literature at all, but in gardening." This revolt, which began about 1710 as a criticism of the formal garden, Professor Lovejoy has aptly described as "horticultural Romanticism."[1] Yet if my interpretation of the significance of Orientalism be correct, even "horticultural Romanticism" does not represent the first phase of discontent with neo-classical esthetics. Even in the seventeenth century, when classicism became the most authoritative force in architecture and literature, walls hung with Chinese wallpaper and rooms embellished with porcelain and lacquer furniture implied a protest against the principles of symmetry and proportion which gave the art of Renaissance origin its distinguishing character. That protest was not conscious, but was, I think, nevertheless real. The tide of sentimentalism that swept through Europe in the eighteenth century has frequently been accounted for as the natural outburst of emotions that had been repressed and starved by classicism. By a similar reasoning the vogue of Oriental art may be taken as proof that the esthetic instincts were not completely satisfied by the symmetries of the formal garden and the house of axial design and that, in spite of its authority, classicism had not achieved the entire inhibition of the desire for novelty and artistic freedom. In short, Oriental art met a need for variety and playfulness in an environment in which uniformity was the controlling force. That the popularity of this art was regarded as a menace to their standards of beauty is evident from the ridicule to which the classicists repeatedly subjected it. Since from the very outset of its importation Oriental art represented a challenge to classicism and a potential force of reaction against its influence, it is a question whether it is historically accurate to date the revolt against classicism at a sharply specified moment in the early years of the eighteenth century. Is it not nearer the truth to think of the revolutionary spirit as present even during the Restoration? When Wren was building St. Paul's, the alien art that made the power of classicism less absolute than it wished to be had already taken root in English taste.

With a similar degree of perilous precision it is customary to date what is generally described as the Gothic "revival" near the middle of the eighteenth century. For this "revival," because of the interest which his pseudo-Gothic mansion, Strawberry Hill, excited, Horace Walpole is made primarily responsible. Eastlake characterizes him as an author "to whose writings and to whose influence as an admirer of Gothic art we believe may be ascribed one of the chief causes which induced its present revival."[2] Professor Beers remarks that

> one service that Walpole and his followers did, by reviving public interest in Gothic, was to arrest the process of dilapidation and save the crumbling remains of many a half-ruinous abbey, castle, or baronial hall. . . . "The restorers of churches, the manufacturers of stained glass . . . should think of him with kindness."[3]

As recently as 1928 Mr. Kenneth Clark has ventured to call Walpole and Gray "the real revivalists."[4] I cannot believe that Walpole deserves as much credit as these writers generously give him, nor do I think that interest in medieval art was a phenomenon that abruptly manifested itself in the middle of the eighteenth century. This interest never "began" or "revived" in any true sense, but existed throughout the classical period in an inconspicuous but nevertheless genuine form. The antiquaries, who carried on the traditions of Leland and Camden, preserved a veneration for the past, and cherished the buildings which had been inherited from the Middle Ages even when Gothic architecture was losing its prestige among those who responded with enthusiasm to the new Italian art of Inigo Jones and his successors.

The activities of the antiquaries have been recognized as not without influence in bringing about the "revival" and in preparing the way for Walpole; yet it has been the habit to belittle that influence and speak of it in a depreciatory tone. To discount the antiquaries as dull, unimaginative workers, boring like moles and blinking like owls, with neither any esthetic appreciation of the edifices they were investigating nor any emotional response to the historic past of which those edifices were a part, is to do them scant justice. Their books, to be sure, are frequently dull compilations requiring a heroic nerve for their perusal — the age in which they wrote inferred that the more massive a volume the better it must be —, but the fact is that even when classicism was at its height the antiquaries anticipated the moods of Thomas Warton, Gray, and Walpole, and that these three men instead of being forerunners were the products of an interest in the Middle Ages of which the continuity had never been broken in the classic period. An unprejudiced reading of the antiquaries, and especially of their letters, leads to the pleasant discovery that they were every whit as human as those who have misinterpreted the spirit in which they worked.

To throw the opinions of the antiquaries into bolder relief, let me first place over against them Evelyn's denunciation of Gothic architecture. It is the more necessary to do this, as he has very lately been credited by Mr. Clark with a "sincere admiration" for the buildings of the Middle Ages. It is true that on more than one occasion he does express what appears to be a cordial appreciation of Gothic architecture, but it is noteworthy that almost without exception these brief passages of commendation occur in his *Diary* previous to the Restoration.[5] Yet when in his *Account of Architects and Architecture*, which he wrote as an introduction to his translation of Fréart's *Parallèle de l'Architecture Antique et de la Moderne*, he undertook to formulate his considered opinion, he expatiated vehemently and at length on what impressed him as the gross deficiencies of medieval architecture. The artistic poverty of England had stirred Evelyn's national pride, and, having traveled in Italy and France, he returned dazzled by the ideal of King Charles and the nobility as grandiose patrons of art. But he had to confess the indifference of the English aristocracy to architecture — an art which "the most noble Youth of *Italy*" valued as part of their culture and about which they could converse in technical language with discriminating intelligence. Evelyn regarded as proof of this indifference of the English upper classes the old mansions in which they were content to live — "those irregular Congestions, rude and brutish Inventions, which generally so Deform and Incommode the several Habitations of our Gentry, both in City and Country."

But more significant than this opinion is Evelyn's contemptuous disapproval of what is now esteemed a masterpiece of Perpendicular Gothic:

I dare Report my self to any Man of Judgment, and that has the least Taste of Order and Magnificence; If after he has look'd a while upon *King Henry* the VIIth's *Chappel* at *Westminster*; Gaz'd on its sharp *Angles*, *Jetties*, Narrow Lights, lame *Statues*, *Lace* and other *Cut-work*, and *Crinkle Crankle*; and shall then turn his Eyes on the *Banqueting-House* built at *White-Hall* by *Inego Jones* after the Antient manner; or on what his *Majesties* present *Surveyor* Sir *Christopher Wren* has lately advanc'd at St. *Paul*'s; . . . I say, let him well consider, and compare them judiciously, without Partiality and Prejudice; and then Pronounce, which of the two *Manners* strikes the Understanding as well as the Eye with the more Majesty, and solemn Greatness . . .

Evelyn proceeds to specify even more definitely what offends him in the design of Henry VII's Chapel:

then the Universal and unreasonable Thickness of the Walls, Clumsy Buttresses, Towers, sharp pointed Arches, Doors, and other Apertures, without Proportion . . . Turrets, and Pinacles, thick set with *Munkies* and *Chimaeras* . . . dissipate, and break the Angels of the Sight, and so Confound it, that one cannot consider it with any Steadiness, where to begin or end; taking off from that noble *Aier* and *Grandure*, Bold and Graceful manner, which the *Antients* had so well, and judiciously Establish'd . . .

From this scorn of one Gothic edifice Evelyn with unflinching logic advances to the indictment of other great medieval buildings, Continental as well as English:

But, in this Sort have they, and their Followers [i.e., the Goths and Moors] ever since fill'd, not all *Europe* alone, but *Asia* and *Africa* besides, with Mountains of Stone, Vast, and Gygantic Buildings indeed; but not Worthy the Name of *Architecture*: Witness . . . what are yet standing at *Westminster*, *Canterbury*, *Salisbury*, *Peterborow*, *Ely*, *Wells*, *Beverly*, *Lincoln*, *Gloucester*, *York*, *Durham*, and other *Cathedrals* and *Minsters* . . . at *Amiens*, *Paris*, *Roan*, *Tours*, *Lyons*, etc.

in *France* . . . and compare them (almost numberless as they are) with *One* St. *Peter*'s at *Rome* . . .[6]

My condensation of these passages has, in fact, weakened their violence, yet the character of this tirade is all too clear. With the blindness of a fanatic Evelyn has completely lost his usual sense of proportion. It is astonishing to find him pleading for impartiality of judgment when he is himself incapable of it, damning without reservation all the greatest monuments of the Middle Ages. His *Account* is one of the earliest and most unsparing criticisms of Gothic in English. As his work was widely read and went through a considerable number of editions, it gave the cue, I suspect, to many a subsequent eighteenth-century critic of medieval architecture, and scattered in the minds of countless readers the seeds of prejudice against any type of architecture that did not obey the Vitruvian canons.

This admiration for classic architecture, accompanied by an indifference and even contempt for that of the Middle Ages, was a fashion as much as a sincere judgment based on a genuine understanding and appreciation of Italian architecture. When it was approved by the King, the court, and people of wealth and power who had taken the grand tour and were forming collections of Italian pictures and antique sculpture, classic architecture came to enjoy social prestige, but one may well believe that even for a good many years after the Restoration the great body of Englishmen whose taste had not been cultivated by travel and who lived at a distance from London remained loyal in spirit as in fact to the architecture to which their eyes had always been accustomed. Many cities and towns, as is clear from the diary of Celia Fiennes, retained, except for a few new houses, their ancient appearance. Even in 1742, to judge from its description in Defoe's *Tour*, Newcastle was still a medieval city: "The town is defended by an exceeding strong wall, wherein are seven gates, and as many turrets. . . . The buildings being very close and old, render it incommodious." [7] Coventry was equally medieval:

The buildings are very old, and in some places very much decayed; the timber-built houses project forwards into the street towards one another, insomuch that in the narrow streets they almost touch at the top; a method of building formerly much practised in London.[8]

Moreover, the number of ancient houses that in towns and villages all over England have survived until to-day indicates that the country did not undergo any sudden and complete architectural transformation. College buildings erected at Oxford during the seventeenth century are, of course, a remarkable example of the continued employment of the Gothic style in what was one of the building centers of England. It is indicative of the same conservatism that when one of Wren's wooden models for St. Paul's was under consideration, some did not "relish" it on the ground that "it deviated too much from the old Gothic form of cathedral churches which they had been used to see and admire in the country." [9] Those who confine their reading to books written by men of letters and members of the traveled classes are too ready to infer that the opinions of a man like Evelyn were representative of those of the great majority of his fellow-countrymen, whereas he probably expressed the tastes of only a relatively small, but articulate, minority.

By contrast, what the antiquaries thought of Gothic architecture is important as the judgment of learned Englishmen who lived outside the social circles that were most strongly affected by currents of fashionable taste. It is this body of antiquarian opinion that we shall now examine.

During the summer of 1656, when Dugdale's *Antiquities of Warwickshire*, a work which signalized an epochal advance in the study of local history, arrived in Oxford, one of its first readers was Anthony à Wood. As anyone capable of sympathizing with such an experience will recognize instantaneously, Wood's account of the impression made upon him by Dugdale has the ring of absolute authenticity. His "tender affections and insatiable desire of knowledg" were kindled "by the reading of that book," and "his life, at this time and after, was a perfect Elysium." [10] Catching the flame of antiquarian enthusiasm, Wood undertook to do for Oxford and its environs what Dugdale had done for Warwickshire. It is in his diary and narrative of his research that Wood proves himself to have been no sluggish investigator of medieval monuments. Speaking of the Bocardo, or old North Gate of Oxford, he assures us of "its pristine beauty and strength, not only for fortifications but for battlements statues and armes theron," and in a tone of exasperation he records that in his own time the gate was used only as a common prison. He regrets that the Castle of Oxford and "those faire imbattleled structures" that surrounded it have also lost their "beauty" and are falling into decay. In particular he laments that in 1649 the Parliamentary garrison pulled down the four "stately towers . . . which were great or[nament] to that end of the city." [11] Even if Wood's epithets are more limited in range than the florid conventional vocabulary which the eighteenth-century romanticists popularized in such descriptions, is there not present in these passages a feeling for the picturesque effect of towers and battlements that to-day lures tourists to Carcassonne and San Gimignano? It was its varied silhouette, due to its turrets and pinnacles, that provided one reason for Evelyn's impatient criticism of Henry VII's Chapel, and with such an attitude Wood, at all events, had no sympathy. He also appreciated the decorative embellishments of medieval edifices. At the ancient abbey of Dorchester he notes that "the walls of the chancel have been all painted very gloriously with several sorts of beasts," and he rejoices that the figures of a lion, a griffin, and a leopard are still visible. He resents that the Cromwellians "daubed over with paint" the representations of prophets, apostles, and saints "in various and antique shapes" with which the backs of the stalls in the choir of Merton College had been decorated in the time of Henry VII. Nor was he alone in his regret at this wanton destruction, for it was lamented by "curious men that were admirers of antient painting."

More than fifty years before Walpole was adorning Strawberry Hill with bits of medieval decoration, Wood makes it plain that he felt the rich, somber beauty of stained glass. In 1693, when the newly elected chief of Merton College removed "the old windows in the warden's dining roome and hall under it, containing rebuses, fantasticks, devices, in almost all the paines" and replaced them by "square glass," Wood was very bitter. For although the Warden restored the armorial glass, Wood complained that "the majestick light of the room was lost." This folly would not have been committed, Wood whimsically alleged, if the Warden had been a bachelor, but as it was, he had a fastidious wife and six or seven daughters who induced him not only to dismantle the ancient windows, but also "to set up a coach having had none before." Wood's feeling for the emotional values of dim light is equally evident in his account of the abbey of Osney. Commenting on "the exquisiteness and variety every window did represent," he says that

> In the windows were the effigies of saints, kings, bishops and abbats most artificially (according to that age) depicted. Every payne almost therin being employed with the fancy of the limner, in such places (as it hath bin observed) where the light was diminished, did impose a more aufull reverence upon the adorer or religious apprehensions resembling therin the antient Romanes who for the most part made choise of shady places for their devotion.[12]

In the middle of the eighteenth century the popularity of *Il Penseroso* made "dim, religious light" one of the commonplaces of romantic rhapsody, but Wood felt the imaginative suggestiveness of such a light before the imitators of Milton converted it into a stage property of the poetry of gloom. To rate Wood's sentiment at its true worth, one should bear in mind that to a classicist like Wren a dimly illumined interior was repugnant. He praised the windows of Salisbury Cathedral simply because the light was not excluded by heavy mullions and tracery. Their designer was, in Wren's opinion, aware that nothing could be more beautiful than light.

On more than one occasion in the presence of ancient buildings and ruins Wood's spirit was chastened and pervaded by that feeling of pleasurable melancholy which is generally regarded as the peculiar development of the eighteenth century. Frequently he visited a secluded house "situated in a romancey place" in Bagley Wood, "to refresh his mind with a melancholy walke and with the retiredness of the place, as also with the shady box-arbours in the garden"; it was, he says, an ideal retreat for "a man that is given to devotion and learning." In 1657 he went to Eynesham:

> He was there wonderfully strucken with a veneration of the stately, yet much lamented, ruins of the abbey there, built before the Norman Conquest. . . . He spent some time with a melancholy delight in taking a prospect of the ruins of that place. All which, together with the entrance or the lodg, were soon after pulled downe, and the stones sold to build houses in that towne and neare it. The place hath yet some

ruins to shew, and to instruct the pensive beholder with an exemplary frailty.

Here, in these last phrases, is the seed of that fatal romantic tendency to extract from decay the cheerless but not unexpected truth that life is short. More important is it that Wood should on the eve of the Restoration regret the obliteration of a monument of Gothic architecture at the hands of mercenary vandals. In 1678 Wood visited the ruins of the abbey of Malmesbury:

> The porch . . . is the most stately and costly carved piece of work that my eyes ever beheld, carrying with it also a very venerable face of antiquity. It is broad withoutside and by degrees as you enter is lesser, and upon the columns that so lessen the entry are well carved little scripture stories in every little part of each column . . . When I entered into the church I had a strange veneration come upon me to see the ruins of such a majestic and gigantic pile, with windows over windows and walks over walks in the walls, stately pillars, curious carved work every where.

The recessed doorway and especially the succession of lateral columns enriched "in every little part" with sculptured incidents from Biblical history were a source of gratification to Wood; but to a classicist they would have been distasteful. The classicist was invariably irritated by what he regarded as the exuberant detail of Gothic decoration because such detail was contrary to antique simplicity. Undoubtedly the "curious carved work" which Wood observed in the interior of the abbey would have been sneered at by Evelyn as mere "crinkle-crankle." It is not surprising that Wren's favorable impression of Salisbury was partly due to its absence of abundant ornament, which he thought tended to "glut the eye." Unhampered by the dogmas of classicism, Wood, on the other hand, sensed the dignity of medieval architecture and was stirred mysteriously by its grandeur even in decay.

In the seventeenth century there were evidently many persons who, although they did not possess Wood's antiquarian interests to predispose them in favor of Gothicism, yet admired the old buildings which the classicists were energetic in discrediting. According to Wood, strangers who entered Oxford by the North Gate took "great delight" in its battlements and statues, and foreigners who viewed the noble roof of the Divinity School grew enthusiastic over "its great variety of exquisite sculpture"; even Charles II, when he visited Oxford in 1681, "spent some time" in examining it. As a facile journalist, Ned Ward could not resist the temptation of flamboyant statement; yet, after due allowance has been made for his idiosyncrasy, his praise of medieval buildings is another interesting example of a judgment made in complete independence of the architectural taste of the aristocratic classes. The author of *The London Spy* could not behold Westminster Abbey "without reverence and amazement. Which was raised to that stupendous height, and beautified with such ornamental statues, that the bold strokes of excelling artists . . . will always remain visible." When Ward describes Henry VII's Chapel, the building Wren mildy commended as "a nice piece of embroidery work," he spreads the wings of his rhetoric. He does not hesitate to say that it might

> justly claim the admiration of the whole universe, such inimitable perfections are apparent in every part of the whole composure, which looks so far exceeding human excellence that a man would think it was knit together by the fingers of angels, pursuant to the directions of Omnipotence.

When, moreover, in the course of his wanderings about London Ward came face to face with old Northumberland House, the mansion of the great Percy family near the Strand, he confessed that he "beheld with satisfaction the handiwork of our forefathers." Then he adds significantly that in the antiquity of this edifice, scarred though it was by time, he "could discern much more beauty than my genius can discover in any modern building." [13]

In other words, although Ward was aware that the person of taste was supposed to prefer structures in the Italian style, and had made an effort to appreciate them, his liking for England's older architecture had proved too strong to be dislodged at the behest of the newer fashion. In this mood of loyalty to the past and with a pang of regret Ward recalls that Northumberland House, "so magnificent and venerable," is no longer the scene of such hospitality as dignified it in days gone by. To be sure, Ward's dithyrambic praise of medieval architecture is too general to suggest that he had any real specific knowledge of it, but it does convey to us the certainty that he, as well as Anthony à

Wood, still cherished what many of his more sophisticated and more traveled contemporaries held in contempt.

At the outset of the eighteenth century the interest in England's historic past was consolidated by the establishment of the London Society of Antiquaries. The Society was, in reality, a revival of a similar group which, after an existence of some years, had been suppressed for unknown reasons when James I came to the throne. At first meeting informally in 1707, the members of the new Society were regularly organized under elected officers in 1717 and met weekly at the Young Devil Tavern in Fleet Street. The principal concern of the gathering was the study of the antiquities of Great Britain, by which term was to be understood all memorials of British culture antecedent to the reign of James I. The movement, once started, gained ground. At Spalding, Lincolnshire, the first and most famous of the provincial societies was founded in 1712.[14] As Lincoln Cathedral, Croyland Abbey, and other monastic remains as well as memorials of Roman civilization made Lincolnshire a particularly rich field for antiquarian investigation, there was every reason why the Spalding Society should flourish. Although entirely independent of the London Society, it maintained closest communication with it.

Similar societies were in turn formed at Peterborough, Stamford, Doncaster, Wisbeach, Lincoln, Worcester, and Dublin. For a time the Peterborough Society met appropriately in the ancient gate-house of the cathedral, just as that at Spalding assembled, in later years of its history, in a former monastery fitted up as a library and museum. While the scope of the different societies varied, including as a rule Celtic and Roman antiquities as well as medieval, that the latter should be considered at all was a sign that there was no prejudice against the Middle Ages. In fact, in a list of possible undertakings drawn up at some date in the first quarter of the century by a member of the London Society, phases of medieval civilization were very far from being neglected. Such items as castles, costumes, chivalry, heraldry, weapons, instruments, manufactures, and handicrafts, as well as architecture, painting, and sculpture were specified as deserving of research. Moreover, the writer of the memorandum urged that properly qualified persons should be sent to travel over England and abroad "to draw ancient fortifications, castles, churches, houses, tombs, inscriptions, epitaphs, painted glass, etc. and, if need be, to buy up the most curious for the Society." Of course this was an ideal plan, and is not to be taken too seriously. However, the prospectus does indicate that these early investigators had a vision of what it would be both interesting and important to know about medieval civilization.

The antiquaries, to be sure, were at first indiscriminate in their interest, and with naive impartiality moved back and forth from the period of Roman occupation to the Middle Ages. To their contemporaries many of the matters which excited their concern seemed trivial, even grotesque — a mere fussy "busyness" over a carving, a sculptural fragment, or a dusty manuscript. But only by the collection of beads can a necklace be put together. As the century progressed, antiquaries gradually accumulated a great body of facts about castles, churches, stained glass, heraldry, baptismal fonts, coins, manuscripts, inscriptions, and costumes. Thus they helped dispel the mist of ignorance and prejudice that enveloped the Middle Ages. Before such knowledge the scorn of the classicist ultimately had to give way. The traveler of classical training and taste had for decades been going to Italy to refine his culture, to confirm by observation what he had read in the authors of antiquity, to study faithfully and reverently, and to draw and to paint with ardor the remains of Roman civilization. The antiquarians by degrees taught their fellow-countrymen that there were at home in England churches, castles, and works of art worthy of respectful examination, reproduction, and preservation. By monographs on individual monuments and by county, municipal, and parochial histories they fostered local pride, developed the historic sense, made the medieval past more real and vivid, and slowly created a sensibility to the artistic values and the emotional appeal of an art not classical in conception and feeling. All this was a work of time, but in the end knowledge, supplanting indifference and contempt, flowered into a sympathetic understanding of the Middle Ages.

Yet even in the seventeenth century, as we have seen, long before the revival of the Society of Antiquaries, men like Anthony à Wood and Ned Ward expressed genuine enthusiasm for the monuments of England's architectural past. This feeling was communicated to the following century in spite of the vogue of classicism. Thomas Hearne's account of his walks in the countryside of Oxfordshire discloses attractive glimpses of a scholar indulging his taste for archeology and the consolations of the wayside inn — by no means an incompatible combination of interests. In June, 1718, for example, Hearne walked from Oxford to Ditchley to see the ancient seat of the Earl of Lichfield. Here are bits of his simple narrative:

It being a very fine morning, I walked gently on, and made observations. . . . From Aristotle's well I passed over pleasant meadows and other ground between both Wolvercotes.

He visited the ruins of the nunnery at Godstow and lingered at the George Inn in Woodstock:

My ingenious, excellent friend told me last night, that he would ride to Ditchley, and stop at this inn, where, if he met me, he would leave his horse, and walk with me to Ditchley. I staid therefore and smoked a pipe here. But he not coming, I went on before, and left word that I was gone.

He climbed over a stile, crossed Woodstock Park, and

walked a mile and an half through a very pleasant country, in a good measure adorned with marvellous pleasant woods, till I came against Ditchley House . . . This old house is a very notable thing, and I think I was never better pleased with any sight whatsoever than with this house, which hath been the seat of persons of true loyalty and virtue. . . . I was mightily delighted with the sight of this old hall, and was pleased the more because it is adorned with old stags' horns, under some of which are . . . inscriptions on brass plates.

He saw the armor belonging to the Earl's ancestors, viewed with interest the small bedroom which Queen Elizabeth had at one time occupied, and examined all the old family portraits in the Long Gallery on the first floor.

About four o'clock, Mr. Calvert and I returned home. I went on foot the horse way, Mr. Calvert riding my pace, and sometimes walking with me. . . . We stopped and refreshed ourselves at Woodstock, at the Bear Inn, which is now the principal inn in Woodstock.[15]

From this pleasant narrative of a day's outing it is evident that the antiquary was not always such a ridiculous figure as contemporary satire would lead us to suppose. His pedantry was not, at all events, so great as to chill his response to the historic appeal of an ancient edifice. Ward's regretful recollection of the former hospitality of Northumberland House and Hearne's pleasure in the old hall of Ditchley, reminiscent of the day when it was the center of household life, anticipate the sentiments which a later generation was to express more self-consciously, and often, I suspect, less sincerely.

William Stukeley, another famous antiquary of the first half of the eighteenth century, resembled Chatterton in his youthful enthusiasm for medievalism. As he was born in 1687, when classical architecture was daily gaining greater authority, one might suppose that Stukeley would automatically have become a fervid admirer of the Italian style, but such was not the case. Although he matriculated at Cambridge in 1704, when he was only seventeen years old, even before that date the archeological interest that was to enrich his life had manifested itself. When as a boy he accompanied his father to the assizes at Lincoln, he neglected the proceedings of the court to roam through the town, delighting in the cathedral, the ruins of the Bishop's Palace, and the ancient monuments. About this time he made a habit of visiting the remains of Barnwell Abbey "to sigh over" its decay and to engage in the more practical task of cutting tobacco-stoppers out of pieces of the old yew trees. When he was finally settled in Cambridge, Stukeley haunted King's College Chapel to contemplate the glories of that incomparable Gothic building.

In 1709 — he was at the time twenty-two years old — while on a visit in Northamptonshire in company with a friend's sister, he took antiquarian rambles in the vicinity:

> We traveled together like errant virtuosos, and when we came to an old ruined castle, etc. we climbed together through every story and staircase, mutually helping one another and pulling each other over gaping arches and rugged heaps of rubbish, and when I had occasion to draw a view of them out, as we sat upon a stone or the grass, she held my ink horn or my paper and was very serviceable and assistant in taking my designs, and all without any reserve or immodesty; nor

could any aged philosophers have conversed together with more innocent familiarity or less guilt even in thought or intention. Nor could travailing [*sic*] curiosity or antiquarian researches be rendered so agreeable as with a fair and witty companion and fellow-laborer, and when we returned home, my young disciple could entertain the family with so very curious relation of the curiosities we had seen, that it would be difficult to say whether so nice a taste in the remains of ancient time most recommended a young lady or that refined study became more lovely and delightful for her sake. She is since married to a gentleman in Wales.[16]

These excursions in the cause of medievalism, rendered, to be sure, immeasurably more enjoyable by the charm of Martha Lucas, were undertaken in the very year that the youthful Pope, publishing his *Pastorals*, introduced himself to the literary world as the bard of lovesick classical shepherds. Even if, at the moment, fashionable society was more inclined to listen to the sorrows of Strephon and Daphnis, it was only a question of time before the interest which made Stukeley draw ruined abbeys would crystallize and become the dominant note in poetry. Thomas Warton was only seventeen when he depicted in *The Pleasures of Melancholy* (1745) the allurement of "some wasted tower," but thirty-six years previously young Stukeley would have been in sympathetic agreement with the lines which Warton was to write on a blank leaf in Dugdale's *Monasticon*:

> Nor rough, nor barren, are the winding ways
> Of hoar Antiquity, but strown with flowers.

Much has been made of the archeological tours which Thomas Warton undertook whenever he could escape from the academic sterilities of eighteenth-century Oxford. But Anthony à Wood and Thomas Hearne already knew the pleasures of such antiquarian rambles, and Stukeley discovered them even in his boyhood. The habit which he had happily acquired in his early years Stukeley retained through life. While Warton was still in his teens, Stukeley was with undiminished zest visiting and studying the architectural remains of the Middle Ages. In 1735, 1743, 1744, 1746, and 1747 he made journeys to the ruins of Croyland Abbey — an enterprise which he described as "a religious pilgrimage."

Stukeley's enthusiasm was, moreover, not without its practical results. Professor Beers has remarked that admirers of stained glass are indebted to Walpole for its preservation. But in the seventeenth century Anthony à Wood had felt the beauty of the "majestic light" of a medieval interior, had known the fascination of armorial devices and grotesque figures as decorative features of ancient glass, and had deplored the replacement of the latter by glass of modern manufacture. Nearly fifteen years before Walpole had revealed his interest in medievalism by the rebuilding of Strawberry Hill, Stukeley was concerned over the destruction of old glass in the churches of Stamford and was active in his effort to save as much of it as possible. In 1736 "with great regret" he noted "what miserable havoc is made daily," in particular at "St. John's and St. George's, where the most painted glass is left." He explains that parishioners tear out old glass in the belief that a church is too dark, and that when they discover that they get more light than they bargained for, they are forced to cover the window with curtains. Taking advantage of the indifference of the townspeople, the glaziers encouraged this destruction so that they might profit by the installation of new glass. Stukeley's account of what took place at St. Martin's in 1737 is illustrative of the situation. As the minister, Mr. Popple — his name has a Dickensian connotation — was opposed to wearing spectacles, he ordered the old glass to be removed, but when plain glass was put in he complained of the glare and insisted that the light should be shut out with hangings. It was, moreover, the custom of the glaziers, it appears, to break up the pattern of the old windows and to sell the pieces of glass to whoever would buy them. If Stukeley heard in time of what was being done, he went from glazier to glazier and purchased such fragments as he could find. He records his disappointment when, on one occasion, he discovered that he had arrived too late to save all the founder's window of St. George's, which had been taken apart with the exception of the founder's figure. This figure he immediately bought. Much of the old glass which his alertness and taste rescued from destruction Stukeley either gave away to friends or used himself in the enrichment of the windows of his own house at Barnhill.[17] In 1753, when Walpole wrote to Sir Horace Mann that he had "amassed such quantities of painted glass, that every window in my castle will be illuminated with it," [18] he was only describing what Stukeley had previously undertaken, perhaps much more wholeheartedly.

But Stukeley was not alone in his solicitude for medieval buildings. Indeed, in his taste for Gothic architecture, the printer and topographer Thomas Gent was no less conspicuous. In 1733, when Walpole was only sixteen years of age and Gray only seventeen, Gent was expressing fervent appreciation of the somber beauty of an ancient ruin. It was the remains of Kirkstall Abbey, Yorkshire, that occasioned his enthusiasm:

> A Place, once so famous, excited my Curiosity to ride thither one Morning, in order to view it. No sooner it appear'd to my Eyes at a Distance from a neighbouring Hill, but it really produc'd in me, an inward Veneration. Well might the Chief of the Anchorets leave the Southern Parts for this pleasant Abode; and the Abbots also desire so delightful a Situation. I left my Horse at a Style; and passing over it, came down, by a gentle Descent, towards its awful Ruins; which, Good God! were enough to strike the most harden'd Heart, into the softest and most serious Reflexion. . . .

In this mood Gent felt impelled to comment on "its ancient beauty," noting that "stately Gate North West of the Abbey, (now converted to a Farm-House, as may appear by the magnificent Arches on each Side, but wall'd up) thro' which they were once us'd to pass into a spacious Plain, at the West End of the Church. . . ." He observed "the stately reverential Isles in the whole Church," the cemetery of the monks, "now made an Orchard," with lofty trees "casting an awful, gloomy Shade"; and he regretted that, at the time of the Dissolution, "this stately Building" was destroyed when it had "arrived to its full Perfection and beauty. . . . Now only is it a meer Shell, with roofless Walls; having yet a well-built but uncover'd Steeple; the Eastern Parts embraced by its beloved Ivy; and all about the whole Pile desolate, solitary, and forlorn." [19] In such a passage as this there is no note of perfunctory regret. Like Anthony à Wood and Stukeley before him, Gent was anticipating the mood of romantic melancholy that a few decades later was to be the stock-in-trade of even the most mediocre poets.

If the power to appreciate the English cathedrals be a fair test by which to discover the presence of romantic feeling, it is a criterion which can be employed in the present discussion to great advantage. An examination of books evidently rarely read makes clear that when Evelyn and Wren spoke disparagingly of medieval ecclesiastical architecture, their opinion did not represent the universal judgment. The classic grandeur of St. Paul's did not, in fact, have the effect of silencing those who still admired "the old way of building." Although the writers of books of travel were unenlightened by any real knowledge of Gothic architecture, and summed up their esthetic judgments in a sentence or two, their descriptive epithets make it perfectly evident that they were free from the classical contempt for ancient churches. At the close of the seventeenth century and for some time after, no word of praise in behalf of Gothic art can be neglected entirely. In *The New State of England* (1691) Guy Miege makes short, but approving, comment on most of the great English cathedrals. Lincoln, he declares, is "one of the stateliest Piles in England, and perhaps in Christendom; high seated on a Hill, and from thence discerned all over the Country." Lichfield is "a fair Cathedral, and that sufficient of it self to renoun the Place," and Salisbury is "indeed one of the principal Ornaments of England" and "a most stately and magnificent Church."[20] In *Travels over England, Scotland, and Wales* (1700) James Brome is equally brief, but commendatory. In *A New View of London* (1708), the anonymous author (Edward Hatton) is less restrained; he describes Henry VII's Chapel as "this unparallel'd Edifice," "a Pattern of Ingenuity," "the Admiration of all Travellers," and the possessor of an "Incomparable Roof."[21] In *A Journey through England* (2nd edition, 1722) John Macky praises the interior of Winchester, the tower and the cloisters of Gloucester, and the choir and the chapter-house of York. In *A Survey of the Cathedrals* (1727–30) Browne Willis has scattered through his vast accumulation of antiquarian lore phrases of approval for which he deserves recognition in an age reputed to be anti-Gothic.

In *A Tour through the Whole Island of Great Britain* (1724–27) Defoe, like his predecessors, limits his commendation of ecclesiastical buildings to a few brief sentences until he has occasion to describe the cathedral at Lichfield. His enthusiasm for this edifice is at this date remarkable. It is, he says,

> one of the finest and most beautiful in *England*, especially for the Outside, the Form and Figure of the Building, the carv'd work'd [i.e., work], Imagery, and the three beautiful Spires; the like of which are not to be seen in one Church, no not in *Europe*.
>
> . . . the *West* Prospect of it is charming, the two Spires on the Corner Towers being in themselves perfect Beauties of Architect [i.e., Architecture], in the old *Gothic* Way of Building, but made still more shining and glorious by a third Spire, which rising from the main Tower in the Body of the Church, surmounts the other two, and shews itself exactly between them.
>
> It is not easy to describe the Beauty of the *West* End; you enter by three large Doors in the Porch or Portico, which is as broad as the whole Front; the Spaces between the Doors are fill'd with carv'd Work and Imagery, no Place being void, where (by the *Rules* of *Architect* [i.e., Architecture]) any Ornament could be plac'd.
>
> . . . between these Pinnacles, on the Top of each Tower, rises a Spire equal in Height, in Thickness, and in Workmanship, but so beautiful no Pen can describe them.

Notwithstanding that Defoe regarded Lincoln as "a very noble" structure in a situation superior to that of any other cathedral in England, he declared that its western towers were "mean, small, and low, and not to be named with those at *Litchfield*."[22] Such a eulogy of Lichfield must have had a wide, even if intangible, influence. It sanctioned a taste for medieval architecture among those who were already inclined to prefer it, and fostered appreciation among those who had previously been indifferent by attracting their attention to its more remarkable features. Finally, it reminds us that even in the first quarter of the eighteenth century all currents of contemporary taste were not flowing in classical channels, and that Campbell's *Vitruvius Britannicus*, with the publication of which Defoe's *Tour* was virtually coincident, is not the sole index by which to judge what Englishmen were thinking about architecture.

If we make, moreover, a reasonable allowance for differences of individual opinion, it is noteworthy that subsequent editors of the *Tour* maintained the sympathetic spirit of Defoe's comments on cathedrals, and as the accounts of them were frequently amplified, one can only infer that these additions are indicative of a corresponding increase of interest in the cathedrals on the part of both those who described them and those who visited them. At times the later editors significantly modified Defoe's judgments. He had, for example, slighted the grand Norman cathedral of Gloucester, describing it with wretched inadequacy as "well built," "plain," but of "a very handsome appearance." The writer of the third edition (1742) warms to his subject and is eloquent on the vista of the nave through the finely vaulted choir, the splendor of the great east window, and the "exquisitely beautiful cloisters." [23] Although Defoe admired the Chapter-House at York, he thought the inscription "Ut rosa flos florum, sic est domus ista domorum" an overstatement. The second editor (1738) deletes Defoe's qualifying phrase, asserts that the inscription is deserved, and maintains that the Chapter-House "exceeds anything of that kind in the world for magnificence and curious workmanship." [24] That pains should be thus taken to do justice to the cathedrals, where, in the opinion of the successive editors, these buildings had previously been neglected, is testimony that the sentiment in favor of Gothic architecture, which, indeed, had never died but had been only temporarily eclipsed, was growing stronger and more articulate as the mid-century approached.[25]

Scarcely had Defoe completed the publication of the *Tour* when Thomas Gent issued in 1730 his *Ancient and Modern History of the Famous City of York, and in a particular Manner of its Magnificent Cathedral.* Written, as he tells us in the Preface, so that visitors, having this guide to "the inimitable Beauties" of the edifice, might be able to talk more intelligently of them, he cruelly inflicts upon the reader, it is true, much dull information about sepulchers, epitaphs, and the identity of the entombed; but he redeems himself by his sense of the importance and grandeur of the Minster. It is in Gent's description of the Chapter-House, however, that he shows the unusual individuality of his judgment. His enjoyment of the humorous whimsicality of the sculptured decoration of the stalls is at this date really extraordinary. There is

> so great a Variety of delectable Fancies, as shall confound him who shall go about to determine which among the rest is most curious.
>
> Here are antick Postures, both of Men and Beasts; In one Place, and in another, is a Man cut out half Way, as if he was thrusting and striving, with all his Strength, to get out of a Window, or some narrow Passage. In another are several Faces, having different Aspects, as

one crying, another laughing, a third making wry Mouths, &c. And, what is also very ingenious in another Place, is to be seen an old bald pated Fryer kissing a young Nun in a Corner: And in the Chapiters [capitals] of the Pillars near it, are the Faces of several other Nuns, as well old as young, peeping and laughing at the old amorous Fryer.

Other Chapiters represent the Leaves of several Trees, Fruits, and Flowers; and the Pendants also, with such wonderful and admirable Variety, that strike Wonder in the Beholders, the most of them gilt, and some painted.[26]

His judgment warped by his desire for simplicity and his indifference to the number of "streaks of the tulip," the classicist was generally prone to dismiss summarily the beautiful details of Gothic decoration on the ground that there was too much of it. As this decoration was, he thought, all more or less "crinkle-crankle" and distracted the eye by its very abundance, he never examined it long enough to catch its spirit or to appraise its execution. Then, too, the classicist was always in danger of priggishness in his artistic judgments; when he did fall a victim of this bias, he loftily disapproved of descents into playfulness and frowned upon humorous ornament as out of keeping with architectural dignity. Evelyn, it will be remembered, had only scorn for the "monkeys and chimeras" that disported themselves upon Henry VII's Chapel. From these esthetic handicaps Gent was singularly free. He had the audacity to express his relish of the Chaucerian mood in which the medieval carver with satiric malice had depicted indiscreet nuns and wayward friars. In the course of all my reading I recall no similarly striking instance in which an eighteenth-century writer has cared to show that he had examined medieval sculptured decoration with minute attention and perceived its incidental humor with delight.[27]

Stukeley's enthusiasm for York Minster, expressed on the occasion of his visit in 1740, was so fervid that he thought it superior — his impression of the Roman buildings, to be sure, was based on prints, as he had never been in Italy — to either the Pantheon or St. Peter's. Even Lord Burlington, the great Palladian who reproduced the Villa Rotonda at Chiswick, conceded that a Gothic cathedral might achieve greatness. In view of the usual conception of him as a leader of the classical "die-hards," his tribute is remarkable. It occurs in an address which the ardent and scholarly Gothicist, James Essex, made before the Society of Antiquaries. Glad to secure Burlington's support for his own ideas, Essex cited the Earl's opinion of Lincoln Cathedral as quoted in a letter of a Mr. Simpson:

> I have his Lordship's leave to say that this is by far the noblest Gothic structure in England, and York in no degree comparable to it. He even prefers our west front to anything of the kind in Europe, and says that whoever had the conducting of it was well acquainted with the noblest buildings of old Rome, and had united some of their greatest beauties in that one work.[28]

It is not important that Burlington's explanation of the grandeur of Lincoln is without historical foundation; he was in this emergency employing only the characteristic method by which the classicist placated his artistic conscience whenever he found himself liking a work of medieval origin, whether a ballad or a building. His acknowledgment that the cathedral possessed such qualities of architectural excellence as to put it, in a measure, on a basis of esthetic equality with classic edifices is what makes Burlington's criticism surprising. Another point deserves remark. The date of Simpson's letter is 1740, a year after Gray's often-quoted description of Amiens Cathedral:

> a huge Gothic building, beset on the outside with thousands of small statues, and within adorned with beautiful painted windows, and a vast number of chapels dressed out in all the finery of altar-pieces, embroidery, gilding, and marble.[29]

Beside Defoe's eulogy of Lichfield, Gent's praise of York, and Burlington's commendation of Lincoln, Gray's opinion appears rather anemic, being superficial in observation and marking no advance in appreciation. Indeed, his further comment that the cathedral at Siena was "laboured with a gothic niceness and delicacy in the old-fashioned way"[30] creates the suspicion that he was at this time tainted with the "crinkle-crankle" theory of medieval decoration. Gray is not, then, to be listed among those who stimulated enthusiasm for the Gothic cathedral during the first half of the eighteenth century. But even if he be eliminated from consideration, the admiration of others for this great type of medieval construction suggests that an appreciative attitude was more common than has generally been supposed. Nor was this appreciative attitude confined to the antiquaries. They, it might be contended, had what might be described as a professional prejudice in favor of medieval building that predetermined their preference. The writers of travel-books, Defoe, Gent, and their lesser brethren, also extolled the cathedral, and voiced what may justly be taken, I think, as the sentiments of the average intelligent Englishman who was not afflicted with the superiority complex of the man of taste. For these reasons Sir Leslie Stephen's claim that to Walpole belongs the distinction of being among the first of his countrymen to discover the beauty of the English cathedrals is patently at variance with the facts.[31]

Regret for the progressive destruction of ancient buildings was the natural accompaniment of this interest in medieval architecture. Even in 1657 Anthony à Wood lamented that the ruins of the abbey at Eynesham were pulled down to furnish cheap building material for houses in the vicinity. In 1699 Ned Ward, who "beheld with satisfaction the handiwork of our forefathers," acknowledged that nothing affected him with greater distress than the annihilation of some relic of antiquity. In 1718 a friend in Gloucester reported to Hearne "with grief" that "great havoc" had already been wrought in the cathedral and that the destruction of "a very beautiful stone arch," a small chapel, and an attractive altar was unfortunately in contemplation. In 1735, when he was at Croyland Abbey, Stukeley denounced the owners of the ruin, a Mr. Hunter and a Mr. Butler, for countenancing the demolition of the impressive pile. On subsequent visits he viewed with indignation the great gaps in the wall where magnificent windows had been torn out, and bitterly records that in 1712 "hundreds of loads of the religious stone" had been disposed of in Spalding after a fire in that town.

The editor of the third edition (1742) of Defoe's *Tour* enlarges upon the previous accounts of Glastonbury,[32] and what he adds has to do with the gradual and wanton dismantling of the remains of the abbey. When the editor formerly visited Glastonbury, he found "magnificent ruins" there, but since then a Presbyterian tenant had rifled the edifice for building material, which he sold to the highest bidder. "And they were actually stripping St. Joseph's Chapel for that purpose, and the squared stones were laid up by lots in the Abbot's kitchen." Although a superstitious fear of the founder's curse generally prevented the townspeople from using the stones in their houses, they were willing to tempt his wrath when occasion arose to build a road, a barn, or a stable. Nevertheless, throughout the town the editor observed "the tattered remains of doors, windows, bases, capitals of pillars, etc. brought from the Abbey and put into every poor cottage." He was especially incensed that the Abbot's lodging had been torn down and that out of its stones had been erected an incongruous house adorned here and there with the armorial insignia of kings and princes. He also noted that St. Mary's Chapel, formerly roofless, had been provided with a thatched covering, and was degraded into a stable. The walls of St. Edgar's Chapel "are overgrown with ivy, which is the only thing here in a flourishing condition, every thing else presenting a most melancholy, though venerable aspect." His conclusion is that the townspeople should spare the ancient buildings for their own profit, if for no other reason, for they were largely supported by "the great concourse of strangers" who went there "purposely to see this Abbey." This is an extremely interesting comment: even in 1742, in the blessed days before the charabanc, the number of sightseers who were interested in a Gothic ruin was sufficiently large to make the care of tourists the "greateşt trade" of a town.

Concern for old buildings was not manifested merely in regret at their reckless demolition. In many instances it led to their restoration. In 1739, when the rains which had penetrated the roof of Roslyn Chapel threatened to do it serious injury, Sir John Clerk, a gentleman with an affection for antiquities, persuaded the owner, Lord Sinclair, to undertake its repair. As Roger Gale informed Stukeley, the work was entirely supervised by Sir John, and there was every expectation that the famous chapel, "a most noble Gothic structure," would be "as beautiful as ever." [33] When the ruins of Roche Abbey, Yorkshire, picturesquely hidden amid woods and boulders, were gradually disappearing in consequence of the depredations of persons who wanted stones to rebuild churches or put up houses, the Earl of Scarborough intervened and saved the remains from complete annihilation. Then the dying sunlight playing over the shattered nave, the broken arches, and the tombs enveloped the scene with solemnity and, according to the editor of Defoe's *Tour* (1742), inspired "a contemplative melancholy, oftentimes pleasing as well as proper to indulge." [34] In a similar spirit of solicitude for the relics of the past Mr. Child of Farnham, Surrey, rescued what remained of the ruins of Waverley Abbey from a marauding farmer in want of stones to mend a road.[35] Sometimes when the repair of an ancient building was undertaken, it was no more successful than the eighteenth-century attempts to "improve" Shakespeare. Very modern in tone and reminiscent of many a protest of our own time is Stukeley's indignation at the defiant disregard of architectural fitness evident in Peterborough Cathedral in 1747:

> They are new whitewashing, or rather dawbing the cathedral, and new painting the roof in ridiculous filligree work, party-coloured, that has no meaning in it; and above all they have, for greater ornament, as they fancy, painted the ceiling over the high altar in imitation of marble. They have made a new quire of paltry fir, painted over, in a most tastless and mean manner, and after laying out a great sum of money have really deformed this most august and venerable structure.[36]

Manifestly in the eighteenth century the ways of the restorer were viewed critically by those who had a sympathetic acquaintance with medieval architecture.

These matters would not, perhaps, need so much remark if in previous discussions of the Gothic "revival" misleading statements had not been made in regard to the restoration of ancient buildings as a phase of that movement. Professor Beers has credited "Walpole and his followers" with the preservation of "many a half-ruinous abbey," but in this laudable enterprise Walpole was, as I have pointed out, anticipated by Viscount Weymouth, Sir John Clerk, Lord Sinclair, the Earl of Scarborough, and Mr. Child. Further search would, no doubt, bring to light additional instances of restoration in the early decades of the century. Moreover, indignation at the shameless demolition of old buildings, the feeling, after all, which must antedate any practical effort to save them, was not unknown even in the seventeenth century. Wood and Ned Ward, and after them

Stukeley and the editor of Defoe's *Tour* (1742), make it plain enough that to them the decay of medieval edifices was by no means a matter of indifference. Finally, Mr. Kenneth Clark's surprising statement "that soon after 1780 men began to notice that the old Gothic buildings were falling down" and "tried to prop them up" or to rebuild them implies that not until the ninth decade of the century was any attempt made to check the deterioration of such buildings.[37] Obviously it is just because historians of English culture in the eighteenth century have slighted or ignored the earlier evidence of Gothicism that they have been able to refer to the interest in medievalism as subsequent to the development of naturalistic gardening or as "reviving" at the approach of the mid-century.

Professor Havens is assuredly correct when he contends for a wider acknowledgment of the romantic elements in the age of Pope.[38] If he has erred at all, it is in not observing that those elements were existent at an even earlier period. Battlements, medieval painting, stained glass, ruins, old houses, and cathedrals were not, to be sure, the dominant preoccupations of the late seventeenth and early eighteenth centuries, for classicism was in full tide among the wealthy, traveled classes; but these memorials of the past were objects of concern to a sufficient degree to make it clear, I think, that there was no real interruption in the enjoyment of Gothic architecture.

If the imposing folios of *Vitruvius Britannicus* suggest the belief that England was now weighed down only with vast Palladian mansions, a survey of the numerous views of ruined abbeys and castles which Samuel Buck was engraving at this time, and his long list of titled subscribers, including, indeed, the Earl of Burlington himself, show us that in the third decade of the century architectural taste had another aspect. The same impression of diversity is strengthened at Oxford: in the first quarter of the century Hawksmoor built the twin towers in the Quadrangle of All Souls' College in a mongrel Gothic style, and in 1737, only a few yards away, Gibbs began Radcliffe Camera, crowned with a dome that is the cousin of St. Paul's. The point need not be labored further. Clearly classicism did not enjoy an undisputed monopoly of favor. If a Battle of the Styles was not actually in being, it was, at all events, imminent.

A curiously paradoxical and absurd phase of Gothicism was the erection of ruins in gardens and parks. Their practical purpose was to form a picturesque terminary for a view. Their ideal purpose, in the opinion of the eighteenth-century sentimentalists, was even more important: to stimulate the emotions harmlessly by a salutary reminder of the transitory nature of all things raised by hands of mere flesh. It would be interesting, as Mr. Clark says, to know when the first of these ruins was built. He regards the Gothic tower erected in 1746 by Sanderson Miller — he always refers to him as "Millar" — on the top of Edgehill as the earliest for which there is an exact date.[39] However, it is possible to point out some few previous instances of ruins employed as garden-decorations. Sham classical buildings called "perspectives" and frequently merely painted upon a wall were, as we saw, of common occurrence in the formal garden of the seventeenth century; even a man of taste like Evelyn was capable of praising them. But their popularity, according to *La Théorie du Jardinage*, ultimately waned because of their liability to dilapidation. Nevertheless, Batty Langley favored them in his *New Principles of Gardening* (1728) as a means of closing a vista. Yet his ruins were not Gothic, but "after the old Roman manner . . . which ruins may either be painted upon canvas or actually built in that manner with brick and covered with plastering in imitation of stone." Then in all seriousness he conscientiously presents a number of designs (Fig. 53) for such "eye-traps," as these architectural fakes ultimately came to be called after the analogy of "clap-trap," a stage trick for inciting applause. Furthermore, in a letter dated 1733 and addressed to Swift, Mrs. Pendarves, afterwards Mrs. Delany, described an early example of architectural shamming which succeeded in producing the desired impression of age. Lord Bathurst, it appears, had converted a wood-house which formerly was "not a bit better than an Irish cabin" into "a venerable castle," and so well had he contrived his deception that an antiquary had mistaken it for a genuine relic of the days of King Arthur. Mrs. Pendarves regretted that her skill in drawing was not sufficient to enable her to send Swift a sketch of it.[40]

In the same year, in *The Man of Taste*, Bramston, satirizing the colossal scale of Vanbrugh's classic architecture, implies that ruins were at the time recognized as an effective element in a landscape:

> Substantial walls and heavy roofs I like,
> 'Tis Vanbrug's structures that my fancy strike:
> Such noble ruins ev'ry pile wou'd make,
> I wish they'd tumble for the prospect's sake.

Moreover, Rocque shows in his *Plan of the House and Gardens of Wanstead, the Seat of the Earl of Tylney*, of which the date is 1735, a mount upon which stands a ruined obelisk and a shattered Roman arch.

It is apparent that the taste for a Gothic ruin was not yet established and that Lord Bathurst's example was not everywhere followed. In 1738, after a journey through the grand mountain scenery of Wales, Bishop Herring wrote:

> I am afraid, if I had seen Stow in my way home, I should have thrown out some very unmannerly reflections upon it; I should have smiled at the little niceties of art, and beheld with contempt an artificial ruin, after I had been agreeably terrified with something like the rubbish of a creation.[41]

In this last phrase, which is plainly an echo of Burnet's theory of the origin of mountains, Herring sums up his feeling for the difference between ruins made by man and by nature or God. Unfortunately he does not specify whether the "artificial ruin" was classic or Gothic; but it is probable that it was Gothic, for I cannot recall any subsequent allusion to a classic ruin in any of the innumerable accounts of Stowe. The sham edifice Herring had in mind may have been that of which an account was given in 1742 in the third edition of Defoe's *Tour*; there the Gothic building which still stands at Stowe on the crest of a hill is fully described. Finally, it is to be noted that in 1744 Stukeley gratified the Duke of Montagu with a design of "a Gothic bridge with three arches, a temple in the middle," which was to span his great canal, sixty feet wide, in the park.[42]

It appears reasonable to believe, at all events, that before Sanderson Miller gained a reputation as an amateur Gothic architect the custom of erecting medieval buildings to add interest to a park or garden was in a fair way to become a fashion.

The developing taste for this sort of thing naturally put Miller in great request. He designed the ruined castle at Hagley which so delighted Walpole that he declared it had "the true rust of the Barons' Wars." [43] He also designed a ruin for Chancellor Hardwicke at Wimpole, a crumbling castle for Lord Chetwynd, a Gothic front for the stables of a friend of Lord Deerhurst, and rebuilt the Great Hall of Lacock Abbey, which upon completion its owner, Ivory Talbot, opened with "a grand sacrifice to Bacchus." It is not surprising that when he ran for office Miller was satirized in a skit called *The Canvassing Couple, or, A Trip to the House of Commons . . . with scenes, machines, and other decorations. Particularly a new scene in the Gothic Taste by Mr. M-ll-r.* [44]

Additional evidence of the regard for medievalism at a time when it is believed to have been in complete disrepute is to be found in the attitude toward the sash-window. While it made for light and comfort, facilitated the rental and sale of houses, and was the means by which travelers were in the habit of judging the prosperity of provincial English towns, the sash was more or less discredited by those who liked Gothic buildings. In the first quarter of the century Addison with half-humorous disapproval and Defoe with something like anger had looked upon the sashes in the shop-fronts of London as reprehensible proof of the spread of luxury and of foolish, needless expenditure. This type of window was, indeed, identified in the popular mind with classic architecture and was looked upon as the last word in convenience and modernity. In consequence of this conviction, England was dotted with old houses the owners of which in an effort to keep up with the times had partially modernized by the replacement of Gothic windows by sashes. But those that cherished a feeling for the beauty and historic charm of medieval buildings were anxious that those buildings should be preserved in their integrity. They resented the presence of such a foreign, incongruous element as a sash-window in a house or a castle that otherwise in plan and construction finely exemplified Gothic architecture. The sash-window was unwelcome; it was an intruder and destroyed the architectural harmony.

Horace Walpole's appreciation of Gothic architecture was a

form of shallow estheticism. But almost ten years before Strawberry Castle began to take shape, that is, in 1740, the Countess of Hartford and the Countess of Pomfret exchanged letters in which was expressed a genuine feeling for both the grandeur and the traditions of which the great homes of the older time were the impressive embodiment. The Countess of Hartford's comment on the vicissitudes of the sash-windows of Longleat, Wiltshire, is much to the point, and its interest warrants quotation:

> I think your reflexions on the modern rage for pulling down the venerable castles and abbeys which were built by our ancestors, are very just. I confess there always appears to me more true grandeur in these piles, than in any of the new-fashioned edifices. I am perhaps partial to them, from the circumstance of having passed the first years of my life at Long-Leate, which I believe is allowed to be the finest shell now remaining of the houses built in the reign of Edward the Sixth. Though I was only nine years old when my father died, I still remember his lamenting that my grandfather had taken down the Gothic windows on the first floor, in one of the fronts, and put up sashes, in order to have a better view of his garden from a gallery that occupied almost all that side of the house. As soon as the present Lord Weymouth married, and came to live here, he ordered the sashes to be pulled down, and the old windows to be restored. I flattered myself that this was a good omen of his regard to a seat which for two hundred years had been the delight and pride of his ancestors.[45]

As Henry Thynne, the father of the Countess of Hartford, died in 1708, his protest against the sash-windows is really remarkable evidence that even in the first decade of the eighteenth century, when the prestige of classic architecture is generally believed to have been unquestioned, owners of a great Tudor mansion like Longleat were capable of prizing their inheritance and, possessing some appreciation of historic architectural values, wished to retain unchanged such a distinctive feature as long ranges of ancient mullioned windows. Moreover, be it noted that the Countess, like her father, favored the maintenance of architectural consistency and did not approve of the modernization of ancient buildings. Her opinion has all the greater weight because it is expressed with moderation, whereas other and especially later admirers of Gothic architecture vent their preference with such sentimental exaggeration that their sincerity is immediately under suspicion. That the second Viscount Weymouth soon after his marriage in 1726 proceeded to tear out the sashes at Longleat leaves no doubt as to the unanimity of the family in this matter of taste.

The prejudice against sashes is echoed elsewhere. In 1752, when Dr. Lyttelton took a horseback tour through Cornwall, he observed that there were very few cottages, no matter how dilapidated, which were without sash-windows. As an antiquary he regretted this incongruity in humble thatched houses; yet in this case he was willing to overlook the modern feature; but what he could not forgive was the sashing of the churches, "which ill suits the Gothic simplicity of these ancient buildings." [46] Six years later Mrs. Montagu visited Lumley Castle; she recognized that it had once been an impressive building, but now her enthusiasm for it was very cool, for it had become in her eyes merely "a good house," too "modernized by sash-windows and other fashionable ornaments." [47]

This distaste for a sash-window in an old building is reflected in literature. As a rule Richardson is so preoccupied with the perturbations in the hearts of his characters that he gives only an occasional hint about the environment in which their agitations occur. But what he has to say about the sash-window is a descriptive detail of unusual explicitness. In one of the epistles which the delectable and tireless Pamela penned for her worthy parents she told them with the utmost unction that Mr. B., their benefactor, her "dear master," wished to repair and improve their "pretty dwelling." But to preserve the amenities of the cottage, Mr. B. planned to keep "the old oaken floors of the bed-chamber," and as he was also anxious to retain "the old bow-windows" overshadowed with woodbines, jessamines, and vines, his intention was not to sash the windows, but merely to put in larger panes of glass "to let in the sweet air and light." [48] Here even the stodgy Richardson forgot his platitudes long enough to record his indifference to the fashionable sashes and his pleasure in a bow-window in the style of other days.

Assuredly the zeal of the antiquaries in the investigation of historic monuments, the admiration for the cathedrals, the regret for the decay and demolition of ancient edifices, the melancholy inspired by the ruins of castles and churches, and the eagerness to collect old glass and to preserve the remains of crumbling medieval buildings were manifestations of a deep and genuine attachment to the earlier architecture of England. They provide ample grounds for believing that in the late seventeenth and throughout the first half of the eighteenth century there flowed a steady, even if at times inconspicuous, current of taste in favor of the Middle Ages and its art. In any proper sense, then, can it be said that the interest in Gothicism "revived"? Was it not an interest which was continuous even in the face of the vogue of classicism? The sentiments expressed by an unknown letter-writer when, in 1744, he was visiting the Archbishop of York were cherished, it may well be claimed, by many another conservative Englishman who refused to be swept by the tide of fashion into an admiration for the formal splendors of Palladianism which he did not feel. This writer, whose words are much to the point, incisively remarks that the house in which he was staying

> was built at a time of day when men paid more regard to convenience than to uniformity. . . . The rooms are very large and furnished in character; and that apartment where I now sit to write, is ornamented with the "Adventures of Sampson," curiously wrought in old tapestry, the work, perhaps, of some religious dame. . . . Upon the whole, it is a most agreeable house; and pleases me more than if it had been designed by Lord Burlington or any other genius of the age.[49]

II. Strawberry Hill, Vauxhall, and Chippendale's Furniture

In 1747, when he was thirty years of age, Walpole took over the lease on the property of Strawberry Hill from Mrs. Chenevix, the fashionable toywoman, and in the following year he purchased the site and the insignificant house that stood upon it. For the next few years his letters brim with references to the progress he was making in remodeling the building into "a little Gothic Castle." In 1750 he asks Horace Mann to send him "any fragments of old painted glass, arms, or anything" that he can pick up in Italy. In 1753 he is still in the midst of "brick and mortar," but he is able to announce that "the castle" is

Fig. 53 — Avenue with an Artificial Roman Ruin as a Terminary (1728). Designed by Batty Langley

Fig. 54 — Strawberry Hill

near completion and that it will have no less than thirty-two windows of ancient glass. Oddly enough, while he was immersed in these medieval preoccupations Walpole visited Mereworth Castle, and he has to confess that the perfection of its Palladianism weaned him from Gothicism.[50] But the disloyalty was only temporary. As Strawberry Hill, moreover, reached only the first stage of its development in 1753, Walpole was able to amuse himself at intervals for many years in making additions to the original building. In 1760 and 1761 he added the Gallery, Round Tower, and Great Cloister, in 1770 the Great Bedchamber, and in 1776 the Hexagonal Closet and Beauclerc Tower. Just because for over twenty years it was thus growing by a process of accretion, Strawberry Hill is, with no intention on Walpole's part, in one respect more medieval than the Gothic imitations of his contemporaries. Whereas their houses were symmetrical Palladian edifices with Gothic trimmings, Strawberry Hill (Fig. 54) is in the medieval fashion irregular both externally and internally. No attempt having been made to achieve coordination of space by an axial plan and an arrangement of apartments *en suite*, the rooms are simply detached units having no real formal relationship. In going through the house one gets, as one does in many ancient buildings, a confused impression of a series of rooms connected merely haphazardly by narrow, unattractive passageways.

For the medieval details of Strawberry Hill Walpole, assisted by his friend Bentley, copied and adapted bits of ancient buildings; but his pursuit of authenticity was in vain, for in the gay irresponsibility of ignorance he has jumbled together architectural features of varied origin. To medieval tombs he was especially indebted for many of his ideas of interior ornament. The design of the Gothic wallpaper in the entrance hall and on the staircase was taken from the screen of Prince Arthur's tomb in Worcester Cathedral; the ceiling of the China Room was by Müntz after one in a Borghese villa at Frascati; the walls were covered with blue and white Dutch tiles, and the floor with tiles from Gloucester Cathedral. The roof of the Tribune was suggested by that of the Chapter House of York Minster, and in its center was an unmedieval star of yellow glass which filled the room with "a golden gloom." The ceiling of the Holbein Chamber was from a royal dressing-room in Windsor Castle; the chimney-piece imitated a tomb at Canterbury; and the entrance screen embodied ideas from the choir of Rouen Cathedral. The ceiling of the Gallery (Fig. 55) was an imitation of that in Henry VII's Chapel; the large door at the end of the room was adopted from one at St. Alban's; and the "gold network" incongruously placed over the looking-glass was copied from Bourchier's tomb in Canterbury. The walls of the Gallery were hung with crimson damask of Renaissance design, and the chairs and settees were similarly upholstered.

In the various rooms this conglomeration of styles and periods produced, although in a sense in which he did not intend it, what Walpole described as a "fantastic fabric." An uninitiated visitor would infer, I imagine, from the profusion of fussy filigree-work and gorgeous gilding that the decoration was Oriental. Yet Walpole took these features seriously; he states that one of the purposes of his published descriptions of Strawberry Hill is to show how medieval detail borrowed from tombs and cathedrals could, in an adapted form, be utilized for chimney-pieces, ceilings, windows, and balustrades. On the other hand, in furnishing his house with modern portraits, French and Chinese porcelain, and classical sculpture — they are very conspicuous, for example, in the photograph of the Gallery in the text —, Walpole realized that he opened himself to criticism. He defended himself, however, on the ground that he had no intention of making his house so medieval "as to exclude convenience and modern refinements in luxury." In other words, he did not wish to "periodize" his rooms; but he could not, in fact, have done so, for neither he nor his contemporaries possessed sufficient knowledge of the interior decoration of past ages to furnish a room with historic congruity.

The architecture of Strawberry Hill has been damned so often that it seems scarcely necessary to send it to perdition again. The total effect of the exterior is mean and paltry. The triangular stepped gable and the absurd little battlemented parapet that fringes the roof are too insignificant to create a bold, unhesitating skyline and are typical of the feebleness that is characteristic of the whole house. The solidity of enduring masonry, whether revealed in wall or pillar or buttress, is the masculine virtue of genuine Gothic architecture, but the unsubstantial construction and the complete neglect of the values of material at Strawberry Hill have deservedly gained it the reputation of a sham. Reluctantly but inevitably one is reminded of the flocks of flimsy, starved-looking houses that have settled on the English landscape since the War. Strawberry Hill is larger in scale, but belongs in the same category. The architectural failure of Strawberry Hill is, indeed, proof of the extent to which the principles of medieval building had been lost during the increasing popularity of classicism. The appreciation of Gothic architecture had not declined to a corresponding degree, and certainly not so much as has generally been supposed, but a knowledge of medieval construction had well-nigh disappeared. Walpole did not realize that carved ornament from tombs and screens, pointed windows filled with fragments of stained glass, and towers and turrets did not make a building Gothic if it did not itself embody the fundamental, integrating architectural ideas of which these features were but specific expressions. But fortunately for Walpole his contemporaries were not in a position to be critical of his work; they went to Strawberry Hill and were delighted. Lady Mary Coke probably expressed the opinion of his more frivolous friends when she declared: "'tis the most amusing house I ever was in; so many pictures and things to help one to ideas when one wants a fresh collection; entertainment without company." As time went by, so numerous were the visitors that Walpole wrote his *Description of Strawberry Hill* to serve as a guide-book, and for his own peace and convenience as the proprietor of a show-place found it necessary to prepare a printed leaflet for the information of persons applying for permission to view the house. One of these leaflets is preserved in the British Museum and runs as follows:

> Mr. Walpole is very ready to oblige any curious persons with the sight of his house and collection; but as it is situated so near to London and in so populous a neighborhood, and as he refuses a ticket to nobody that sends for one, it is but reasonable that such persons as send should comply with the rules he has been obliged to lay down for showing it.

Any person, sending a day or two before, may have a ticket for four persons for a day certain. No ticket will serve but on the day for which it is given. If more than four persons come with a ticket, the housekeeper has positive orders to admit none of them. Every ticket will admit the company only between the hours of twelve and three before dinner, and only one company will be admitted on the same day. The house will never be shown after dinner, nor at all but from the first of May to the first of October. As Mr. Walpole has given offence by sometimes enlarging the number of four and refusing that latitude to others, he flatters himself that for the future nobody will take it ill that he strictly confines the number; as whoever desires him to break his rule does in effect expect him to disoblige others, which is what nobody has a right to desire of him. Persons desiring a ticket may apply either to Strawberry Hill or to Mr. Walpole's in Berkeley Square, London. If any person does not make use of a ticket, Mr. Walpole hopes he shall have notice; otherwise he is prevented from obliging others on that day, and thence is put to great inconvenience. They who have tickets are desired not to bring children.

That Walpole was justified in taking these precautions against the intrusion of hordes of curious visitors is confirmed by one of his letters to George Montagu in which he complains that he has had no time to attend to his correspondence. With affected regret he protests that the villa is

full of people, and has been so from the instant I breakfasted, and more are coming — in short, I keep an inn; the sign, "The Gothic Castle." — Since my gallery was finished I have not been in it a quarter of an hour together; my whole time is passed in giving tickets for seeing it, and hiding myself while it is seen. — Take my advice, never build a charming house for yourself between London and Hampton Court: everybody will live in it but you.[51]

The glamour enveloping Walpole's fantastic "castle" did not readily pass away. It is reflected (dimly, to be sure) in *Strawberry Hill*, a novel by Robert Williams which came from the press in 1847. The author wove his pseudo-historical romance about the miniature of a beautiful girl which he had observed among the articles for sale at the auction of the contents of Strawberry Hill in 1842 — a romance by which he attempted to explain Walpole's indifference to politics and his desire to lead the life of a gentleman of leisure. The last scene of the novel, the only one laid at Strawberry Hill, represents the final meeting of the now aged lovers after years of separation.

In spite of the fame of Strawberry Hill, a number of consider-

Fig. 55 — The Gallery, Strawberry Hill, with Fan-Vaulting in Imitation of that in the Chapel of Henry VII

Fig. 56 — Pavilions and Dining Boxes in the Gothic Style, Vauxhall Gardens

ations suggest that its importance in the history of eighteenth-century Gothicism has been overrated. It has gained its pre-eminence because various writers have belittled or neglected the attitude of Walpole's predecessors toward medievalism. But he was neither first nor alone in the enjoyment of ruins, in the appreciation of the melancholy dignity of ancient buildings, in the sense of the beauty of the great cathedrals, and in an ardor for collecting ancient glass and the relics of the past. These various antiquarian enthusiasms, crystallizing, were responsible for Strawberry Hill, but that does not mean that to Walpole belongs the credit of "reviving" Gothicism. His achievement was the product of historic sympathies which had continued to make their appeal to imaginative minds from the days of Dugdale and Anthony à Wood in the seventeenth century. Moreover, there is no evidence that Walpole himself ever dreamed that he was doing anything remarkable or exceptional in building Strawberry Hill in the Gothic style. If he had been as much of an innovator as some would have us infer, he would assuredly have been conscious that he was breaking new ground, and would not have hesitated to comment on the originality of his taste. But in truth the taste of his contemporaries as well as his own was becoming liberalized. In 1750, when the reconstruction of Strawberry Hill was in its initial stages, Walpole wrote in reply to Mann, who had objected to the Gothic style, that the conservatism of the latter was out of date, that if Mann came to England, he would be surprised at "the liberty of taste into which we are all struck and of which you can have no idea."[52] In other words, the Gothicism of Strawberry Hill was not so extraordinary as to occasion comment except in a country like Italy, where Mann was uninformed about what had been occurring in his native land. The fact, too, that even before the completion of Strawberry Hill in 1753 satire was directed against Gothicism in Cambridge's *Scribleriad* (1751) and in the early papers of the *World*, is an indication that the taste had already attained such considerable proportions as to alarm the classicists into actively opposing the barbarism of medieval architecture. Although clearly not giving the initial impulse to such satire, the subsequent success of Strawberry Hill, without doubt, intensified it.

It has been argued, furthermore, with undue emphasis that, on account of his social position, Walpole's approval of Gothicism so greatly enhanced its prestige that it soon became the fashion. But this is credit which Walpole must share with others even more distinguished than himself. Long before his day antiquarian pursuits had enjoyed aristocratic favor. In 1720, in accounting for the cordial terms on which he associated with the Duke of Montagu, Stukeley said:

> We had exactly the same taste for old family concerns, genealogies, pictures, furniture, coats of arms, the old way of building, gardening, and the like; in a general imitation of pure nature, in the Gothic architecture, in painted glass, in the open-hearted, candid, undesigning, and free manner of conversation.[53]

The Antiquarian Society also enjoyed the support of the nobility. One of its founders was Henry Hare, Lord Coleraine, and for many years Lord Hertford, afterwards the Duke of Somerset, served as president of the Society, to be succeeded upon his death in 1749 by the Duke of Richmond. Stukeley corresponded with the Earl of Winchilsea, Lord Hertford, the Earl of Pembroke, and the Archbishop of Canterbury, and their letters make it plain that their interest in antiquarian matters was far from perfunctory.[54] As Walpole was not the first and only aristocratic sponsor of antiquity, his social influence cannot be held solely responsible for the high tide of favor which Gothicism came to enjoy. One may well suspect that Walpole wrote at such length about Strawberry Hill that modern readers of his letters, hypnotized by his loquacity and learning more about his Gothic mansion than about any other house of the period, have unconsciously magnified its importance more than it deserves.

In truth, Walpole was no more the "father" of Gothicism than Shakespeare, as discussed by the literary historians of the eighteenth century, was the "father" of English drama. Strawberry Hill was the outgrowth of a taste that had long been maturing and represented merely a stage in its evolution. Having wealth and the enthusiasm of a man of leisure eager to discover a hobby with which to amuse himself, Walpole brought to a focus artistic and antiquarian interests that he found already current. As the result of his zeal, Strawberry Hill was the most pretentious effort that had yet been made to assemble architectural and decorative features that were associated with the Middle Ages. As an actual artistic achievement it was worth very little, but it captured the interest of his contemporaries because they were prodigiously ignorant of the Middle Ages and uncritically accepted the amusing novelty which he prepared for them. At the same time I think it would be a mistake to infer that the taste that approved Strawberry Hill was fashionable and nothing more. The type of architecture which Strawberry Hill was supposed to represent did appeal to the English for reasons — we can call them sentimental if we wish — that were rooted in a respect for the traditions and customs associated with the hospitable old mansions of their forefathers. They felt that the formal splendor of the house of Renaissance design was not a native growth, but characteristic of a style that had been imported without regard to its adaptability to English conditions. The older Gothic architecture, on the other hand, belonged to England and was a symbol of her past. Thus it came about that fashion indirectly reinforced by sentiment established the taste for pseudo-medieval houses of which Strawberry Hill was one of the earliest examples.

It was appropriate that Vauxhall, where the jazz spirit of eighteenth-century London was wont to manifest itself most hilariously, possessed a most theatrical specimen of Gothic architecture. Contemporaneous with Strawberry Hill, and indeed slightly antedating it, the Vauxhall creation was as gay externally as were some of Walpole's gilded interiors. In this place of popular entertainment it was the building serving as a commodious open-air restaurant that affected the medieval style to a point of fantastic exaggeration. The great semicircular arcade (Fig. 56) was five hundred feet in length and was divided into alcoves or boxes where pleasure-seekers might sit and enjoy the spectacle of the moving crowds. The three domed pavilions — in the old print in the text these are called with strange ignorance "Chinese" — displayed an irresponsible profusion of pointed, cusped arches, and the connecting arcades were edged with what at the time passed for battlements. The balls, the stars, and the suns with which the domes were studded were thrown in to give decorative effect in good measure, and formed a fraction of that multiplicity of "rich Gothic ornament" which impressed a writer of a contemporary guide-book. The whole building was, in his judgment, "in a noble style of Gothic architecture."

That the central pavilion was flanked on either side by a cluster of four trees betrayed that fondness for symmetry from which the age found it difficult to emancipate itself even in its most frivolous moments. In the mellow light of its hundreds of lamps, for which Vauxhall was famous, the *ensemble* probably produced an impression of tawdry splendor such as we are to-day familiar with in the sham palaces of exhibition-grounds and amusement-parks. In comparison with the barren dignity and sterile conservatism of the classic Rotunda (Fig. 35) of Ranelagh in Chelsea, on the other side of the Thames, the architecture of Vauxhall was recklessness itself. One modern antiquary has, indeed, seen a depressing likeness between the Rotunda and the Reading Room of the British Museum. The pseudo-Gothic pavilions of Vauxhall were more flamboyant; they were akin to the spectacular gilded bookcases of Strawberry Hill.* They contributed to that dazzling magnificence which the writer of our guide-book found irresistible:

A person of an elegant turn of mind, who had never heard of Vauxhall Gardens, and should be conveyed to them in his sleep, might, at his being awaked by the music and the company, be suppos'd to break into the following exclamation:

> Where am I? O what wonders rise?
> What scenes are these that glitter round?
> Some vision, sure, must bless my eyes,
> Or this must be inchanted ground! [55]

But the taste for medievalism was not confined to such architectural vagaries. Accurately gauging the whims of fashionable clients, cabinet-makers set themselves to the task of designing furniture in which Gothic elements were conspicuous. Chippendale's *The Gentleman and Cabinet Maker's Director* (1754) is, in this respect, an invaluable index of contemporary tendencies.

*For the location of the semicircle of dining-boxes in the layout of the Gardens see Fig. 34.

Fig. 57 — Bookcase. Designed by Chippendale in the Gothic Style

Fig. 58 — Chair. Designed by Chippendale in the Gothic Style

Just as he had met the demand for furniture in which pagodas and zigzag lattice work were suggestive of the Orient, Chippendale applied his fertile and flexible genius to the design of chairs, beds, bookcases, and clothes-chests in which pointed arches, pinnacles, and tracery borrowed from stained glass windows were calculated to recall the age of monks, knights, and castles. Very typically the doors of his bookcase (Fig. 57) are embellished with a series of ogival arches terminating in finials after the fashion of a window in the flamboyant style of late Gothic. The four pyramidal pinnacles on the top of the bookcase serve to medievalize it still further. Like the doors of this bookcase, the back of the chair (Fig. 58) echoes the form of a church window, but in this example the designer — we cannot be sure that it was Chippendale himself — has favored not the ogival arch but the sharp pointed arch of the lancet-window of early Gothic.

Obviously such furniture was historically unauthentic. As the number and variety of pieces of furniture in the medieval house were extremely limited (stools, a trestle-table, and some chests and cupboards comprising the household equipment of even a nobleman), Chippendale and his followers were generally medievalizing furniture for which, in fact, no prototypes existed in the Middle Ages. In spite of Gothic trimmings, an eighteenth-century day-bed, bookcase, tea-table, or china-cabinet would have bewildered the doughtiest knight that ever strode within an ancient castle, for he would have been at a loss to divine the exact use of those products of a more complex and more luxurious age. With greater skill than some of his critics are willing to attribute to him, Chippendale adapted Gothic architectural features to furniture that was modern in both form and purpose. On this account his Gothic designs, especially those of chairs, have not met with universal approval. While some authorities have granted that they are "highly successful" and possess "beauty and originality," others have been less generous. It has been said that Chippendale showed no feeling for the Gothic style and that the frame of an ecclesiastical window functions inappropriately as a chair-back. A recent writer, Mr. Kenneth Clark, has even described the medieval designs as "monsters" and "unusually misbegotten."[56] One may fairly suspect that these pieces of furniture have suffered undeserved disrepute from their association with the pseudo-Gothic architecture of Strawberry Hill and its offspring. Assuredly it smacks of pedantry to protest arbitrarily against the employment of a Gothic window-frame as a chair-back. What is important is that Chippendale's adaptation is not obtrusively ecclesiastical, and as a result is in keeping with the domestic interiors for which it was originally designed.

The later phases of Gothicism, especially those which were manifest after 1800, lie beyond the limit set for this study. Much of that subsequent development has been competently treated in one or another of its aspects in two recent and valuable books, *The Picturesque* (1927) by Christopher Hussey and *The Gothic Revival* (1928) by Kenneth Clark. But neither of these writers would claim that the activities of the famous Victorians Pugin, Ruskin, and Sir Gilbert Scott in the cause of medievalism brought the history of Gothicism to a close. Its final chapter, still being written in the United States, has to do with the employment of the vertical elements in Gothic design as an effective means of expressing the immense height of the skyscraper and as a possible solution of that difficult problem of the American architect, the clothing of the towering skeleton of steel. Of this process of adaptation the Woolworth Building in New York City is, of course, an early and admirable example. But as these phases of Gothicism, notwithstanding their very great interest, are concerned primarily with either the esthetics of the picturesque or more purely architectural problems, they carry us away from the purpose of this study, which from the outset has been focused as far as possible upon those particular aspects of English taste which, under the influence of fashionable amateurs and men of letters, had much in common with contemporaneous literature and could on that account be profitably correlated with it.

A brief consideration of one incident in the later history of Gothicism may, however, round out our discussion and properly conclude it. Undoubtedly a spectacular minor climax in that history was the building of Fonthill Abbey (1796–1807) by William Beckford, the author of *Vathek*. Discovering upon his return from a Continental tour that many poor families in Wiltshire were in dire want, he devised a generous scheme for employing them.[57] He commissioned James Wyatt, the famous architect of the Pantheon, to erect on his estate an abbey which, although it was to be in imitation of a ruin, should contain a few habitable rooms. Once started, the plan gradually grew more ambitious until as many as five hundred laborers were sometimes engaged on the enterprise, working in shifts both day and night. Public curiosity was aroused, extravagant tales were circulated as to the nature of Beckford's undertaking, and even though visitors were excluded, a wall twelve feet in height having been built about the extensive domain, persons who, as Beckford said, regarded themselves as gentlemen were so inquisitive as to disguise themselves as ordinary laborers in order to gain admission to the grounds. The fruit of Beckford's megalomania was a vast cathedral-like structure surmounted by a tower two hundred and seventy-six feet in height and provided with a baronial entrance hall seventy-eight feet in height. The huge edifice dominated the countryside, and, as Mr. Clark remarks, "All that the eighteenth century demanded from Gothic — unimpeded perspectives, immense height, the sublime, in short — was present in Fonthill, and present more lavishly, perhaps, than in real mediaeval buildings." He describes Fonthill aptly as a "sudden outburst of romantic rhetoric," and feels that the tower, though "mere trumpery," was capable of submerging the judgment by its sheer "vehemence." [58] Such a grandiose achievement overshadowed Strawberry Hill, which was, in Beckford's opinion, a mere "toyshop," "a miserable child's box." The jealousy of Walpole, now an old man, was roused, especially when it was maliciously reported to him that Beckford's intention was to buy the collections of Strawberry Hill after his death. But all the romantic glamour that enveloped Fonthill and thrilled the imagination of persons ready to be enraptured with the medieval past did not preserve it. The collapse of the tower in 1825 and the accompanying destruction of much of the rest of the building symbolized the architectural insincerity that infected eighteenth-century Gothicism and made it ridiculous. Ashridge, another vast pseudo-medieval mansion, which Wyatt built for the Earl of Bridgewater, illustrates, as Mr. Avray Tipping points out, a similar incongruity. Wyatt's imitation of a baronial hall, which, if correctly employed as in the Middle Ages, should be the principal room in the house, serves at Ashridge merely as a passageway from the entrance to the stairs and is, of course, absurdly large for that simple purpose.[59]

Recalling such works as Gray's *The Bard*, Percy's *Reliques*, and the *Rowley Poems*, one might infer that in revealing in the course of its progress an intensified interest in the Middle Ages the literature of the eighteenth century was more and more influenced by the lyrics, the romances, and other literary types of pre-Tudor England. Yet only in a measure was that true. As Professor Ker has acutely observed, Gothic churches, ancient castles, and all the romantic associations clustered about them stimulated the imagination of men of letters weary of classic formalism, and in consequence affected their own creative works far more deeply than did the gradually increasing knowledge of the actual literature of the Middle Ages.[60] Winchester put its spell upon Thomas and Joseph Warton as much as did their acquaintance with the books of the past. St. Mary Redcliffe, as well as the musty parchments in its muniment room, nourished Chatterton's poetic spirit. The poems, the novels, and the plays which the eighteenth-century medievalists wrote were generally not attempts to imitate literary forms popular in the Middle Ages, but were concerned with reproducing the picturesque life of the time. The chapel, the gloomy vaulted aisle, the crypt, the charnel-house, the embattled wall, the paved courtyard, the dungeon, and the high-arched baronial hall called up a vivid world peopled by knights, ladies, heralds, minstrels, abbots, and wandering priests. It was the progressive depiction of this world by Walpole, Chatterton, and the Gothic novelists that imparted to much of the literature of the second half of the eighteenth century its medieval coloring. What is noteworthy is the fact that it was the architecture and not the literature of the Middle Ages that shaped men's conception of England's romantic past.

CHAPTER XV

CLASSICAL CRITICISM OF "GOTHIC TASTE"

IN JUSTICE to the classicists it must be said that for them pacifism had no attraction. They were staunch fighters. Scorning in matters of culture the role of non-combatant, they refused to accept with complacent tolerance the current state of English taste. As their thinking about esthetics was never confused by any doctrine of relativity which might have permitted them, without compunction, to hover in a comfortable twilight zone of neutrality, counterbalancing objectively the various values of contemporary art, they did not make peace with Gothicism any more readily than with *chinoiserie*. The sentimental tendencies of the eighteenth century in a measure atrophied the sense of humor and paralyzed the muscles of risibility; yet the influence of those tendencies was never so great as to weaken the faith of the classicists in the disciplinary power of laughter. As they had striven to ridicule Orientalism out of countenance, so they relied on satire to check the popularity of Gothicism, which threatened dire hurt to the cherished gods of simplicity and proportion. In a survey of this satire it is difficult to separate the criticism of Gothicism from that of Orientalism, because the classicists attacked them simultaneously, seeing them as the two shapeless heads of a monster possessed of a single body. Men disliking *chinoiserie* disliked medievalism no less, and indicted both as subversive of the eternal verities of art. However, if we are inclined to believe that the eighteenth century pursued its follies without hindrance, this satire restores the balance of our judgment. Checking the too human habit of facile generalization, it reminds us that the age, whatever its vagaries, was by no means without trenchant powers of self-criticism.

Although by no means always specifically anti-Gothic in its aim, the satire to which the antiquary was exposed throughout the seventeenth and eighteenth centuries is not irrelevant to our purpose. As it gives us some idea of the atmosphere in which antiquarian studies of any kind were pursued, it helps to account for that hostility to Gothicism which manifested itself whenever some phase of medieval civilization had incited research. The man who investigated the monuments of the past or cherished merely a sentimental admiration for the customs and manners of a remote age was ridiculed no matter what the object of his interest, classic, Celtic, or medieval. The criticism of the antiquary, following the course of development characteristic of all satire, soon hardened into a formula, and certain grotesque qualities became traditional in the depiction of the type: he appears as a harsh, uncouth, irascible old man, the collector of all kinds of outlandish rubbish — the inventory of his treasures recalls the absurd lists of relics enumerated in medieval satires on the pardoner — and, blinded by his monomania, he is so childishly gullible that he can be easily duped into squandering his money on any fake antique that is brought to his notice. After two centuries of this crude ridicule, Scott with the imaginative balance of genius softened the portrait. He made Jonathan Oldbuck human and lovable, even if a little daft about whatever concerned his hobby.

In 1628 John Earle, seeking to discredit the antiquary's efforts to acquaint himself with the past, put him among the characters of whom he undertook to make a laughing-stock in his *Micro-cosmographie*:

> He is one that hath that unnaturall disease to bee enamour'd of old age and wrinckles, and loves all things (as Dutchmen doe Cheese) the better for being mouldy and worme-eaten . . . Beggers coozen him with musty things which they have rak't from dunghills . . . He never lookes up on himself til he is gray-hair'd, and then he is pleased with his owne Antiquity.[1]

Earle, it is to be observed, also jeers at the medievalist for his willingness to journey long distances to view the architectural remains of the Middle Ages: "He will go you forty miles to see a saints well, or a ruin'd abbey." Samuel Butler, following Earle's cue, also satirized the antiquary in his *Characters*.[2] But the character-writers were not alone in their contempt for the man who dared to be as much interested in some past age as in his own. In 1673 at Oxford a *terrae filius*, John Shirley of Trinity College, publicly ridiculed Anthony à Wood's researches and his book on Oxonian antiquities. With grim humor Wood himself admits that the fellows of Merton "would not let me live in the college for fear I should pluck it down to search after antiquities, that I was so great a lover of antiquities that I loved to live in an old cockleloft rather than a spacious chamber."[3] Dramatists likewise did not neglect to shoot their shafts at the antiquary as a sort of St. Sebastian in the doldrums of old age. In 1636 Her Majesty's Servants performed Shackerley Marmion's satiric comedy *The Antiquary* at the Cockpit. Among the treasures of the absurd hero are the silver box in which Nero kept his beard and the net in which Vulcan entrapped Mars and Venus in a compromising situation. When Veterano goes to court, he wears Pompey's breeches, Caesar's hat — the one he wore when killed by Brutus —, and Hannibal's spectacles. In 1718, upon the reestablishment of the Society of Antiquaries, Marmion's burlesque (with the obvious intention of profiting by the talk of the moment) was revived for two nights, and subsequently it was published in Dodsley's *Old Plays* (1744).

In his comedies Tom D'Urfey directs his laughter not at the antiquary but at the eccentric individual who, out of sympathy with his own age, sentimentally hankers for "the good old days." In *The Bath* (1701) Sir Carolus Codshead, a hearty old fellow, glorifies the times of Henry VIII and King Charles and cherishes a healthy contempt for the trills and quavers of contemporary song in comparison with the "Down derries" of the past. In *The Old Mode and the New* (1703) Sir Fumbler Oldmode is a great lover of the days of Elizabeth. To humor him, his wife dresses in Elizabethan fashion. At the very sight of "that provoking dress" even the exquisite pangs of Sir Fumbler's gout are temporarily allayed. At the close of the play, however, when her effrontery enables her to take matters into her own hands, Lady Oldmode horrifies her spouse by appearing in a costume of their own times. An echo of D'Urfey's satire is heard in Bramston's *Man of Taste* (1733):

> Queer country-puts extol Queen Bess's reign,
> And of lost hospitality complain.
> Say thou that do'st thy father's table praise,
> Was there mahogena in former days?[4]

Whereas Shadwell in *The Lancashire Witches* (1681–82) had delineated the gentleman of the old school, Sir Edward Hartfort, as worthy of admiration, such a man with his preference for the manners of Elizabethan days was merely ridiculous to D'Urfey and Bramston. But it is clear that such a type was by no means uncommon in England even during the decades when classicism looked with haughty disdain upon the Elizabethan era as "barbarous" and "untutored." The interest in the life of England's romantic past survived no doubt as a subterranean stream, the existence of which men of letters and people of fashion studiously ignored.

The drama continued to poke fun at the antiquary. In 1772 in *The Fashionable Lover* Cumberland put Dr. Druid, Lord Abberville's Welsh tutor on the grand tour, in the pillory. Druid's interest in the old buildings of London and regret for their systematic destruction is amusingly contrasted with the crass, unimaginative attitude of Bridgemore, an eighteenth-century English Babbitt. Indeed, their clash of opinion is in all essentials reflected to-day in letters in the London *Times* whenever lovers of the past become involved in controversy with industrialists who have in contemplation some further desecration of the English landscape. In reply to Bridgemore's sneer that the Doctor, if he is so inclined, can take up his residence among the ruins of Palmyra, Druid bursts out:

> Ruins indeed! what are all your new buildings, up and down yonder, but ruins? Improve your own a little further, and you'll drive every man of sense out of it; pless us, and save us, bye and bye not a monument of antiquity will be left standing from London-stone to Westminster-hall. . . . Down with 'em then at once, down with every thing noble and venerable and ancient amongst you; turn the Tower of London into a Pantheon, make a new Adelphi of the Savoy, and bid adieu to all ages but your own; you will then be no more in the way of deriving dignity from your progenitors, than you are of transmitting it to your posterity.

But Bridgemore's self-sufficiency is unshaken. True to the materialistic ideal of his tribe, he puts utility before interest in the historic past: "Well, Doctor, well, leave me my opinion and keep your own; you've a veneration for rust and cobwebs, I am for brushing them off wherever I meet them; we are for furnishing our shops and warehouses with good profitable commodities . . ."[5] And he goes on to say that the Doctor is as much out of place in London as an alderman in Herculaneum. In spite of his learning, or probably because of it, Druid in the course of the play is discredited for his indifference to his fellow-mortals and his inferiority to the man who "has made the human heart his study." His sympathies, in Cumberland's eyes, are as dried up as some of his specimens.

As late as 1808 the anonymous writer of a farce, *Antiquity*, continued to satirize the antiquary in the traditional style. Harvey by his unregulated, unbalanced enthusiasm for the sixteenth century has exasperated his friends and relatives. He dismantles his bedroom because "printed cotton and mahogany weren't used in the days of Shakspeare"; he speculates whether he is the descendant of Gabriel Harvey, the friend of Spenser, and studies Stow and Holinshed with devotion. Resolving to live again the past, he undertakes to give "a true antiquity-supper" at which he and his friends are to impersonate Falstaff, Prince Hal, and their boon companions. Harvey's friends seize the opportunity to exhibit his folly. They come to the tavern in Eastcheap in the proper costume, but at the supper they commit so many intentional anachronisms, talking mercilessly about watches, port wine, Woburn Place, and false teeth, that the historic illusion is woefully shattered. Feeling the sting of their ridicule, Harvey is cured of his fantastic hobby.[6]

This tricking of antiquaries with the design of exposing their ignorance and gullibility was not merely an imaginary contrivance of malicious satirists. George Steevens, the Shakesperian scholar, who had a grudge against Gough, the Director of the Society of Antiquaries, fabricated an inscribed stone, supposedly in commemoration of Hardicanute, on which his sudden death was attributed to over-drinking at the wedding of a Danish lord. After the inscription had occasioned a learned disquisition and had been identified as a work of the eleventh century, Steevens with cruel hilarity exposed the hoax in the *General Evening Post*.[7] Such a trick — and other examples might be cited — was assuredly not calculated to increase respect for the antiquary or any admirer of the "good old days." To-day, realizing that an antiquary's errors were due rather to the imperfect state of archeological science than to his own stupidity, we are apt to think much of this satire as futile and downright silly; but that in the seventeenth and eighteenth centuries the antiquary was almost invariably depicted as a fool and that he carried on his work in the face of the ridicule of an ignorant public must be reckoned with as an influence checking the growth of interest in medievalism.

No doubt involved in this hostility was much of the classicist's contempt for the Middle Ages. It seemed to him a folly akin to madness that anyone should journey to examine either a baron's castle or a ruined abbey, relics of a barbarous architecture which it behooved a more polite and polished age to ignore. Dr. Druid's solicitude for the Tower of London and his belittlement of the Adelphi and the Pantheon, two recent buildings acclaimed by the classicists, were taken in the eighteenth century as proof of his folly and were probably greeted with the loud laughter that is the reward of eccentricity.

As soon as the classicists became aware that the intensified interest in the Middle Ages was affecting contemporary art and assuming proportions that gave cause for alarm, they recognized that it was an occasion for neither delay nor parley. As they had ridiculed *chinoiserie* and antiquarianism, so now, with the vigor of veterans long habituated to the defence of standards of taste, they satirized the Gothic influence that was daily appearing more conspicuous in architecture and furniture. The earliest evidence of this critical attitude occurs, as far as I have been able to discover, in *The Scribleriad* (1751) of Richard Owen Cambridge. When the eccentric hero of this mock-heroic satire consults a Morosoph, the latter in a prophetic frenzy reveals that whereas Scriblerus himself is to set out in search of the philosopher's stone, his companions are to hasten to England. In that country they are to found a state and in all seriousness undertake to revive every "long-lost Gothic art" and to restore "their dress, their building, and their coins." Sarcastically the destiny of the race is described:

Proceed, illustrious race,
And yon fair isle with ancient glories grace.
Let others view with Astronomick eyes,
Yon lucid vagrants in the peopled skies:

Let them the habitable dome design,
Taught by *Vitruvius*, or old *Euclid*'s line;
Carve the rough block, inform the lumpish mass,
Give canvas life, and mould the breathing brass;

. . . .

Be yours the task, industrious, to recal
The lost inscription to the ruin'd wall;
Each *Celtic* character explain; or shew
How *Britons* ate a thousand years ago;
On laws of Jousts and Tournaments declame,
Or shine the rivals of the Herald's fame.[8]

In other words, Cambridge exalts as noble activities the arts of the Renaissance, architecture, painting, and sculpture in marble and bronze. The Gothicists, he thinks, would be far better employed in the erection of buildings in accord with classic taste than in the restoration of medieval structures deservedly forgotten. In a letter to Shenstone Lady Luxborough remarks that *The Scribleriad* "is not calculated to please Mr. Miller, and the rest of the Gothic gentlemen." [9] Plainly at this date such satire was a novelty; so abundant did it become later that it would have occasioned no comment.

The Gothicists could certainly not complain that their critics neglected to give them ample opportunity to grow hardened to ridicule. Imposing upon itself the task of defending conservatism in taste, the *World* (1753–56), which was persistent in making fun of *chinoiserie*, likewise subjected to a gentle rain of irony current manifestations of medievalism. But this mood of gay humor only thinly disguised the bitter conviction of the essayists that English taste was a muddle of perversity. They pointed out that artistic preferences which should be governed by clearly ascertained principles were entirely dependent upon the fluctuations of mere caprice and the fashionable whim of the moment. Such instability soured the wine of the classicist. It must be admitted that the art of which he approved, even in its more mediocre expressions, always possessed a self-respecting dignity owing to its obedience to traditions of which the validity had been tested by the experience and practice of generations. Early papers in the *World*, published in the first months of 1753, even before Strawberry Hill reached the first stage of its completion, disclose the anti-medieval sentiment of the essayists.

In one essay (no. 12), with an inexplicable inversion of chronology, William Whitehead, poet and writer of sentimental comedies, speaks of Gothicism as a fashion that has already passed its prime and regrets that it has been succeeded by the equally foolish fad of Orientalism. The craze for Chinese furnishings was no new thing; it had been increasing ever since the seventeenth century, and Gothicism could scarcely be said to be in a decline at the instant that the plaster of Strawberry Hill was becoming dry. But at any rate, Whitehead's complaint is valuable testimony as to the progress which medievalism had made even before Walpole opened the doors of his villa at Twickenham: "A few years ago every thing was Gothic; our houses, our beds, our book-cases, and our couches were all copied from some parts or other of our old cathedrals." Whitehead regrets, of course, that "the Grecian architecture . . . was totally neglected," and repeats the routine criticisms of medieval architecture: finical ornaments were rampant, awkward buttresses shocked sensitive nerves by their strange proportions, small columns supported great weights, and people trembled "at their entrance into every building, lest the roofs should fall upon their heads." The current defence of such aberration — that "there is something . . . in it congenial to our old Gothic constitution" — Whitehead scornfully rejects. He sees it only as proof that the present is an age of licence in which every individual is free to play the clown.

The essayists are unanimous in their contempt for the small suburban villas that crowded the outskirts of London and swarmed upon the banks of the Thames. In the opinion of Francis Coventry, author of the story of a lap-dog, *Pompey the Little*, they were "fatal proofs of the degeneracy of our national taste." Absurd in design and flimsy in construction, they made a laughable display of the owner's liking for all the odds and ends of medieval architecture. When Squire Mushroom undertook to rebuild a farm-house, it "shot up into Gothic spires, and was plastered over with stucco: the walls were notched into battlements; uncouth animals were set grinning at one another over the gate-posts, and the hall was fortified with rusty sword and pistols." What made these villas of the middle class all the more grotesque in the judgment of the satirists was the frequent habit of mingling Chinese and classic features with the medieval elements in reckless and laughable defiance of congruity. When Squire Mushroom discovered that his house was uninhabitable, he added two rooms in an entirely different style: "Thus while one half is designed to give you an old Gothic edifice, the other half presents to your view Venetian windows, slices of pilaster, balustrades, and other parts of Italian architecture." [10] In the only essay (no. 26) that he wrote for the *World* Joseph Warton also expresses his disgust for the villas that "disgrace the neighbourhood of this metropolis" and is shocked that a classic facade is sometimes "adulterated and defiled by the unnatural and impure mixture of Gothic whimsies."

Addison and Defoe had complained of the pretentious tradesmen who went to the expense of decorating their shop-fronts with the classic orders.[11] Conditions, if we are to believe the satirists, had scarcely improved in the middle of the century. The popular bastard architecture of the time had spread like an infection even to the facade of many a London shop. According to one ironic critic in the *World* (no. 59) "a happy mixture" of the Chinese and Gothic styles was visible on almost every chandler's shop and oyster stall from Hyde Park to Shoreditch, and it was rumored, he slyly added, that the classic portico of Covent Garden Church was to be replaced by one of the Gothic type. It is plain that the thoroughfares of London possessed no architectural harmony, and that a Battle of the Styles was waged perpetually along their length. "Superb colonades, porticos, Gothic arches, and Venetian windows" struggled for the admiration of the passing crowds.[12] So obvious was the conglomeration that it was satirized as grotesque even in a print of the day entitled *The Present Age, addressed to the professors of driving, dressing, ogling, writing, playing, gambling, racing, dancing, duelling, boxing, swearing, humming, building, etc. etc.* (1767).[13] As the print represents the scene, the house on the street along which throng the practitioners of the various follies exemplifies "Modern Architecture: the Corinthian, Venetian, Gothic, and Chinese huddled in one Front." A medieval oriel window projects from a classic facade and a Chinese railing runs before the house.

From such raillery it is not difficult to guess that these satirists would have slighted even Chippendale's composite furniture designs, in which he employed, frequently with the discretion of an artist, rococo, Chinese, and Gothic motives. Perhaps the satirists availed themselves too fully of their privilege of exaggeration; a contemporary French visitor speaks only of the classic fronts of London shops.[14] However, the numerous pattern-books of the time — those of Halfpenny are unintentionally comic — substantiate the critics and amply justify the spirit of their uncompromising ridicule.

It seems odd that Walpole should have identified himself with the *World* — he contributed nine essays to its pages — when some of its writers were thus unreservedly laughing at medievalism. It is true that Strawberry Hill was not an architectural hybrid; as its Chinese and classic features were confined to its furnishings (porcelain, lacquer, sculpture, and *objets d'art*), it was exempt from the most severe criticism, flimsy and fantastic though it was. However, from the complacency with which Walpole describes his house in innumerable letters one would never dream that it was, in reality, a blood-relation of Squire Mushroom's villa, and that the pseudo-Gothicism of which it was the most famous specimen was under a heavy fire of ridicule.

In the decade 1750–60 the attack upon Gothicism, inaugurated apparently by Cambridge in *The Scribleriad* and carried on by the *World*, received support from other quarters. As befitted the intellectual habits of a tory political writer, John Shebbeare was orthodox in his taste. Of Jones' banqueting-house, Whitehall, he said with more than a usual degree of classical prejudice that "a more perfect building in true sublimity of taste is to be seen nowhere." Although remembered today as the man who received from the government a pension simultaneously with Samuel Johnson to the great offence of the latter, who felt himself humiliated, Shebbeare was no more inclined than Johnson to idealize the Chinese. In his contribution to "spy" literature, *Letters on the English Nation* (1755), which he wrote under the name of Batista Angeloni, he introduced a tirade against the craze for Oriental porcelain, wall-paper, furniture, and architecture. Gothicism he ridiculed in corresponding terms:

> The Gothic too has its advocates; you see a hundred houses built with porches in that taste, such as are belonging to many chapels; even door-cases and the fronts of some dwellings, which might be drawn by one horse like a chaise, are fitted up in this manner; not to mention that rooms are stuccoed in this taste, with all the minute unmeaning carvings, which are found in the most Gothic chapels of a thousand years standing. . . .[15]

In the following year Isaac Ware added the weight of his authority as a distinguished professional architect and a translator of Palladio to the anti-medieval satires of the men of letters. On the whole, his judgment of the Gothic was more balanced than his contempt for the rococo. Although he magisterially refused to regard Gothic as architecture, he had the wit to discriminate between it and its modern imitations. He conceded that in the finer cathedrals there was "an air of majesty and grandeur which strikes and affect[s] us, in spite of that profusion of ornaments which so immoderately disfigures them." This was a generous admission for which he deserves credit. But the great error of the modern imitators of the medieval style — and here he confirms the criticism of the satirists — was the employment of Gothic in small buildings. The result was that whatever merits of solidity and strength the ancient style possessed were lost, and it became trivial, fantastic, and "too full of imaginary elegance."[16] Taking his comment as a whole, however, one realizes that Ware's sympathy for Gothic architecture is no greater than was Evelyn's one hundred years before.

From the seventeenth century onwards the critics of Gothicism echo one another with the most monotonous uniformity in thought and expression. The same ideas and the same words and phrases are repeated again and again. How utterly stale, for example, becomes the objection, in itself as a general principle by no means without validity, that in medieval architecture the multiplicity of "meaningless ornament" is destructive of simplicity and obscures the relation of a part of a building to the whole! Classic opinion of Gothic architecture, having in the early stages of its growth flowed into a verbal mold, solidified into a series of formulas that soon, if not immediately, became traditional.

The only modern within my personal knowledge who shuddered at the gloom of a medieval cathedral was a Christian Scientist. The dear lady protested that the interior of Chartres smelt of death and the grave and created a depression of mood of which she, as a professional optimist filled with yearning for only the lovely, cheerful things in life, could not find it in her philosophy to approve. But to the majority of us who have been nurtured in the romantic cult and harbor memories of poetic windows "richly dight," or glorified by innumerable

> stains and splendid dyes,
> As are the tiger-moth's deep damask'd wings,

it comes as a surprise that the beauty of medieval glass and the mysterious enchantment of an interior illuminated by it should ever have been a matter of debate. Yet Wren, unlike Milton and Keats, cared nothing for "storied windows," and by his practice in his own churches testified to the strength of his predilection for clear light.

In 1778 Vicesimus Knox affords a curious example of the persistence of this classical point of view and an epitome of the warping influence of conservatism. Stained glass windows are, in his opinion, an index of the inferiority of taste characteristic of the age that produced them. "Glaring colours, rendered still more glaring by transparency, seem to have constituted, in the idea of those who lived a century or two ago, the perfection of beauty." This is only another way of saying that such colors failed to create that simplicity of effect which the classicist prized, but which often impresses others more romantic than Vicesimus as merely the sterility of imaginative impotence. Many houses built in London squares in the eighteenth century embody this ideal of naked simplicity achieved by the elimination of the cornice and almost every form of architectural enrichment. Knox then proceeds to express astonishment that the twilight of the medieval interior had its admirers:

> It is said to throw the mind into that serious temper, which is peculiarly adapted to the indulgence of devotion. Such an effect it may perhaps produce, in a great degree, on minds subject to superstition and fanaticism, or strongly influenced by a warm imagination; yet, why light, one of the most glorious works of creation, should refriger-

ate the ardour of religion in the rational and dispassionate possessor of it, no good reason can be assigned. . . . A religious dimness may, perhaps, be deemed necessary for the bigoted inhabitants of the convent and the cloyster, whose minds, it is to be feared, are often as dark as their habitations; but light is cheerful, and cheerfulness is the disposition of innocence.[17]

In other words, the dim interior suggested the tainted atmosphere of papacy and made an appeal, in particular, to the ardent imagination, the activity of which the congenital classicist viewed with profound distrust. To Knox, living in an age of hard, self-confident rationalism deficient in spirituality and hostile to any form of mysticism, gloom in an ecclesiastical edifice was distasteful, because he was incapable of comprehending those phases of deep religious feeling with which the somber light of a cathedral was in subtle harmony. The classicist set great store by clear thinking, but he never suspected that frequently his thinking was clear simply because it was shallow. It was inevitable that a man of Knox's mental outlook — he had no liking for the Spenserian imitators and for literary works "of which no archetype could be recognized in the volumes of antiquity" — should align himself with Wren against the poets.[18] By implication, of couse, Knox was slighting all those of his contemporaries who like Stukeley, Walpole, and Gray were indefatigable in the collection and preservation of old glass.

CHAPTER XVI

THE CHALLENGE OF THE ROCOCO

Chinoiserie and medievalism were not the only hornets that disturbed the peace of the classicists in the eighteenth century. The taste for the rococo style was also antagonistic to traditional Renaissance design, weakened its influence, and kept it from enjoying the monopoly of popularity which the admirers of antiquity believed was its inalienable due. Why the French style was inimical to classicism is plain to anyone acquainted with its very conspicuous characteristics; nevertheless, at the risk of expatiating upon what is familiar, a brief explanatory comment may be acceptable.

The word *rococo* is derived from *rocaille*, the term descriptive of the materials — shells, pebbles, and coarse, rough-hewn rocks — out of which were made the fantastically artificial grottos that were to be found in every self-respecting baroque garden of the seventeenth and early eighteenth centuries. Rather incongruously and inexplicably, the term was in time applied to what is the most graceful and refined of decorative styles. A type of design that came to flower during the Regency and the reign of Louis XV and that was in subtle spiritual harmony with the gay, frivolous mood of a pleasure-loving court, the rococo was in its origin a reaction against the symmetry and straight lines that dominated decoration during the period of the Grand Monarch. Rejecting axial emphasis and the rigid uniformity of Louis Quatorze design, which had produced, to be sure, an impression of splendid ceremonial dignity, the rococo exploited the esthetic possibilities of asymmetry. In so doing it frequently achieved effects of exquisite balance by which masses of ornament distributed in a pattern, although not regularly arranged, were kept in sensitive equilibrium. Moreover, instead of the straight line of Louis XIV, conspicuous, for example, in wall- and door-panels and in the backs and seats of chairs, the rococo favored sinuous S- and C-shaped curves (Fig. 59). These curves

Fig. 59 — Ceiling in the Rococo Style, Chesterfield House

Fig. 60 — Silk Brocade. Curvilinear Design, Characteristic of the Period of Louis XV. Cf. Fig. 52

appeared in an infinite variety of forms — in delicate scrolls, undulating moldings, waving vines, and gracefully sweeping branches of acanthus. The borders of panels and the whole frame of chairs and tables became a series of ingratiating curves, melting by imperceptible degrees into one another.

This repudiation of Renaissance formalism was not, however, limited to furniture and interior woodwork; it extended to the whole field of decoration. The grandiose patterns of Louis Quatorze brocade (Fig. 52), large and heavy in the scale of their detail, imposing in their deliberate symmetry, and insistent in their axial stress, were, for example, succeeded by more naturalistic textile designs made up of simple, undulating floral sprays (Fig. 60). On these sprays the smaller, more slender twigs spring from the main stem at irregular intervals, and the flowers and foliage, although exquisitely balanced, seem to possess the spontaneity of nature itself. Whereas the textile patterns of the earlier reign were relatively static, almost majestic, and thoroughly in accord with the spirit of a court governed by an inflexible etiquette and gratified by the elaborate stateliness of formal gardens, the rococo patterns were dynamic, and by virtue of their life and movement were in agreement with the more cheerful temper of the age of Louis XV and its delight in Watteau and the delicate refinements of sentimental literature. What is remarkable is this unity of spirit which in each period pervaded all types of design and by means of line and form gave a brilliant, decisive, individual character to woodwork, furniture, textiles, and every other object upon which artistic feeling chose to spend itself.

It was a sign that the English were breaking away from the strict, disciplinary canons of Renaissance art when, as soon as the new French ideal of beauty defined itself, the asymmetry and curvature of the rococo began to appear across the Channel. This interest did not betoken a transference of allegiance as startling as might at first seem to be the case. Already the greater freedom and naturalism of Chinese decoration had prepared the way for the acceptance of the rococo. Lacquer, porcelain, wallpaper, and other importations from the Orient had accustomed English eyes to irregularity. Textiles, especially chintz, had made familiar patterns of waving lines such as resulted from the realistic treatment of vines and other plants with long stems and delicate tendrils (Fig. 51).

This affinity between *chinoiserie* and the rococo was not, perhaps, so fortuitous as it seemed. Some historians of art have, indeed, argued that in its origin the rococo itself was inspired by Orientalism. Others, rejecting this explanation, have contended that the rococo was a return, after the interruption of the Renaissance, to the characteristic qualities of flamboyant Gothic: its indifference to exact symmetry and its love of the flowing lines that pulsate in the tracery of innumerable Gothic windows and in the delicate shafts which sweep upward to the intersection of vaults. Whether or not the rococo was historically a blood-relation of either Chinese or medieval art is a question that lies outside our province. It is, at all events, a significant coincidence that in England in the eighteenth century the taste for *chinoiserie*, for Gothicism, and for the rococo perfectly synchronized. However different their obvious physical characteristics, there existed between them no fundamental opposition. These three modes of artistic expression possessed in common qualities of design — asymmetry, movement, variety, freedom, spontaneity — by virtue of which the influence of one reinforced that of the others. Singly and together they militated against the classical ideals of repose, sobriety, and discipline.

The evidence of the influence of the rococo in England is abundant and various — far greater, indeed, than one would infer from those English writers who are always inclined to slight the presence of foreign elements in the native style. At Vauxhall, adjacent to the semicircle of dining-boxes (Fig. 56), which was, as we saw, the most spectacular of eighteenth-century Gothic edifices, was the Music Room, or Rotunda (Fig. 61), decorated in a rococo style of vulgar exuberance. The window-frames, the sconces for the candles, the ornate brackets supporting the busts, and the mirror-frames in the oblong hall, even though sobered by symmetry, were, as the print shows, a dance of S- and C-curves. But in the opinion of a contemporary writer the building was "an edifice fram'd in the highest delicacy and taste." The canopy with its painted floriated sprays looked to him "like the dome . . . of a most august, royal tent." Scarcely in harmony, to be sure, with this gay scheme of decoration were the plain classic portal on the right and the severe rectangular panels on the left. At the end of the vista the pointed Gothic archway marked the exit to the open-air restaurant. Such a curious juxtaposition of the classic, the medieval, and the rococo was of frequent occurrence in the middle of the eighteenth century. Yet this bespangled architecture, like that of Strawberry Hill, secured admirers in its own time. It moved the contemporary writer I have quoted to a higher literary flight. The rococo Music Room was, he thought, "the Temple of Pleasure, whose architect must be a genius," and, in general, he said, "an intelligent spectator, of a warm imagination, is so variously delighted here, that he need not envy the transports felt by the antient Greeks, in their Idalian, Cnidan, or Paphian temples of Venus."[1] Very fittingly one of the silver season tickets designed for Jonathan Tyers, the owner and manager of Vauxhall, was provided with a delicate border of characteristic rococo curves encircling the figure of Amphion on a dolphin.[2]

In the middle of the century, when the French style enjoyed its greatest popularity, rococo ornament with impish perversity sometimes invaded strange places. At Oxford it is found disporting itself on the ceilings of the Bodleian Library and the Christ Church Library. In the London Museum it plays in several of the diminutive rooms of the elaborate Georgian doll's house designed about 1740. At the Foundling Hospital the Court Room was embellished with a decorative scheme that also reflected Gallic taste. Of the great London mansions Chesterfield House was most pronounced in its preference for the rococo. Although the plan of the house was thoroughly Palladian — a central block with two wings — and was designed by Isaac Ware, one of the most cantankerous of the classicists, Chesterfield followed the imported French mode in the decoration of his drawing-room and music-room (Fig. 59). Like Chesterfield House, Hagley Park, familiar to readers of Thomson and famous for its natural garden, exemplified the range of contemporary taste. Although Lord Lyttelton himself, the friend of the amateur Gothic architect Sanderson Miller, had a hankering for pseudo-medievalism, at the behest of his wife he built the house in the approved Italian style with a monumental external staircase entirely unfit for the English climate; but he saw to it that within the mansion the lighter French style prevailed in the principal apartments.[3]

The graceful waving lines which in such interiors played over the surface of walls and ceiling were likewise echoed in English furniture. For his designs in the rococo which Chippendale, in addition to his Chinese and Gothic designs, illustrated in *The Gentleman and Cabinet Maker's Director* he has indeed been frequently and often justly criticized. They are altogether too often a frenzy of curves which weary the eye by their incessant meanderings and produce an unpleasant feeling of instability. Although the commode illustrated (Fig. 62) is one of Chippendale's more reposeful conceptions, its curvature is amply sufficient. Whereas classic taste required that a table or commode should be strictly square or oblong in form, Chippendale's design is one of studied curvature. The edge of the top is straight only at the back, where the necessity of placing the commode against the wall made a curve impossible. Moreover, the sides instead of being flat present a series of undulating planes, as if some vibration in defiance of the inflexibility of the material were passing in waves through the wood. As these curved diagonal planes at the corners avoid the sharp angles of a rectangular commode, they render the transition from the sides to the front more gradual and the rhythmic movement more conspicuous.

The classicist, furthermore, guided by his architectural feeling for function, was careful to distinguish between the leg and the body of a piece of furniture. This feeling even Chippendale himself reveals in the design of his Chinese chair (Fig. 48). But when as a designer of rococo he was desirous of long flowing lines, he treated furniture plastically, so that one part merged gradually into another. Accordingly the ornament that borders the base of the commode is fused with that of the curving legs, resulting in a continuity of line in place of incisive structural differentiation. Finally, the rough serrated ornament that is applied to the front of the commode and forms its legs has a resemblance to the sharp irregular edges of shells which gives the style its name.

Contemporary painters and engravers undertaking to repro-

Fig. 61 — Music Room, Vauxhall Gardens. Rococo Decorations

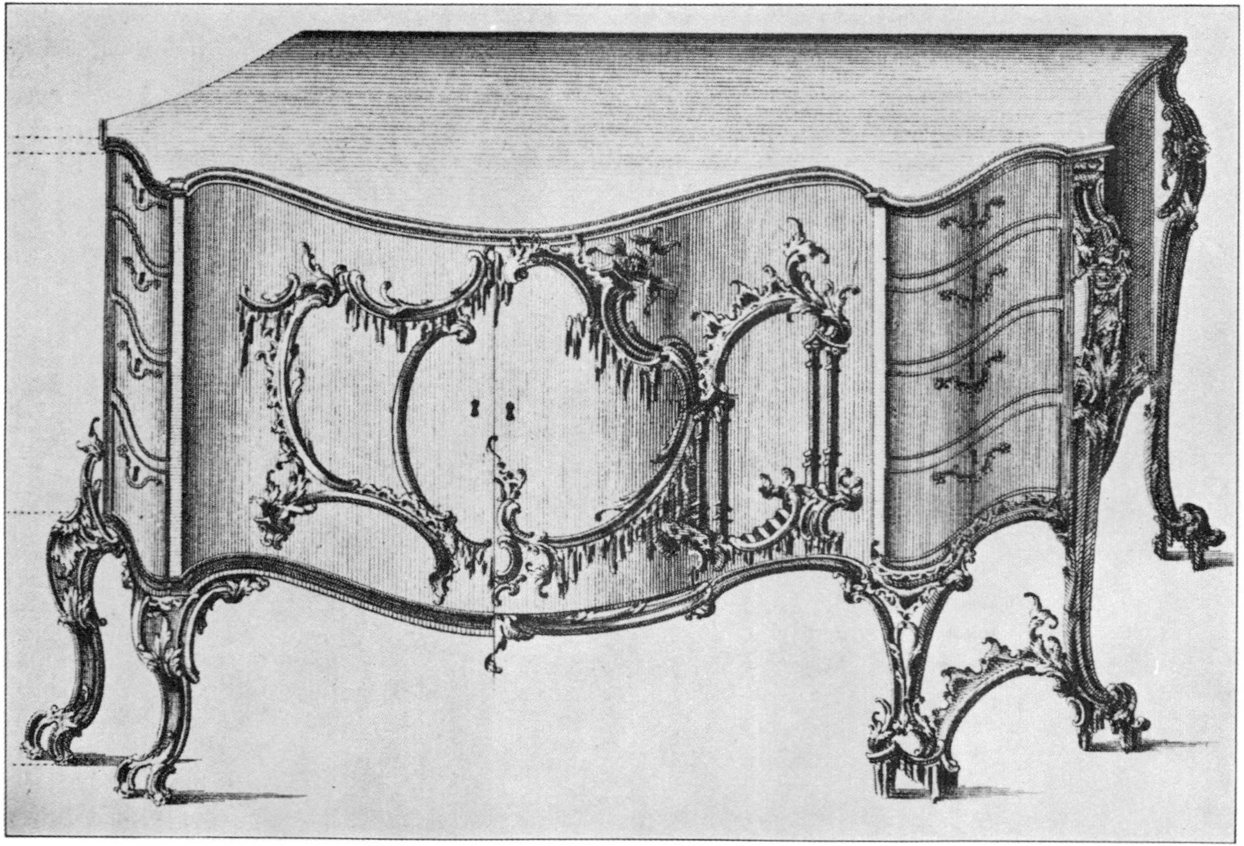

Fig. 62 — Commode in the Rococo Style. Designed by Chippendale

duce faithfully the rooms of their own time represent numerous interiors which, like the Georgian doll's house, have rococo furnishings. As might be expected, Hogarth's realistic work is rich with examples. In plate 2 of *The Harlot's Progress*, the wench quarreling with her Jewish protector kicks over in anger a Louis Quinze table, and in plate 6 in the same series the name-plate on the coffin is an unsymmetrical rococo cartouche. In plate 8 of *Industry and Idleness*, the virtuous apprentice, having become sheriff of London, feasts in a hall hung with pictures in frames in the French style. In other plates in *The Rake's Progress*, *The Election*, and *Marriage à la Mode*, the evidence of rococo influence is plain. Then, too, as the illustrators of Theobald's edition (1740) of Shakespeare were light-heartedly indifferent to historic congruity, they repeatedly introduced rococo details. As they have engraved various scenes of the plays, chairs in *Henry IV, Part II*, door-frames and picture-frames in *The Taming of the Shrew*, and great candle-holders in *Othello* rejoice in interlacing S- and C-curves. Even Desdemona is done to death on a rococo bed.

Gay serpentine forms likewise disported themselves on the English porcelains that decked the cabinets, mantelpieces, and dining-tables of the time. The curving edges of plates, the unsymmetrical vases, the pitchers with capricious handles, and the fantastic bases of *rocaille* on which stand figures of Watteau shepherds, smiling, love-making, or fingering a lute, all declare the French style. Indeed, from 1759 to 1770, when the influence of Vincennes and Sèvres porcelain was paramount, rococo ornament is the most characteristic feature of Chelsea and Bow ware.

Finally, it should be borne in mind that the English ladies and gentlemen who lived in rococo rooms, sat in rococo chairs, and sipped tea from rococo porcelain were at the same time dressed in silk, either imported or of native manufacture, of which the pattern was made up of the familiar waving sprays of foliage. English taste in textile design had succumbed to the charm of the wayward curve. To such an extent is this true that it is possible for anyone visiting the English costume collections in the Victoria and Albert Museum and in the London Museum to recognize immediately the suits and dresses of the mid-Georgian era by the pattern of the rich fabrics.

English designers were not troubled by antiquarian compunctions. Frequently, when they took their pencil in hand, whatever historic sense they possessed went to sleep. Without apology they employed in the same room or on the same piece of furniture rococo details and other types of ornament from such totally different sources as the Orient and the Middle Ages. This fusion of decorative ideas separated in time and space marks the uncertainty of taste in the middle decades of the eighteenth century, when romanticism was developing into a conscious hostility to the Renaissance. The room from Wotton-under-Edge (Fig. 47) is illustrative. The English wallpaper in the Chinese style, the plain rectangular panels that would be appropriate in a room of classic design, and the graceful rococo ornament over the mantelpiece, noticeably symmetrical and constructed so as to support small porcelain objects, do not create an impression of harmonious unity. To such an extent does the rococo decoration and its studied arrangement fail to "tie up" with the more naturalistic pattern of the Oriental wallpaper that the chimney-piece is detached from the rest of the room and stands in isolation. Of all the rooms set up with such skill in the Victoria and Albert Museum, this is the least attractive. It probably represents fairly the esthetic muddle of an age uncontrolled by any dominant artistic principle. If one compares this room with the earlier one from Clifford's Inn (1686) (Fig. 9), it is clear how beautiful an integration of an interior the earlier designers accomplished by the simple restful repetition of straight lines and rectangular forms. Such an interior was the product of an idea of order firmly grasped by the intelligence and carried into practice with conviction — an idea of order which was as evident in the garden plan of the seventeenth century as in the preference for the heroic couplet. On the other hand, the Chinese-rococo room and the Gothic vagaries of Strawberry Hill are growths of an inchoate taste when the standards of the Renaissance were in the melting-pot and no one knew in what direction he was going artistically.

Much more satisfying are some of Chippendale's furniture designs in a composite style. On his Gothic bookcase (Fig. 57), midway between the four pinnacles, the lattice-work that forms a sort of crest is pierced by a group of unusually concave C-curves. It would be pedantic to object to them, for they do not clash with the medieval tracery of the doors. Although the fine chair (Fig. 58) is definitely Gothic in its employment of ecclesiastical window-tracery as a pattern for the back, the whole frame of this admirable piece of furniture is molded by a feeling for the beauty of the gently undulating line. Indeed, from that point of view it may be said that the chair is actually more rococo than Gothic. Whereas in a chair of which the design was controlled by the classicist's sensitiveness to architectural values there would be a careful discrimination between the vertical uprights of the back and the horizontal connecting bar at the top, the frame of this chair slights such distinctions of function and consists virtually of one line that flows across the top and down each side of the frame in a wave-like rhythm. The same affection for the unbroken line is evident elsewhere in the design. Perhaps even more conspicuously than in Chippendale's commode the beautifully modulated curves of the seat-frame melt into the tapering legs, and produce that plasticity of form which is the delight of the rococo and which it is willing to secure at the expense of structural emphasis.

This tendency of the rococo to slight functional values in design has added significance if, digressing a moment, we recall that the literature of the time exhibits in terms of its own technique an identical phenomenon. The classic critic, dominated by a clear perception of fundamental differences in purpose between the various literary types, required for his intellectual satisfaction that those differences should be objectively reflected in a characteristic and appropriate form. Just as the classic designer differentiated through construction between the seat and leg of a chair, a table, or a commode because he recognized that their function was obviously not the same, so the classic critic wished, for example, to keep apart comedy and tragedy because their emotional intention was dissimilar. When he condemned tragi-comedy, he did so because it audaciously mixed together laughter and tears and produced, in his opinion, only esthetic chaos. For both the classic designer and the classic critic form was a means of clarifying and externalizing ideas of function. Later when, as the reaction against the critical standards of the Renaissance developed, the romantic dramatist rebelled against the principle of decorum and the three unities, he was, in reality, like the designer of rococo, who sought for a greater plasticity of form in a desire to express linear rhythms of more varied range and complexity. Was it not more than a mere coincidence that in England at the same moment literature and design manifested a growing indifference to architectonic values?

Of the numerous pattern-books which streamed from the press, Chippendale's is the most famous and one of the few that are taken seriously to-day. But a host of others by lesser men illustrate the confusion of English taste between 1740 and 1780. Their authors were no idealists, inspired by a wish to force their own artistic predilections upon the public, but they industriously drew and published without discrimination classic, Chinese, Gothic, and rococo designs because these various styles were what the unsettled taste of the time demanded and what workmen, whether architects or cabinet-makers, wished to know about if they were to secure clients. It is necessary to make only the briefest comment on these books individually. Their long titles, generally not distinguished by modesty of statement, display their scope and make evident against what competitors for popular favor classicism was now contending. For anyone who is not familiar with such books the titles of a few will be amusing and illuminating:

The Universal System of Household Furniture consisting of above 300 designs in the most elegant taste, both useful and ornamental. . . . The whole made convenient to the nobility and gentry in their choice, and comprehensive to the workman by directions for executing the several designs, with specimens of ornament for young practitioners in drawing. By Ince and Mayhew, Cabinet-makers and Upholders, in Broad Street, Golden Square, London, where every article in the several branches treated of is executed on the most reasonable terms, with the utmost neatness and punctuality. *c.* 1762.

(The designs are Gothic, Chinese, and rococo.)

The Nobleman and Gentleman's Director and Assistant in the True Choice of their Wheel-Carriages. 1763.

(In many of the designs for closed carriages the frames of the panels and windows consist of simple rococo curves employed with English restraint. However, the French influence is unmistakable.)

The Chimney-piece Maker's Daily Assistant, or, A Treasury of New Designs for Chimney-pieces: Beginning with the most plain and simple and gradually ascending to the most grand and magnificent in the antique, modern, ornamental, and Gothic taste; proper to be executed in halls, salons, vestibules, guard-rooms, state rooms, parlors, dining-rooms, drawing-rooms, ante-rooms, music rooms, cabinets, bed-rooms, etc. . . . From the original drawings of Thomas Milton, John Cruden, and Placido Columbani, architects. London, 1766.

(The designs are both classic and fantastically rococo.)

The Joiner's and Cabinet-Maker's Darling, or, Pocket Director. Containing sixty different designs, entirely new and useful. Forty of which are Gothic, Chinese, Mosaic, and ornamental frets proper for friezes, imposts, architraves, tabernacle frames, bookcases, tea-tables, tea-stands, trays, stoves, and fenders. And twenty new and beautiful designs for Gothic, modern, and ornamental fan-lights for over-doors in the most elegant taste. Calculated for the universal use of carpenters, joiners, cabinet-makers, masons, plasterers, smiths, etc. etc. And intended to assist the nobility and gentry in their choice. The whole designed and engraved by John Cruden, architect. London, 1770.

The Cabinet and Chair-Maker's Real Friend and Companion, or The Whole System of Chair-Making Made plain and easy. Containing upwards of one hundred new and useful designs for all sorts of chairs amongst which are some very elegant in the Chinese and Gothic taste . . . grand French settees . . . and also a geometrical view of the five orders of architecture, adjusted by equal parts with full explanation, whereby the meanest capacity by inspection may delineate and work an entire order or any part, of any magnitude required. The whole invented and drawn by Robert Manwaring, Cabinet Maker. London, 1775.

If one looks over the numerous admirable plates in Heal's *London Tradesmen's Cards of the XVIII Century*, the impression of sprawling eclecticism in matters of taste suggested by the pattern-books is repeatedly confirmed, sometimes with unconscious irony. As the purpose of these cards, really valuable though minor social documents, was to set off to greatest advantage the information they conveyed (the name of the tradesman, his business, and the location of his shop), the statement of facts in the center of the card was generally framed with a carefully engraved design, more or less elaborate and frequently genuinely beautiful. But whether the design should be classic, rococo, Chinese, or Gothic was, of course, a matter of choice. However, it cannot, unfortunately, be said that the decision was always determined by a sense of fitness as to what sort of decorative pattern would most appropriately glorify a given trade. A vendor of ass's milk, a dentist, and a chimney-sweeper selected a classic design. D. Negri, a confectioner, and Robert Legg, an undertaker, preferred the Chinese-rococo style. Dr. James advertised his famous powders for fever with rococo accompaniments, and Matthew Darly in a frame of similar design proclaimed his stock of wallpaper "in the modern, Gothic, or Chinese Tastes." They were by no means alone in their preference. A bookseller, a cabinet-maker, a carpenter, a watch-maker, an engine-maker, and a hatter also chose rococo design. All these cards are not of the same date, yet it is evident from their decoration that the bulk of them belong to the third quarter of the century and that they are contemporaneous with the pattern-books.[4]

Although the practice of mixing together Gothic, Chinese, and rococo ornaments called up incongruous historic and geographical associations, the product was not always such a ridiculous hybrid as might be imagined. If this juggling with motives was managed clumsily and stupidly, as in the designs of third-rate English cabinet-makers like Batty Langley and John Halfpenny, the result was often grotesque. But if this play with motives was guided by intelligence and artistic feeling, the outcome was the exquisite fantasies of Huet and Pillement and some of the more enduring examples of Chippendale's genius.

The inherent qualities of the rococo, its asymmetry and its curvature, encouraged extravagance in design and excessive multiplication of ornate detail if the hand of the artist was not held in check by common sense and good taste. No doubt because of the English passion for moderation and the accompanying distrust of audacity, the rococo never exercised over English decoration any such authority as it secured in France and especially in Germany, where, as in the palaces of Potsdam and in the Residenz at Würzburg, the style attained its apotheosis. Although England has, in consequence, no example of rococo decoration which possesses the incredible extravagance of the church of St. Johannes Nepomuk in Munich or the sheer loveliness of the Silver Room of Amalienburg in the gardens of Nymphenburg, the prevalence of the style in England from approximately 1740 to 1775 is certainly sufficient testimony that the straight lines and rectangular forms of the Renaissance were at a discount. The ingratiating mood of the rococo, its pleasure in movement and variety, the alluring grace with which it invites the eye to travel through the intricacies of a delicate pattern, were calculated to make the elegant repose, the dignified symmetries, and the measured rhythms of classical design seem dull and monotonous if not actually unimaginative.

A comparison, a literary one, makes clear the divorce of the rococo from classicism. The literature of the Renaissance, developing from an assimilation of ancient culture, demanded an acquaintance with the classics for its appreciation. To relish fully the irony of even such a delicate morsel as *The Rape of the Lock* required a familiarity with the conventions of the Homeric and the Virgilian epic. Similarly the art of the Renaissance was in its own way essentially a learned style depending upon a knowledge and intelligent adaptation of ancient forms and ornamental motives. The dome of Chiswick House, for example, recalled the Pantheon and the portico of St. Martin-in-the-Fields was reminiscent of a Roman temple. The more vividly the eighteenth-century man realized the ancestry of these buildings, the more his enjoyment of them was heightened and his self-complacency flattered. The rococo, on the other hand, repudiated any such ideal of imitation. Its charm was its own, existing in and for itself and entirely detached from any historic associations. Fundamentally romantic in spirit, it individualistically emancipated design from its bondage to Greece and Rome and joyously followed its own impulsive intuitions.

Classicists were continually sneering at the prevalence of French taste in all phases of English life, and no doubt they had in mind the rococo as one pernicious example of it. But unfortunately, as they were not always as specific in their satire as they might have been, they fail to make any definite disclosure of their opinion of the rococo. That the hostility to *rocaille* was not more articulate may partly be accounted for by the fact that, although evident enough in its influence upon interior decoration, furniture, Sheffield silver, porcelain, and *objets d'art*, the rococo did not affect English architecture. Had any English architect ventured to erect on a London street a façade like that of the house of the brothers Asam in Munich, we may be sure that the classicists would have trained their guns upon him without mercy, and with some justice on their side. The charming conceits of the rococo, its appealing grace, and its fluidity of movement are attuned to a boudoir or a ballroom, but they do not create that impression of permanence and stability which is essential to architecture. What is attractive as decoration in the intimacy of an interior becomes trivial and childish on an exterior.

But Isaac Ware made no such discrimination. Liking *rocaille* neither inside nor outside a house, he delivered against it an unequivocal broadside. Coming only two years after Cochin's famous attack upon the rococo in *Mercure de France* (1754), Ware's criticism, imbedded in the depths of his huge work, *A Complete Body of Architecture* (1756), signalizes the resolve of the classicists, whether in France or England, to recall taste from the S-curve into the path of rectitude. But whereas Cochin discharged only light shafts of penetrating irony, Ware employed a blunderbuss. Moreover, as if to convince us of his obtuseness and malice, he allowed his anti-Gallicism to run away with him and mingled his pertinent critical comment with irrelevant sneers at the French intelligence. Altogether Ware impresses one as an intolerant and thoroughly disagreeable person.

The strictures which Ware passes even on forms of classic architecture are a warning that he will not deal tenderly with manifestations of the romantic spirit. He pushes to extremes, for example, the argument from nature to which on occasion the classicist, paradoxically enough, was as fond of resorting as his arch-enemy, the apostle of Rousseau. To both the square and the fluted column Ware objects on the ground that the tree of which the column is a development is neither square nor fluted. To treat the column thus without the sanction of nature is, Ware declares, nothing less than a false practice. Then with pride in his intellectual courage he adds: "This is judging with severity, but it is judging with truth." [5] His conservatism is patent elsewhere. He regrets that wallpaper has driven sculptured interior decoration out of fashion; he deplores that on recent houses Chinese railings have replaced the classic balustrade; and, referring to Gothic "building," he self-righteously explains that "we will not descend to call it architecture."

His criticism of *rocaille* is in keeping with these opinions. He sees the sound scientific principles of architecture undermined by "the caprice of *France*." To offset encouraging indications that neither *chinoiserie* nor Gothicism is as popular as formerly, Ware has to confess that "the *French* are more difficult to conquer." This "frivolous people whom we are apt to imitate" he holds responsible for the loss of favor formerly enjoyed by "those ceilings which a *Burlington* had taught us to introduce from *Roman* temples, and those ornaments of doors" in which Inigo Jones had followed classic models. The "very childish taste" of the French is now visible on the entablatures of the orders as well as on the frames of mirrors, and has secured "the most universal footing in the finishing of rooms." The style "consists in crooked lines like C's . . . ; the Gothic is hardly more contemptible." This

> unmeaning scrawl of (C's) inverted, turned, and hooked together, take place of *Greek* and *Roman* elegance . . . This is not because the possesser thinks there is or can be elegance in such fond weak ill-jointed and unmeaning figures: it is usually because it is *French*.

Ware believes that "a ceiling straggled over with arched lines, and twisted curves, with . . . C's, and tangled semi-circles" is fitted only to "please the light eye of the *French*, who seldom carry their observation farther than a casual glance."

What does Ware advise should be done in this crisis? The architect, if he is judicious, ought to discourage the adoption of the rococo. When he discovers that a client is "captivated . . . with foolish fancies," the architect, relying on the common sense of the Englishman, should point out that "this is reviving the decoration of Goths and Vandals." Generally the client will recognize the truth of this statement, and will express his gratitude for his enlightenment. Those who, however, persist in their preference for the French style should be allowed to have their way; "they deserve no better." This remark Ware may have barbed for Chesterfield's special benefit. Although that noble lord had been willing to have the entrance hall and stairway, the library, and the sitting-rooms of his London house decorated in the classic style, he had seen to it that his drawing-room and his music-room were rococo.

Finally, in addition to his specific advice to the architect, Ware resorts to exhortation against the French. It is true that they are

> difficult to conquer; but let us rouse in every sense the national spirit against them; and no more permit them to deprave our taste in this noble science, than to introduce among us the miseries of their government, or fooleries of their religion.
>
> Upon the most impartial review we shall find that nothing in greatness, or in grace, can compare with the *Greek* or *Roman* architecture; therefore let us employ nothing in the place of them.

This battle-call to lion-hearted Britishers to rush to the defence of the cornice and Ionic column sounds like Voltaire's panic-stricken manifesto against the corruption of French taste by Shakespeare. However, it must be admitted that in spite of his vehemence Ware turns out to be more practical than one might expect. He follows a chapter on the classic compartmental ceiling (Fig. 10) "in the true taste" with one entitled *Of decorating a ceiling in a fanciful manner.* Here he undertakes to lead the reader into the "wildernesses" of fancy. In other words, accepting the inevitable, he favors the discreet adoption and modification of rococo ornaments. He suggests in particular that their luxuriance be curbed until they have been reduced "into a more decent appearance." Thus John Bull solemnly sets about the task of teaching this wayward, chic French miss to behave herself in the presence of the English. It is not difficult to believe that Ware's compromise was crassly conceived as a means to placate those aristocratic clients who still yearned for the grace and charm of the rococo. But Ware's own loyalty to "the manly noble orders" was unshaken.

CHAPTER XVII

THE SECOND REVOLUTION IN GARDEN DESIGN

I. Experiments in Naturalism

At the beginning of the eighteenth century the debt of English art and literature to the Continent was immense. The debt had been accumulating for centuries during which Englishmen, according to their spiritual need, had enriched the national inheritance by the continuous assimilation of foreign culture. But close as had been this artistic and intellectual relationship between England and the Continent, it had never become parasitic. Consequently there never was any occasion in England for a definitely nationalistic movement such as developed in Germany in the eighteenth century and in Russia in the nineteenth century in a deliberate effort to break the dominance of French civilization. The English were relieved from the necessity for such a purgation by a fortunate circumstance: their capacity for the absorption of Continental culture was counterbalanced by a similar capacity for the adoption and modification of what they had borrowed without any loss of their own intrinsic character. England, in the meantime, exercised no corresponding influence upon Continental civilization; in the eyes of Europeans she was a country inhabited by barbarians. That a change of attitude took place in the eighteenth century is a commonplace. Europe was swept by a wave of Anglomania; the French, Germans, Italians, and Russians idealized England and her institutions, extolled her poets and philosophers, and in varying degrees adopted her customs and fashions. For the first time England was repaying her debt to the Continent. In this liquidation of culture one of the principal items was the natural or landscape garden. Developed in England, it passed to the Continent, became the fashion, and in popular esteem replaced noble Italian and French gardens of Renaissance origin.

The vogue of the English garden, like that of *chinoiserie*, medievalism, and the rococo, arose obviously out of dissatisfaction with the standards of classic design and a desire to emancipate the garden plan from symmetry for the sake of greater irregularity and variety in the treatment of water, the planting of trees and flowers, and the laying out of walks and avenues. Taste now required not the ideal beauty of axial arrangement, but the spontaneity and freedom of nature itself. Such a revolution in esthetic feeling could be only of slow growth. The natural garden is identified with the eighteenth century; yet its development was influenced in a measure by such seventeenth-century writers as Bacon, Milton, and Temple.

Indeed, in this connection, Milton's description of Paradise in the fourth book of *Paradise Lost* cannot escape comment. The garden which Milton has depicted with evident delight plainly has nothing in common with the formal garden of the period in which the epic was written. The waters of Eden neither rest in the unbroken calm of a long rectangular canal nor shoot upward from marble basins in a gleaming shower, but flow through the garden in "many a rill," or as rippling brooks meander like the serpentine of the eighteenth century through the deep shade of overhanging boughs. In their course they refresh flowers which are not, as Milton assures us, confined "in beds and curious knots" in accord with the principles of "nice Art," but scattered luxuriantly "on hill and dale and plain." In the placid surface of a lovely lake — not a canal — are reflected the myrtles that fringe its bank. Elsewhere are grottos and caves overgrown with vines heavy with luscious grapes, and between flourishing groves stretch "lawns and level downs" where flocks graze peacefully. This last unobtrusive pastoral detail Milton has detached from the English countryside, but the vegetation he has envisaged flourishes only on the shores of the Mediterranean or in the clear air of the tropics. We hear of palms crowning the hilltops, "rich trees" shedding "odorous gums and balm," and "fruit burnished with golden rind." In a manuscript note Addison has remarked that "Milton would never have been able . . . to have laid out his Paradise, had he not seen the . . . gardens of Italy." [1] This is perhaps true if Addison had in mind only the myrtles and palms, oranges, lemons, and grapes which struck Milton's imagination as they do any traveler from the bleaker North, but aside from their sumptuous, exotic vegetation it is impossible to discover anything that such grandly formal gardens as those of Lante or Caprarola could have contributed to Milton's conception of Eden.

This brief passage of description is the center of a very respectable little tempest of controversy. Writers on the garden in the eighteenth century, Cambridge, Joseph Warton, Walpole, William Mason, and Hayley — to name no others —, saw in Milton's Paradise an anticipation of the natural garden, which was then in the height of its vogue, and they hailed the poet as a "herald," a "founder," and a "prophet." In their eagerness to enlist such an adherent for the style of garden design which they themselves admired, they misinterpreted the spirit of Milton's attitude, and implied in him a conscious, almost belligerent, reaction against the formal garden of his age. They ignored the simpler explanation that it is possible that Milton had enough sense to realize that the representation of Paradise as a formal garden would be a conspicuous and objectionable anachronism. It is plain, moreover, that in this matter of taste in gardens Milton was no bigot. The poet of spacious imagination who was able to feel the placid loveliness of the English countryside and the sensuous beauty of the Mediterranean shore also praises in *Il Penseroso* "trim gardens" and a "dry smooth-shaven green." But in spite of this passage it is assuredly obscuring the facts to assert dogmatically, as Sir Reginald Blomfield has done, that Milton "of all men loved the formal garden." [2] Although Sir Walter Scott, to whose fair statement of the case Sir Reginald has done scant justice, admits his own personal preference for the formal garden, he has the frankness to acknowledge that Milton "has anticipated the schemes" of later designers of natural gardens.[3]

The truth is that Milton's ideas had no influence whatsoever upon his contemporaries. It is significant that the stage directions of Dryden's *The State of Innocence* (1674) seem to indicate that Paradise was set as a formal garden. A fountain is in the very center of the scene, and "at the far end the prospect terminates in walks." Adam tells Eve that their easy morning's task is to trim "the dangling boughs" in their "alleys." Some fifty years had to pass before a single garden appeared in England which imitated even in a limited degree the irregularity of nature. Later William Pitt, an eager amateur gardener, undertook, to be sure, to lay out a friend's grounds after the model of Milton's Bower of Bliss.[4] But Milton's influence upon gardening was, after all, indirect and only in a general sense of utilitarian value. After the acceptance of the natural garden in England his description of Eden gave encouragement to a generation for whom the citation of authorities had become an intellectual habit. It was a comfort to discover that a great poet sanctioned the preference for unadorned nature.

In one respect especially various writers on gardens have been in error. They have made Milton's originality appear all the greater by creating a false contrast between his conception of Eden and that of his contemporaries. They have repeatedly implied, if not actually asserted, that Milton's idea of Eden as a wild landscape was quite exceptional in his day. When Walpole remarked that a Frenchman, thinking of Eden, imagined it to possess all the characteristics of Versailles — "clipped hedges, berceaus, and trellis-work" —, he made a gratuitous assumption that did not necessarily have any foundation in fact.[5] In his *Essay on Pope* Joseph Warton also produced a wrong impression when he contrasted Milton's Eden and that pictured in the woodcut illustrating Andreini's dramatic poem, *L'Adamo*, which had appeared in Milan in 1617. The woodcut (Fig. 63) of the Italian poem represents Eden in the elaborate full dress of a formal garden: a fountain and a tall tree, cut into three shelves or tiers, accent the axis of the design, and railed beds with a tree in the middle of each are laid out symmetrically on either side of these central features. Even the animals have been made to cooperate in the interest of symmetry: a monkey squats on the axis in line with the fountain and two crows on his right balance two rabbits on his left. This woodcut Warton interpreted as evidence of the usual conception of Eden current in Milton's own century.[6]

Warton's ideas were perpetuated when he was quoted with approval and the Italian woodcut was actually reproduced in

Fig. 63 — Garden of Eden, as Illustrated in *L'Adamo* of Andreini, Milan, 1617

Fig. 64 — Garden of Eden. Rubens and Jan Brueghel, Mauritshuis, The Hague

Loudon's *Encyclopaedia of Gardening* (1850). Moreover, in that recent and excellent book *Mediaeval Gardens* (1924) Crisp followed the precedent of the *Encyclopaedia*, giving side by side the illustration from *L'Adamo* and one of John Martin's plates as a naturalistic representation of Eden typical of the nineteenth century.[7] To say that the two pictures exemplify "the difference in treatment of the same subject at different periods" implies that the woodcut from *L'Adamo* represents the general practice of the seventeenth century whenever it undertook to delineate Eden. If that were true, then Milton's conception would, indeed, be original.

Milton was, in fact, in no sense exceptional in his delineation of Paradise as a picturesque region in which neither had the trees submitted to the shears nor had the flowers felt the confinement of a parterre. In the first place, Warton himself should have noted that even in Andreini's work two of the other illustrations, the temptation of Eve and her offer of the apple to Adam, present the incidents as taking place in a natural landscape. The *Adamo* (1606) of Giovanni Soranzo contains, furthermore, three illustrations depicting the story of our first parents, and in no one of them is the slightest suggestion of a formal garden. In the first is a landscape of rolling, irregular hills; in the second Adam reclines under a twisted, gnarled tree; and in the third rugged hills rise in the background and in the foreground is a massive, misshapen tree about which the serpent crawls.[8] The truth is that long before Milton had begun the composition of his epic, painters, both Italian and Flemish, had represented Paradise as a glorious natural landscape. They were allured by Adam and Eve as subjects because the nudity of the figures gave the artist opportunity to delineate full, warm tints of the flesh against a background of rich vegetation. True to this interest of the Renaissance artist are such pictures as Titian's *The Original Sin* (the Prado), Tintoretto's *Adam and Eve* (Academy, Venice), Domenichino's *The Original Sin* (Palazzo Barberini, Rome), and a painting by an unknown Flemish artist at Parma. In the Mauritshuis at The Hague is another glowing picture (Fig. 64) of Eden, in which Rubens painted the two nude figures, and Jan Brueghel, with the exquisite detail and solicitude that were the tradition of his country, the luxuriant landscape and brilliantly colored fruits and flowers.

It is, of course, impossible to say that Milton saw any of these pictures, but it is by no means outside the range of probability that he did see pictures like them, as they were sufficiently numerous in the seventeenth century. However, I am not concerned with finding a new source for Milton's representation of Paradise; I wish merely to point out that his conception of Eden was, in his day, by no means an extraordinary phenomenon. The imagination of some of the great pictorial artists had also dreamed of Eden as a lovely region in which was none of the features of a formal garden. Indeed, the painters were not alone in so conceiving Paradise. Designers of cartoons for tapestry and decorators of majolica in Italy and of Limoges enamel in France in the sixteenth century likewise pictured Adam and Eve in a landscape of untouched beauty.[9] Finally, bringing the discussion nearer home, we should recall the important general circumstance that in his own time Milton was not the only Englishman who felt that the genuine charms of nature were often sacrificed to the devices of "nice Art." Cowley had no desire for "whole Woods cut in walks" and declared water was "every whit as clear and wholesome" even if it did not flow "from the breasts of a marble Nymph, or the Urn of a River-God."[10] Two years before the publication of *Paradise Lost* John Rea asserted that "a green Medow" was "a more delightful object" than a garden without flowers, because there nature displayed herself "without the aid of Art."[11] Twelve years later John Worlidge repeated with vigor this criticism of garden sculpture, grass plots, and gravel walks.[12] Obviously Milton's depiction of Eden was in accord with that contemporary English taste which, in defiance of fashion, deplored the excessive elaboration of gardens of "the new model." That such a native current existed is a fact which hitherto has been, I believe, completely overlooked.

What was the practice of the early illustrators of separate editions of *Paradise Lost*? The fourth edition, that of the year 1688, was the first to contain illustrations; Medina was responsible for most of the designs, and Burgess engraved them. The style is heavy and grandiose with no power to move us. However, the various views of Eden present a rugged, hilly, thickly wooded landscape; the "bowers" or arbors of woven branches in which Milton says our first parents dwelt are the only evidence of man's unholy tampering with nature. These views are repeated in the sixth (1695), the ninth (1711), the tenth (1719), and the thirteenth (1727) editions; and although in representing Paradise as a beautiful but uncultivated landscape, the designers have merely followed Milton's text, it is not without significance that these illustrations continued to appear at a time when the formal garden was still in vogue. It may, moreover, be surmised safely, I think, that the designers as professional artists were familiar with the pictorial tradition and that this knowledge assisted them in realizing Milton's verbal description. In Hayley's edition of Milton's poems (1794–97) Eden becomes at the hands of Westall a retreat of cool forest depths where streams wander silently through the shadow, but, in response to the taste of the age, the sylvan scene as well as the fair, graceful Eve herself have been sentimentalized into unimpressive prettiness. Greuze would have admired these engravings, and Paul and Virginia would have been at home in this Eden. But before it received adequate embodiment, Milton's universe had to wait until 1827, when John Martin engraved the plates of *Paradise Lost.* Martin was the first who possessed gifts equal to his task and who sensed the grandeur, mystery, and terror of his subject. His living creatures are no longer large figures occupying the center and foreground of his scene, to which the landscape is merely a background, but, completely changing the scale of relationship, Martin reduces the figures, whether human or supernatural, to a diminutive size, so that they seem pitiably lost and helpless in the vast, mysterious spaces that envelop them. The chiaroscuro is frequently profound, except here and there where it is pierced by blinding light or where in the penumbra of shadow are dimly visible the tumult of chaos and the thronging of multitudes of spirits. Eden itself, as Martin conceives it, is a place of dense, exotic vegetation and shadowy open glades, bounded in the far distance by mountains luminous with a strange radiance. Here assuredly is the first arresting and memorable embodiment of the shapes and forms of Milton's imagination.

Milton's description of Eden passed completely unnoticed in the seventeenth century, and the naturalness of the first garden apparently made no impression upon readers of *Paradise Lost* until other writers had inaugurated a campaign against the formal garden and eagerly cited the Miltonic passage in support of their taste. Sir William Temple's casual reference to Chinese gardens in his essay *Upon the Gardens of Epicurus* (1692) also passed unnoted in the author's lifetime. He had pointed out that in the layout of their gardens the Chinese followed principles diametrically opposed to those of Europe: they scorned symmetry as an inferior form of beauty and as something that a boy might achieve, and showed in the decoration of their screens and porcelain as well as in the plan of their gardens that uniformity and the regular disposition of parts were not an element in their conception of the most artistic design. Although Temple was not unsympathetic to this idea, he felt it to be too revolutionary to carry into practice. In the eighteenth century, when his statement was recalled, the example of the Chinese no longer had a mere academic interest but afforded a model worthy of imitation. To adopt their idea of a garden was not an extraordinary procedure at a time when Chinese wallpaper and furniture were, as Mrs. Malaprop might say, "the very pineapple of fashion."

In 1709, in *The Moralists*, Shaftesbury was the first to declare definitely, without doubt or equivocation, that wild nature was superior to "the artificial Labyrinths and Wildernesses of the Palace" and "the formal Mockery of Princely Gardens." [13] He does not, however, suggest even by so much as a hint that the regular mode of the garden should be abandoned or even remodeled in a more naturalistic style. Nevertheless, it is a point scored in favor of such a style that a man like Shaftesbury recorded his judgment that in departing from nature the garden had become less beautiful. But probably much more influential than this specific opinion, which I do not remember ever to have seen quoted by any subsequent eighteenth-century writer, was the whole purport of Shaftesbury's philosophy. In all the books with which cultivated readers of the early eighteenth century were familiar nature generally appeared in the role of a lady whose reputation was under suspicion. Lucretius, for example, regarded the wild disorder of the natural landscape as proof of the non-existence of God, and Thomas Burnet took its amazing lack of uniformity as the outward sign of God's curse put upon the world at the moment of man's fall.[14] Shaftesbury, on the other hand, rejecting this dark interpretation of the physical environment of man, felt that there was in nature much more than met the eye: a spiritual revelation that glorified even the more irregular, wild forms of the natural world, and filled the beholder with mysterious reverential emotions that exalted him and created within him the mood of a worshipper before a shrine. In other words, Shaftesbury argued that nature shared in and expressed the divine order of the cosmos, and in *The Moralists*, in prose that he meant to be lyrical and that is certainly out of accord with the classic tradition, he hymns the praise of the all-pervading harmony of the natural world even in its most forbidding aspects. Such a vindication of nature untouched by the hand of man tended inevitably to discredit the conscious manipulation of trees, rocks, and water in the formal garden of the period. Nature, it appeared, was better and more beautiful than she had been thought to be, and need not be twisted, tortured, or "methodized" by man in an effort to improve or restrain her. Indeed, it was almost a sacrilege to make her the victim of human whim.

Addison's references to gardens were neither casual nor incidental, but formed the substance of several essays which did much to injure the prestige of the formal garden.[15] When he played, as he did in these essays, on the obvious antithesis between nature and art, the latter always emerged from the comparison with her credit damaged. Of art Addison speaks slightingly as something disciplinary, trivial, and finical in contrast to the luxuriance, the breadth, the variety, and the grandeur of nature. "The nice touches and embellishments," "the curiosities," and the "elegancies of art" seem insignificant by the side of the "bold and masterly" qualities "in the rough, careless strokes of nature." This esthetic point of view was exploited to the limit by the later romanticists — witness Warton's *The Enthusiast* —, but in Addison's time it was a novelty and set up an unfamiliar scale of values. As the specific result of his distaste for "the checks and restraints of art" in a garden

Addison, perhaps with a backward glance at John Rea's *Flora*, which he may have read, prefers flowers growing in profusion in a meadow to their orderly arrangement in a border or parterre; he admires a tree flourishing with luxuriant foliage rather than one clipped into the shape of a cone or a pyramid; and he takes pleasure not in a long, placid, rectangular canal but in a stream that wanders through a field between willows and beds of violets and primroses. Judged by such ideas, the power of organization and the technical skill that were displayed in the planning and execution of a formal design were rated as misspent ingenuity.

Addison contended, moreover, that the contemporary garden failed to yield one of the keenest of imaginative pleasures: the astonishment and thrilling sense of liberty derivable from greatness or vastness of extent when the eye is conscious of no boundary to its vision short of the horizon itself. Confined in space, the attractions of "the most stately garden," unlike those of "the wide fields of nature," are soon exhausted, and the imagination craves for the relief of variety. So Addison hazards the suggestion that the whole estate be turned into "a kind of garden," embracing even the meadows and "fields of corn." The idea was revolutionary; the garden was no longer to be regarded, as it always had been from the earliest times, as a walled-in, self-contained enclosure, but as a landscape including in effect, if not in actuality, the whole countryside in its compass. This conception led in practice to the tearing down of all walls and fences and to the concealment of every boundary of an estate so as to give it the spaciousness, variety, and imaginative appeal of a natural landscape. The immediate connection between the origin of the landscape garden and Addison's conception that vastness of prospect was one of the sources of imaginative pleasure has, I believe, hitherto not been observed, or, at least, not emphasized. His preference for an irregular garden may have been stimulated by his knowledge that the Chinese held symmetry in contempt; at any rate, he was glad to cite their opinion in support of his own ideas. Like Shaftesbury, although on very different grounds, Addison undertook to rehabilitate the reputation of nature.

Pope's famous paper in the *Guardian* (no. 173) in which he ridicules the fantastic clipping of trees, and his fourth epistle on taste in which he scoffs at the deadly symmetry of Timon's vast garden, add little to Addison's criticism, but echo its spirit satirically in phrases of brilliant incisiveness. It is ironic, however, that Addison and Pope, who from many points of view symbolize the age of classical authority in its more brilliant moments, were chiefly instrumental in dislodging from its position in popular esteem the garden of axial design, which impressively embodied the Renaissance ideal of order. To realize the validity of their criticism, one should bear in mind that they were not ridiculing such a formal garden as the tourist sees, for example, at Versailles to-day. Except for some indispensable trimming, the trees at Versailles are now allowed to grow with much of their natural luxuriance so as to form long, glorious, cool tunnels of green light under over-arching and entwined boughs. As any old print (Fig. 24) will show, the Versailles of Pope's time was a very different affair. Along their whole length the straight avenues were bordered with lofty, dense hedges trimmed perfectly flat on the top and sides. Since in the absence of overhanging branches shade was reduced to a minimum, the walks must have often been intolerably hot and resembled passageways between unbroken walls. To-day in Germany at Veitshöchheim and especially at Schleissheim, where high hedges scores of feet in length still line the avenues, it is possible to appreciate the monotony of interminable, straight walls of verdure and understand why they should incite a protest and create a longing for variety and the exhilarating expanse of a less confined view. This dissatisfaction with a garden dominated by architectural ideas of form was only another manifestation of the rebellion against uniformity that accounted for the vogue of *chinoiserie* and *rocaille.* It is remarkable evidence of this discontent that the curving line or serpentine, frequently accompanied by asymmetry, appeared simultaneously in gardens, furniture, interior decoration, and textile patterns.

Never before in the history of art did the fashionable amateur exert such an influence as he did in the eighteenth century. Even in such a technical field as architecture the non-professional man of social position did not hesitate to try his hand at design. Vanbrugh, a dramatist, was responsible for Blenheim and Castle Howard; Burlington did all in his power to advance the cause of Palladianism; and Sanderson Miller was always ready to oblige his friends with Gothic ruins. In gardening the situation was similar. As the revolution in taste precipitated by Shaftesbury, Addison, and Pope progressed through various stages of development, poets and men of fashion guided its destiny: Shenstone, Mason, Walpole, Pitt, Knight, and Sir Uvedale Price. It is, of course, this close relation between the arts and men of letters that accounts for the innumerable allusions to the arts, especially architecture and gardening, in eighteenth-century literature, both prose and poetry.

London and Wise were the last important professional gardeners to devise plans entirely in the formal style. Their skilful transformation of the unsightly gravel-pit in Kensington Gardens into a sunken garden (Fig. 65) embellished with rows of evergreens led even Addison to describe them in the *Spectator* (no. 477) as the "heroic poets" of their craft, and inspired Tickell to compose the graceful narrative poem *Kensington Garden*. Switzer's two books, *The Nobleman, Gentleman, and Gardener's Recreation* (1715) and *Ichnographica Rustica* (1718), the latter being an amplification of the former, are interesting, if for no other reason than that they are the earliest work of a practical gardener to reveal the influence of the literary men. It must not on that account be inferred that Switzer, conscious of his indebtedness, suffered from an inferiority complex. He reminds us that "the sole and manual operation and contrivance of Omnipotence in the beautiful portraiture and harmonious distribution of Paradise" is evidence that from the very beginning of things gardening enjoyed Divine approval; and, in proof of the fact that in the development of the arts gardening was prior to surgery, he cites triumphantly the historical circumstance that gardening was already in existence before the catastrophic removal of the rib from Adam's side.

However, in spite of his pompous estimate of his profession, Switzer makes his debt to literature perfectly plain. He quotes from Milton, Addison, and Pope and urges the garden designer to cultivate his taste for rural scenes and to stimulate his imagination by reading the poets. Homer, for example, will develop the gardener's feeling for grandeur, and in time he will come to appreciate "huge forests, misshapen rocks, and precipices" —

FIG. 65 — THE GRAVEL PIT, AS ILLUSTRATED IN *Kensington Garden*, T. TICKELL, 1722

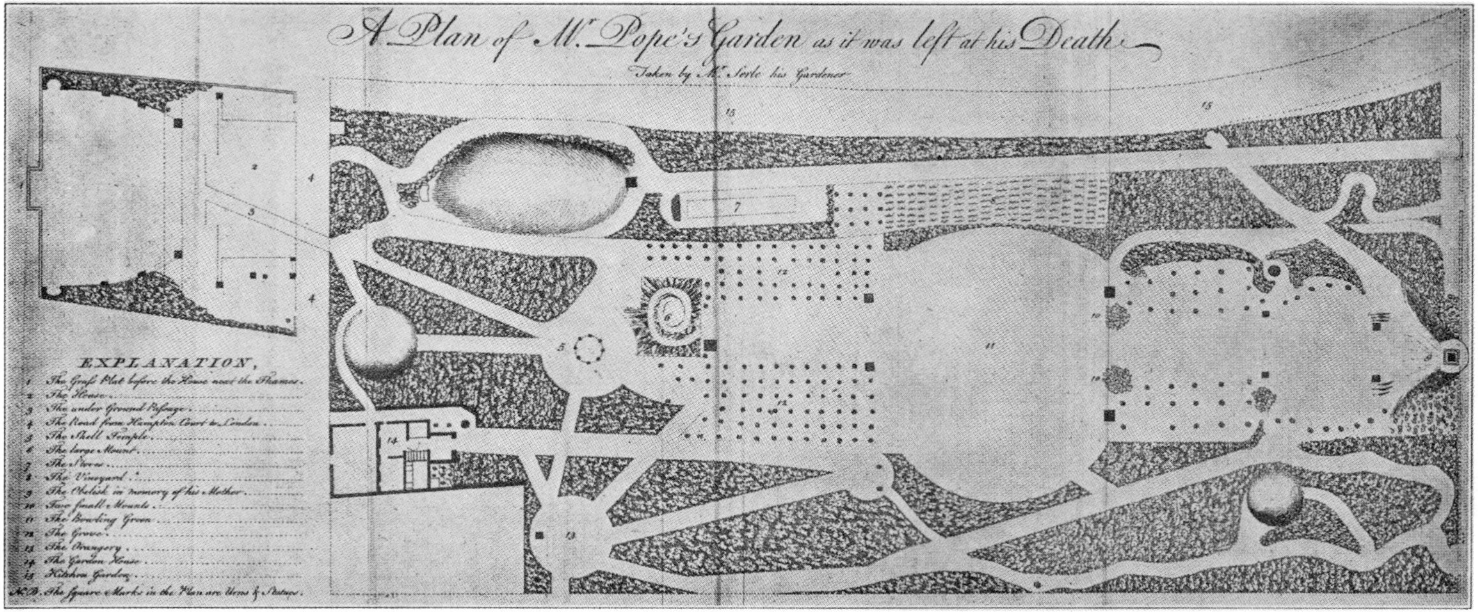

FIG. 66 — SEARLE'S PLAN OF POPE'S GARDEN

features of the landscape which he should make every effort to incorporate into his design. Unfortunately Switzer betrays mental confusion when he supplements this advice by suggesting the perusal of Pope's *Windsor Forest*, an epitome of artificiality which would only stultify a love of nature if it did not actually foster a dislike of it.[16] Switzer, furthermore, makes Addison's ideas more explicit and practicable when he urges as a matter of cardinal importance that

all the adjacent country be laid open to view and that the eye should not be bounded with high walls, woods misplaced, and several obstructions that are seen in too many places, by which the eye is as it were imprisoned and the feet fettered in the midst of the extensive charms of nature and the voluminous tracts of a pleasant country.[17]

As this statement was made in 1716, a year before Kent returned from his long sojourn on the Continent, it appears that Walpole's much quoted remark that Kent first "leaped the fence, and saw that all nature was a garden" is inaccurate.[18] It ignores Switzer's prior realization — a development, in fact, of Addison's thought — that the beauty of the natural landscape should be merged into that of the garden and that this object might be achieved by a reduction in the height of walls and by the elimination of intervening obstacles. In the feat of leaping the wall of the formal garden Switzer anticipated Kent, but since Walpole's witty essay on gardening will always secure more readers than the clumsy book by Switzer, the latter stands little chance of having justice done him.[19]

Not only by bringing the estate and its environs into relation with one another did Switzer strive to achieve the variety of which Addison had deplored the absence in the formal garden. If the woods of an estate covered a landscape of irregular contour, Switzer contended it was the greatest error to cut down noble old beeches and oaks and to level eminences in order to conform, at the sacrifice of variety, to some arbitrary design of straight walks. Let the walks be adapted to the character of the country, and wind, first in one, and now in another, direction. "The natural gardener" will not insist on some mathematical pattern with pedantic obstinacy, but will make "his design submit to nature, and not nature to his design." [20] In other words, if he would avoid the fault of the symmetrical garden which wearies the beholder by the continual repetition of one part by another, the gardener should not impose his will upon the landscape but adjust his plan so as to take full advantage of the hills, dales, cornfields, and trees at his disposal. A garden laid out in accordance with such a design will afford innumerable surprises and keep the curiosity on the alert because its very irregularity will make it impossible to anticipate how and when its natural beauties will be disclosed. This is, in Switzer's opinion, the outstanding merit of the serpentine line. Its windings maintain keen interest because, unlike the straight walk which makes objects visible from a great distance, it stirs expectation and does not reveal a scene until one has rounded the final bend and is suddenly face to face with it.

What are the more fundamental reasons for the fact that an incipient romanticist like Switzer cherished a preference for curvilinear design and the surprise that is resident in a varied composition? Surprise as an element in art, whether it be in the grimace of a carven face peering from the foliage of a capital or a verbal audacity in verse or prose, springs, indeed, from originality; it is the challenge of an enterprising individuality. Surprise is not, then, a dominant element in the art of an age that does not wish its emotional tempo increased beyond a discreet moderation and dislikes the shock of the strong, sudden contrast. The experimental spirit rarely stirred through neoclassical art. Standardized diction, deference for decorum and tradition, solemn fussiness about inconsequential matters of form, inexplicable patience with platitude repressed those effervescences of personality that are creative of surprise. The desire for variety which Switzer repeatedly voiced was the herald of the new age. In a sense, the straight and the curved lines were symbolic of the periods in which they had greatest esthetic authority: the former connoted simplicity, uniformity, reserve, stability, and the absence of the unexpected; the latter connoted complexity, multiplicity, energy, and the expressiveness of a resurgent vitality. The curved line, whether it occurs in furniture design or a garden plan, delights the eye by its movement, excites the curiosity, and stimulates the imagination because its course and its destination are unknown. Its encounter with other lines surprises us, and its subtle fusion with them lures the eye to pursue new adventures into unexplored regions of the design. It creates a romantic illusion of waywardness of purpose that is remote from what I may call the clear, firm resolve, the sheer will of the straight line to reach its objective. Even in the case of an ornamental pattern, with the intricacies of which we are already familiar, acquaintance does not impair its power to rouse and maintain our interest. As the eighteenth century progressed, the romanticist cared less and less for the rhythmic repetitions of classic art — his rejection of the heroic couplet in favor of more complex rime schemes is typical — and for that reason he found refreshment for his spirit in the adventures of a *rocaille* pattern as well as in the winding paths of a naturalistic garden.

Switzer's praise of the serpentine is sincere and indicative of a more liberal esthetic sympathy. But his attitude may mislead us. As is almost always the case when eighteenth-century writers extol nature and variety, it is necessary to be on one's guard. With admirable precision they state their reasons for admiring nature and variety, and we concur heartily. But when they cite specific examples of their principles, we experience a shock of surprise; they unconsciously reveal that, after all, they like their wine only moderately watered, and turn out to be far more conservative than their general statements lead us to suspect. Principles that on the surface seem to imply a repudiation of classic conventionalities are responsible for correct, unimpeachably traditional judgments. The *furor poeticus* is in theory exalted, in practice discreetly shackled. In his *Analysis of Beauty* (1753) Hogarth eulogizes diversity in design, but specifies St. Paul's as "the most judicious application of every principle that has been spoken of."[21] In his *Essay on Taste* (1759) Gerard lauds variety in art, but finds beauty in "the straight and parallel sides of a canal," regards admiration for the profuse ornament of Gothic architecture as a discreditable preference, and approves of the "superior elegance in the more *simple* symmetry and proportion of *Grecian* architecture."[22] Similarly with Switzer. When we examine his own designs and read his favorable account of Mr. Blathwayt's garden, we are considerably disconcerted to discover that they are still very formal and that terraces, canals, straight avenues, and parterres adorned with statues are their outstanding features. Batty Langley's *New Principles of Gardening, or, The Laying out and Planting Parterres, Groves, Wildernesses, Labyrinths, Avenues, Parks, etc. after a more grand and rural manner than has been done before* (1728) illustrates the same contrast between principle and practice. The fountain, the canal, and the geometrically shaped basin are still in the ascendant, and statues of Rucima, the goddess of weeding, Agerona, the goddess of silence, and Bubona, the goddess of oxen, are cordially recommended as garden ornaments if the supply of the better known deities becomes exhausted. Only the paths through the wilderness are allowed to roam; the avenues centering upon the house are still absolutely straight.[23]

Pope, like Switzer and Langley, admirably illustrates the gap between theory and practice during the transition period. To Joseph Spence he remarked that

> All the rules of gardening are reducible to three heads: — the contrasts, the management of surprises, and the concealment of the bounds. . . . I have expressed them all, in two verses; (after my manner, in very little compass) . . .
>
> He gains all ends, who pleasingly confounds,
> Surprises, varies, and conceals the bounds.[24]

As these are obviously the principles of the new cult, we might expect the writer of the fourth epistle to reject formalism whenever he was free to treat nature in accordance with his own ideas. But our hopes are disappointed. In spite of his protests Pope was not inclined to let nature be herself. At one time he thought of planting a Gothic cathedral of poplar trees, their white trunks properly stripped of their foliage to represent the columns. He told Spence that he had long wished to carry out Dinocrates' proposal of fashioning a gigantic figure of Alexander the Great from a mountain. All that he needed was the gift of a Welsh mountain and some munificent person to pay the laborers. Trees, Pope thought, could be used to represent Alexander's hair and eyebrows, and he suggested that if a stream could be contrived to appear as if gushing from his hand, the effect of the whole figure would be greatly enhanced.[25] In 1722, when he visited Lord Digby at Sherborne, he was delighted with the gardens. Although their "beauty," he wrote to Martha Blount, was due to their "irregularity," by some legerdemain he managed to reconcile this irregularity with a T-shaped canal and five "green terraces." Then, in phrases that might have been coined in some romantic mint, he describes with enthusiasm the ruins of the ancient mansion:

> On the left, full behind these old trees, which makes this whole part inexpressibly awful and solemn, runs a little, old, low wall, beside a trench covered with elder trees and ivies; which being crossed by another bridge, brings you to the ruins, to complete the solemnity of the scene.

But "these venerable broken walls" and "views which are more romantic than imagination can form them" need, nevertheless, in Pope's opinion, to be helped out by the hand of man. To give them "a prodigious beauty," he favors the embellishment of the scene by means of geometry and the compass and the line. He suggests that the space between different parts of the ruins might be enriched with "greens and parterres," that "circles or octagons of grass or flowers" might be laid out in "the open courts," and that "little paths of earth or sand" provided with seats at the proper intervals might be made among the ruins to render the views more accessible; finally, to complete this dressing up of nature, he advocates the building of a temple on an adjacent hill and the erection of a commemorative obelisk beside the ruin itself.[26] The letter closes with an affectation of candor that indicates how readily, in the atmosphere of Sherborne, Pope succumbed without resistance to the sentimental illusion of the "good, old days." It is the mood of many a later romanticist: "Believe me ever yours, with a sincerity as old-fashioned, and as different from modern sincerity, as this house, this family, and these ruins, are from the Court, and all its neighbourhood." The duplicity of Pope's personal conduct is admirable evidence of the extent to which he conscientiously strove on all occasions to maintain the standards of "old-fashioned" integrity.

Pope's own five-acre garden (Fig. 66) at Twickenham belied his own principles of naturalistic design as much as, if not actually more than, his schemes for the beautification of Sherborne.

Its artificiality, although frequently mentioned, has not been specifically described. His house (2) and the grass-plot (1) that sloped down to the Thames were located on the smaller half of his property, and by means of a subterranean passage (3) leading under the London–Hampton Court Road (4) were connected with the garden proper, which lay on the far side of the intervening highway. As the plan published by Searle, Pope's gardener, reveals, the concessions to naturalism were not conspicuous. The Shell Temple (5) and the large mount (6) have, to be sure, no formal relationship, and some of the walks in the more remote, less visible parts of the garden serpentine through the woods surreptitiously as if in fear of being caught in such an unorthodox proceeding. The body of the garden is, however, unapologetically regular. The axis runs from the large mount (6) between two uniformly planted groves (12) across a symmetrical bowling-green (11), and then passes between two smaller mounts (10) and two more uniformly planted groves until it reaches, at the end of the garden, the terminary of the vista, namely, the obelisk (9) in memory of Pope's mother. The ornaments, it is to be noted, are distributed in pairs; urns, statues, and mounts on one side of the axial line are carefully balanced on the other side by similar urns, statues, and mounts.[27] Moreover, the Shell Temple (5) and the Orangery (13) are equally the center from which radiate straight walks as might be the case in any French garden. The space between the house and the river is also regular; the lawn (1) is decorated with pairs of urns and statues, and on either side, next to the bank of the river, is a semicircular niche or alcove. In this rather grudging fashion Pope obeyed his own injunction —

In all let nature never be forgot.

But to show that Pope scarcely observed his own principles is not to prove that his garden was unattractive. As my own preference is nearly always for a formal plan, I am inclined to think that his garden was, indeed, all the better for his inconsistency. It had the interest always possessed by an intelligent design. Pope's problem was a special one; the separation of his garden from his house deprived him of the usual focal center by which his plan might be integrated and its principal lines might be determined. For this purpose he utilized the large mount, which in bulk was probably comparable to a house, and made it the point from which the axis started. Along the line of the axis for the sake of variety he skilfully arranged an alternation of narrow rectangular and wide circular spaces, and by means of statues and mounts he carefully accented the transition points in the axis as it passed from the narrow to the wider areas or *vice versa*. As a result the eye was led forward from object to object, and at the farther end of the garden the prospect contracted so that the attention was unescapably focused upon the terminal obelisk. But these merits of coherent design are due to Pope's appreciation of formal values, and are not to be put to the credit of his dictum that nature was an infallible guide.[28]

The mania for grottos was widespread, and probably Pope's famous cave, which strikes us as a creation of childish artifice and whimsical affectation, was no worse than most of its kind. Although Pope assured Edward Blount that if he could see the grotto he would realize "how little it owes to art," Searle's formidable list of minerals and Pope's own reference to "shells interspersed with pieces of looking-glass in angular forms" give one a perturbing feeling that nature had very little to do with the construction of this cave, illuminated by its "orbicular" lamp of "thin alabaster."[29] Nevertheless, we must believe that in his own time Pope was something of a radical in his method of laying out a garden. Robert Dodsley, of whose playlet *The Toyshop* Pope had been the sponsor, ventured to predict in *The Cave of Pope*[30] what he imagined would be the fate of the fantastic grotto. When oblivion shall envelop "the names of heroes and of kings" and "their high deeds" shall be "amongst forgotten things,"

> Grateful posterity, from age to age,
> With pious hand the ruin shall repair:
> Some good old man, to each inquiring sage,
> Pointing the place, shall cry, "The Bard liv'd there,"
>
> . . . .
>
> With awful veneration shall they trace
> The steps which thou so long before hast trod;
> With reverend wonder view the solemn place,
> From whence thy genius soar'd to Nature's God.

Then, some small gem, or moss, or shining ore,
  Departing, each shall pilfer, in fond hope
To please their friends, on ev'ry distant shore,
  Boasting a relic from the Cave of Pope.

When Lady Montagu became involved in her notorious quarrel with Pope, she retaliated in a satire, *The Court of Dullness*,[31] in which the grotto was represented as the dwelling-place of the goddess of stupidity and her attendant nymphs, Profanation and Obscenity:

Adorn'd within with shells of small expense,
(Emblems of tinsel rhyme and trifling sense)
Perpetual fogs enclose the sacred cave,
The neighboring sinks their fragrant odors gave.

But Lady Montagu's pointless attack notwithstanding, Pope's house and garden, as Dodsley predicted, did become something of a shrine. Edward Pugh reports that in 1809 two weeping willows which, it was believed, Pope had planted on the bank of the Thames with his own hands were carefully propped up to preserve them as long as possible. Slips from the finer of these trees were frequently presented to the poet's admirers, and even to so great a personage as the Empress Catharine of Russia, who planted some of them in her garden in St. Petersburg.[32]

The later history of Pope's house and garden is not without its ironies. Sir William Stanhope, Chesterfield's brother, who bought the estate after the poet's death, made some very necessary additions to the small, uncomfortable house, in Walpole's words, "hollowing out that fragment of the rock of Parnassus into habitable chambers." Then Stanhope ravaged the garden. By his skilful, thick planting of trees along its boundaries Pope had shut out the three public lanes that bordered his property, and had succeeded in achieving a delightful seclusion in the midst of his impenetrable woods. After Stanhope had mercilessly cut through the groves and laid out new paths, he discovered that he had been extraordinarily successful in destroying his privacy. "There was," as Walpole says, "not a Muse could walk there but she was spied by every country fellow that went by with a pipe in his mouth."[33] Stanhope was then compelled to put up a wall to protect both himself and the Muses.

As it turned out, Dodsley, in a sense he did not intend, forecast correctly the ultimate destiny of the grotto. In time curious visitors, in order to secure mementos, virtually dismantled it by tearing out of the walls "spars, ores, and even the common flints."[34] To-day, in a sadly degenerate form, Pope's spirit broods over the neighborhood. Ousting Walpole, Pope has provided the neighborhood with the name of its telephone exchange, and if one wishes to communicate with Strawberry Hill, now a college, he must ask for "Pope's Grove 1240." Within a few steps of his former garden is a dingy, uninviting brick building called Pope's Grotto Hotel, and in a place named Grotto Hall a lady, estimable, no doubt, and I hope industrious, gives instruction in dancing. It would take the courage of an eighteenth-century platitudinist to make the trite comment that such a decline obviously suggests.

The development of the natural garden proceeded with all due circumspection on the part of land-owners who professed a sympathy with the new ideas. Pope's friend Lord Bathurst is said to have constructed at Ryskins the first winding stream to take the place of the traditional canal. Queen Caroline herself was responsible for the Serpentine in Hyde Park. But it was her handiwork in the royal garden at Richmond that occasioned comment — comment generally of a very bitter kind. As the two buildings, the Hermitage and Merlin's Cave, which she erected at Richmond, were intended to be garden decorations, and as the references to them in contemporary literature are numerous, an account of them at this point is not inappropriate. The history of gardening has not many comic incidents, but this is one of them.

The two famous structures which came into being under this high patronage were in reality grotesque, and, as in the case of many garden decorations of the period, it was impossible to see much relationship between their names and their design. The materials of the Hermitage were appropriate enough — rocks, massive and rough-hewn —, but classical taste had determined their disposition: the facade of the edifice was symmetrical, and it was crowned with a crude pediment. Within, keeping each other in countenance, were the busts of Robert Boyle, Newton, Locke, Dr. Clarke, and Wollaston. Merlin's

Cave (Fig. 67), built in 1735 by Kent, was no less a hybrid. The ogival arch of the doorway and the buttresses were Gothic, but the central block and the flanking wings of lower elevation, both heavily thatched, revealed in what odd places Palladian design might crop out. Within, in niches framed with Gothic arches, were six figures of wax, representing Merlin and his secretary, Queen Elizabeth and her nurse, the queen of Henry VII, and Minerva. Queen Caroline appointed as custodians of this strange company Stephen Duck and his wife, whose duty it was to show Merlin's Cave to curious visitors. Duck was one of that numerous brood of humble eighteenth-century poets who cultivated the Muses in obscurity until they received the doubtful blessing of patronage from ladies and gentlemen for whom the discovery of talent in a shoemaker or a milkmaid was an exciting experience. Duck himself, who had been a thresher in Wiltshire earning four shillings and six pence a week, had been taken under the protection of the Queen and had had *A Full and Authentic Account* of his life penned by no less a person than Joseph Spence, the Professor of Poetry at Oxford. Duck's appointment as guide to Merlin's Cave was merely another mark of royal generosity.

The Queen's absurd but harmless taste in garden ornament soon attracted the attention of the public. Pope urged Gay, as "every man and boy" was writing verses on the Hermitage, to take his cue and again make an attempt to secure the royal favor which he felt was his due. In April, 1733, the *Gentleman's Magazine* offered a first and a second prize for poems on the Hermitage; it is only charity to spare readers examples of the winning verses. Availing itself of the popular interest in Merlin's Cave, the *Prompter*, Aaron Hill's theatrical periodical, in its eighty-eighth number described an allegorical garden in which were the grottos of Power, Riches, Honor, and Learning. In 1736 appeared Edmund Curll's *The Rarities of Richmond: Being Exact Descriptions of the Royal Hermitage and Merlin's Cave. With his Life and Prophesies*; the work was a piece of mere hack-writing, but there was probably a public even for such a wretched penny-catcher.

The bitterness of party politics, and especially popular anger at the support which Queen Caroline gave to the Walpole ad-

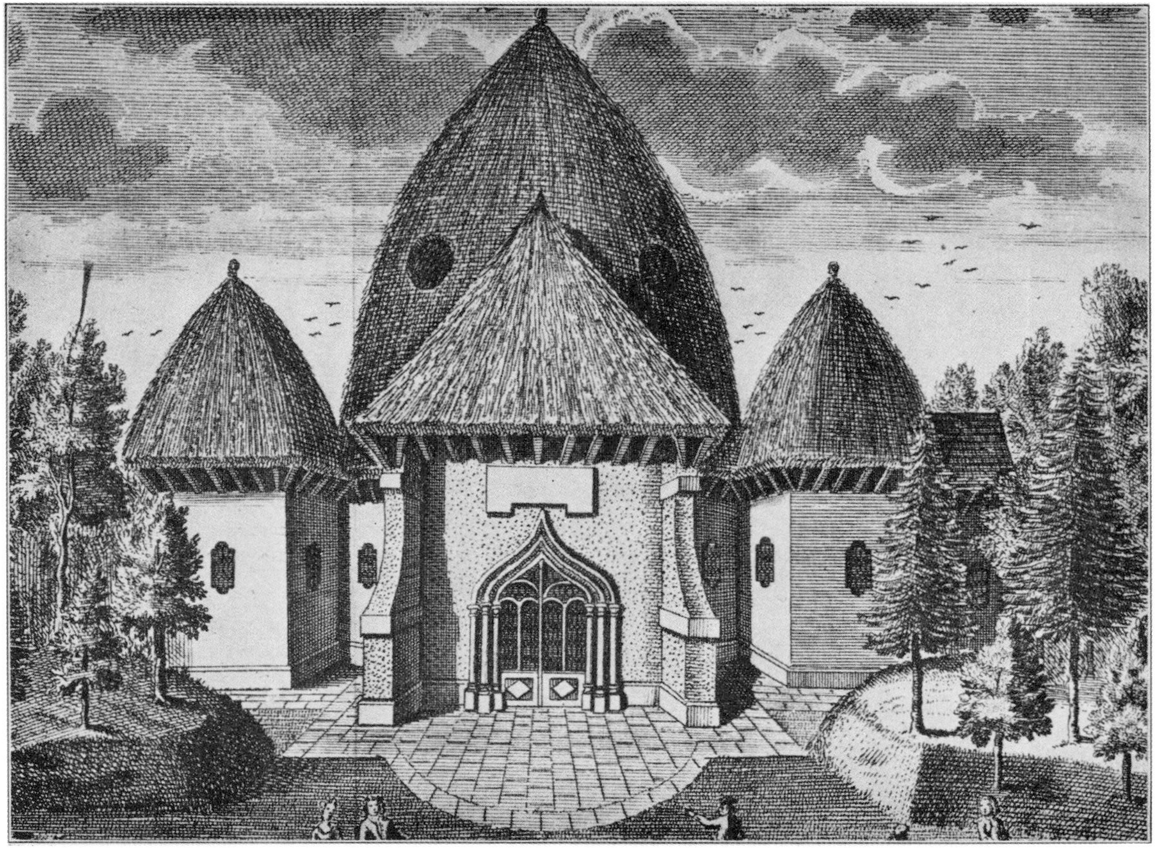

Fig. 67 — Merlin's Cave. Designed by Kent, 1735

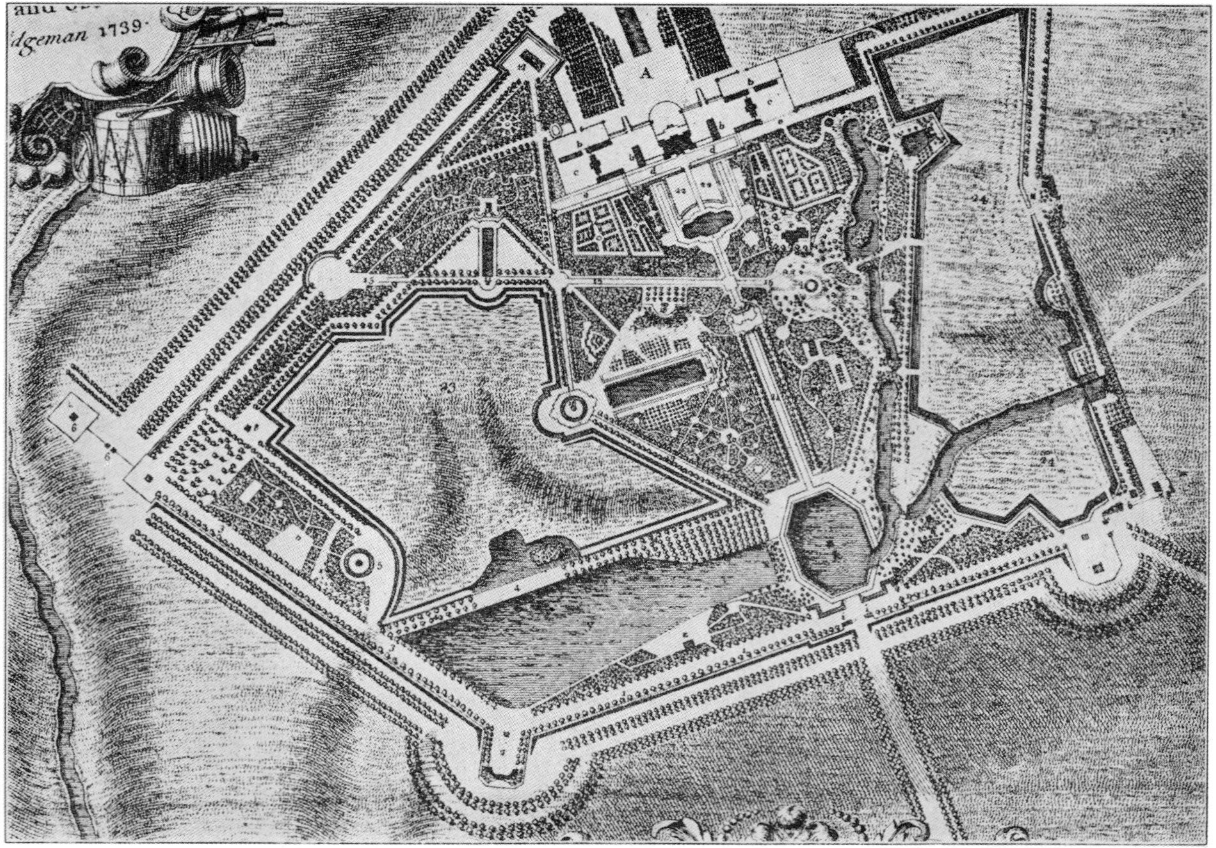

FIG. 68 — BRIDGEMAN'S PLAN OF STOWE, 1739

ministration, intensified the satire of which the Hermitage and Merlin's Cave became the object. Swift wrote some barbed epigrams, inspired by envy of the recognition which Duck had received. The *Craftsman* (nos. 480, 489, 498), the journal sponsored by Bolingbroke in his campaign against Walpole, was merciless. It laughed at the gilded rails that barred the entrance to the Hermitage — proof, it ironically remarked, "that luxury had found its way even into the Hermit's Cell." It laughed at Merlin's abode, a cave "above ground" and "like an old haystack, thatched over." It quoted at length Spenser's description of Merlin and with veiled sarcasm contrasted Merlin's former mode of life and his present one: "The works of the learned surround him, and the celebrated Mr. Stephen Duck is both his housekeeper and his poet-laureate." Speaking for the opposite party, the *Daily Gazetteer* (no. 70) protested against such indecent manners, and, citing passages from Milton's description of Paradise, asserted their applicability to the gardens of Richmond. What must have made matters more uncomfortable for the Queen were the sneers of the King, who, according to Hervey, told her she deserved to be abused by the *Craftsman* for "such childish silly stuff."

In various ways enterprising persons turned to advantage the widespread curiosity which the buildings at Richmond had excited. In the outskirts of London a tavern standing in the midst of gardens and possessed of a skittle-ground opened under the name of Merlin's Cave. In Clerkenwell another tavern soon appeared with the same title.[35] An old undated handbill in the British Museum announces that at the Crown Coffee House in King Street was to be seen *Merlin in Miniature: or, A Lively Representation of Merlin in his Cave, as in the Royal Gardens at Richmond, Being, A New and Entertaining Piece of Moving Machinery, such as never before appeared in Publick.*[36] The stage was equally ready to make money out of the notoriety of the Queen's taste in architecture. At Southwark Fair in 1736 and 1738 and at Tottenham Court Fair in 1738 was revived the droll *The Birth of Merlin*, which, as Nicoll's play-list states, had been first produced in 1724. The regular theaters also undertook to satisfy on a more pretentious scale the curiosity which the satiric papers in the *Craftsman* had undoubtedly done much to whet. At the theater in Goodman's Fields Dryden's opera *King Arthur* was revived in an altered form under the title *Merlin, or, The British Inchanter* (1735/6). At Covent Garden appeared a spectacular entertainment *The Royal Chace*; the first scene revealed the Hermitage and the fourth scene the interior of Merlin's Cave. A few years later, beginning in January, 1740–41, Covent Garden revived *The Royal Chace* for eighteen performances. In February the theater in Goodman's Fields, not to be outdone, countered with *Merlin, or, The British Inchanter*, embellished, as the annoucement in the *London Daily Post* assured the public, with "all the scenes, machines, and other decorations proper to the opera, particularly an exact representation of Merlin's Cave as in the royal gardens at Richmond."[37] In *An Heroic Epistle*, one of a group of anonymous satires in which William Mason attacked Johnson, Shebbeare, and Sir William Chambers for their support of the royal cause, there was described in mocking language the final destruction of Merlin's Cave by the famous landscape gardener "Capability" Brown:

> Come then, prolific Art, and with thee bring
> The charms that rise from thy exhaustless spring;
> To Richmond come, for see, untutor'd Brown
> Destroys those wonders which were once thy own.
> Lo, from his melon-ground the peasant slave
> Has rudely rush'd, and levell'd Merlin's Cave;
> Knock'd down the waxen Wizzard, seiz'd his wand,
> Transform'd to lawn what late was Fairy land;
> And marr'd, with impious hand, each sweet design
> Of Stephen Duck, and good Queen Caroline.

Chief among the transitional gardeners whose designs were a compromise between the formal and natural styles was Bridgeman. As he did considerable work in the royal gardens at Richmond he was, of course, known to Queen Caroline. Although as a lover of power she bitterly resented the authority of Parliament over the King, in her more politic moments she was wont to attribute the greatness of England to the freedom of the government. Without its democratic government, she was accustomed to say, the country would sink into insignificance—an island fit merely to be cut up into gardens by Bridgeman and Kent.[38] Hogarth also paid his respects to the reputation of Bridgeman. In the second plate of *The Rake's Progress* (1735), in the throng of artists, music-teachers, and fencing-masters who crowd around the wealthy young heir in competition for his patronage, is a figure, said to be Bridgeman, who presents a garden plan for inspection.

As I have pointed out, Switzer favored a reduction in the height of intervening walls in order to bring the garden and the countryside into closer relationship. Bridgeman apparently was responsible for a further advance. Walpole blandly ignores Switzer, but he attributes to Bridgeman the ingenious suggestion that by the actual removal of the walls and by the substitution of a deep ditch as a boundary the garden and the country might be merged together and be made to appear as if continuous.[39] Employed with this end in view, such a ditch had great practical value in hastening the realization of the ideal of the natural garden, and came to be known as the "ha-ha!" — the exclamation of persons surprised at this unexpected barrier in the course of their walk in a garden. The belief that the ha-ha was a special device or invention of the natural gardeners is not, however, correct. It was not unknown to French formal gardeners, and the author of *La Théorie du Jardinage* advocates its use at the extremity of avenues to create the impression that they extend out into the park. Such a short, limited ha-ha can be found to-day at the Grand Trianon, abruptly cutting across the alleys within the enclosed garden and yet affording pleasant views into the park beyond. As I recall, when I encountered it for the first time, I expressed my annoyance in a phrase more modern and more American than merely "Ha! ha!" Be that as it may, Bridgeman, it appears, to meet the requirements of the new taste in gardening, extended the use of this sunken fence or ditch, employing it on a greater scale to take the place of long stretches of wall.

Praised by Pope, Thomson, and a herd of minor versifiers, described by Rousseau in *La Nouvelle Héloïse*, eulogized by innumerable letter-writers and diarists, and visited by English and Continental celebrities as well as by persons of less consequence, Stowe, the property of Richard Temple, Viscount Cobham, became the most famous garden in England in the eighteenth century. The bibliography of this estate is really a unique thing of its kind, and is an index of the extraordinary interest which the gardens excited. The earliest work on Stowe listed in the British Museum catalogue is a mediocre poem by George Bickham dated 1732 and addressed to Pope. In 1744, to meet, according to the editor, the constant demand for such a volume and, as he incidentally remarks, to save visitors the trouble of copying the innumerable inscriptions, appeared the first guide-book to the gardens. The latter, as we are informed, "are esteemed by persons of the most exact taste to be the finest in this kingdom and perhaps in Europe." In 1748 this very practical but uninspiring guide-book was supplemented by a more literary effort, *A Dialogue upon the Gardens . . . at Stowe.* As two friends on a summer holiday stroll through the gardens, they rhapsodically comment on the various beauties of the landscape and its architectural embellishments, for the esthetic edification of the reader or the visitor. As the note of rapturous appreciation appealed to a public for the most part sentimental and curious about all matters of taste, it is not surprising that the book reached its third edition in 1751.

Within the next fifty years there were published at least twelve popular handbooks on Stowe, most of them being reprintings of the first guide-book. In 1797, 1817, and 1827 respectively appeared expensive volumes on Stowe provided with special engravings. In 1808 the visit of the Bourbon princes to the gardens was commemorated in a poem of dubious merit, *La Fête Royale.* A more curious book is *A Day in Stowe Gardens* (1825), a sort of sentimental *Decameron,* in which the whimsical author and the ladies and gentlemen he meets during his visit pass the time in story-telling. In 1848 was issued *The Stowe Catalogue* by Henry Forster, and in 1921, in preparation for the sale of the famous domain, *The Ducal Estate of Stowe,* a magnificent illustrated catalogue descriptive of the house, its contents, and its gardens.

At the hands of Bridgeman, Kent, and "Capability" Brown the gardens passed in turn through various stages of development, exemplifying in interesting fashion successive changes in taste. The plan and fifteen views of Stowe published in 1739 by Sarah Bridgeman after her husband's death and sold for four

Fig. 69 — View of the Parterre at Stowe, Enclosed by Clipped Hedge

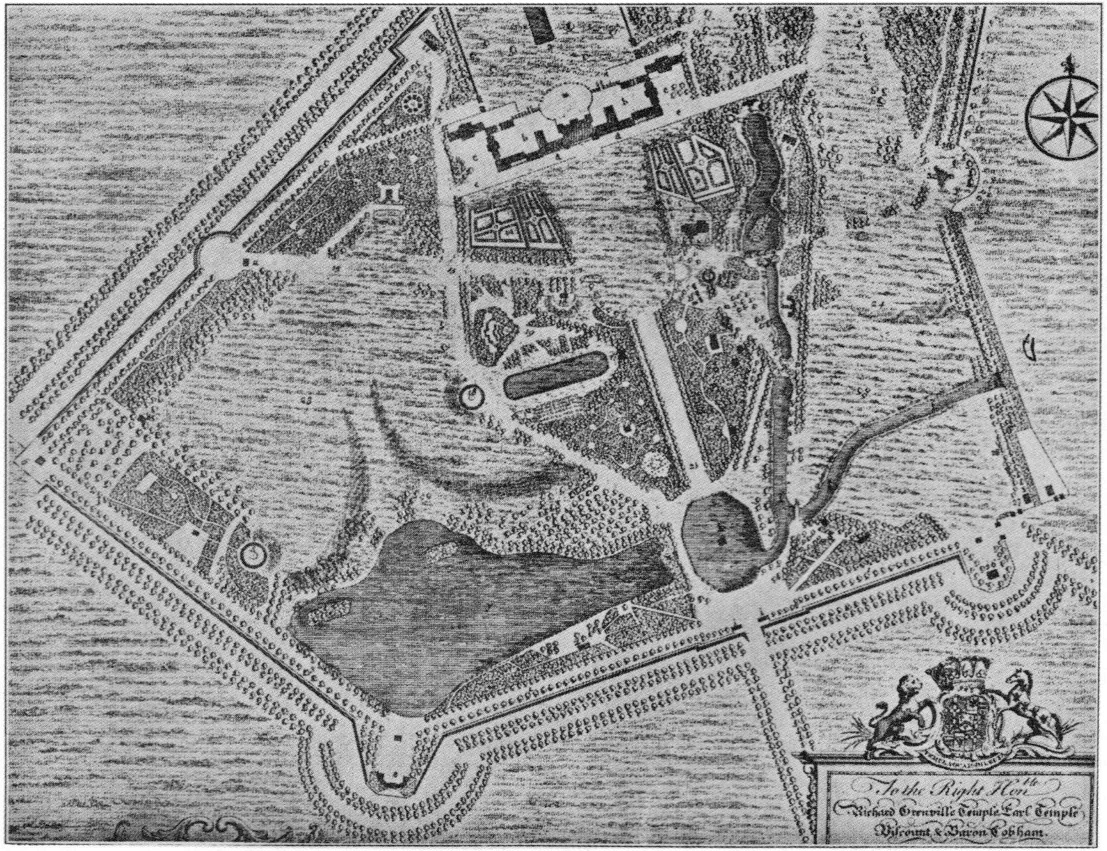

Fig. 70 — Plan of Stowe, 1753, Showing Features of Natural Garden

guineas furnishes an excellent example of his experimental naturalism. The main outlines of the design (Fig. 68) exhibit the clear linking up of the house (b, b) and garden in one axial scheme. Before the house on the north front (A) is a canal, and on the south or garden front is an extremely formal arrangement of which the principal features are treated entirely from an architectural point of view. The grand parterre (22), consisting of two symmetrical rectangular grass-plots and a great polygonal pool, is almost completely enclosed by a high clipped hedge hollowed out at regular intervals into niches for urns and statues (Fig. 69). The spaciousness of the enclosed area, the mirror-like surface of the water, the pieces of sculpture sharply defined against their background of verdure, the play of light and shade in the niches, and the long straight lines of the flat-topped hedge must have produced that effect of imposing dignity which was inherent in Renaissance design. Beyond the pool a long avenue (21) bordered on either side by a double row of trees extends to a great octagonal basin (k) with a lofty obelisk in its center as the terminary of the vista from the portico of the house. Other parts of the garden are laid out with a corresponding regard for the principle of orderly relationship. The lake (y), although irregular in form, has on every side a rectilinear shoreline. The Temple of Bacchus (10) and the Rotunda (16) face an oblong canal, and each is the center from which diverge long straight avenues, linking it with some object of interest in another part of the garden. It is in the region to the right of the axis that Bridgeman has revealed his desire to treat nature with less restraint. A river (v) of varying breadth meanders through an irregularly planted woodland until it reaches the octagonal basin (k). Especially conspicuous for its lack of uniformity is the vicinity of the Temple of Ancient Virtue (q), or the Elysian Fields, as it was called, where in an area of uneven contour trees are scattered at random. Moreover, although all the main avenues are perfectly straight, Bridgeman has allowed a considerable number of paths within the woods to serpentine at will. As Pope died in 1744, it is Stowe in this semi-"naturalized" form as designed by Bridgeman with which the poet was most familiar.

Lancelot, or "Capability," Brown, as he was familiarly

known because of his habit of expatiating at length on the "capabilities" of an estate for development, carried on the process of further "naturalizing" Stowe. The annexed plan (Fig. 70) of 1753 probably reveals his handiwork.[40] On the south front the grass plots, the polygonal basin, and the architectural hedge have disappeared, and the space has been converted into a single great sweep of lawn bordered by trees. The dense woods that formerly separated the axial vista from the Elysian Fields (Fig. 68, q) have been drastically thinned so that the Fields merge into the great lawn. The result is that the naturalistic part of the garden is no longer decisively segregated, as it had been in the earlier plan, but is fused with the former parterre. A similar treatment, on the left, has also destroyed the formality of the planting on that side. The small canal before the Temple of Bacchus (10) has been filled up, a double row of trees has been felled, and the small triangular esplanade, which previously had been noticeably symmetrical, melts into the grassy stretches of the home park (23). The north bank of the lake (y) instead of being a rigid, unbroken straight line has been softened by varying undulations, and the two avenues that radiated from the Rotunda (16) have virtually lost their identity and have been assimilated by the adjacent meadow (23). The disappearance of these avenues and the irregular woods on the curving bank of the lake broke down the distinction between garden and park and made them scarcely distinguishable from one another. Similarly the great field (24) on the right has through the filling of the ditch or moat and the planting of scattered clumps of trees been brought into closer relationship with its surroundings.

Guide-books to Stowe published later than this plan of 1753 disclose additional efforts to imitate nature. The canal in front of the Rotunda (16) is no more, and the body of water (k) at the end of the central vista has become an irregular lake and is referred to as "the late octagon." Two annexed views represent Stowe as it is to-day. The first (Fig. 71) is the glorious vista that opens out before the portico on the garden front, and if compared with Bridgeman's plan (Fig. 69) it enables one to realize the transformation brought about by the "return to nature." Observe how artfully the perspective is narrowed, the woods advancing on either side like wings on a stage. Note also how the beholder's consciousness of distance is intensified by the multiplication of the successive planes formed in turn by the meadowland, the lake, the white temples gleaming against their dark background of trees, and the sunlit fields beyond. The second (Fig. 72) is the first view reversed, that is, the house as seen from the end of the vista beyond the "late octagon." Visible far to the right is the Gothic building which Walpole confessed was enshrined "in the heretical corner" of his heart.

To-day Stowe, like Strawberry Hill, is a great flourishing boys' school. One may regret the tragic necessity which compels their owners to part with such famous estates; yet there is some compensation in the thought that English boys are being educated in an environment rich with memories of the eighteenth-century civilization. It is a noble atmosphere in which to cultivate the national spirit.

II. The Painter and the Gardener

The word *nature* as employed in the eighteenth century is, as I suggested, a trap for the unwary if the exact sense in which it is used is not realized clearly. To infer that in reacting against the formal garden men like Walpole, Shenstone, Mason, or Whately were advocating the lawlessness of a planless garden would be an error. The fact is that, for a second time in its history, the development of gardening was determined by another art: by painting in the eighteenth century just as by architecture in the sixteenth and seventeenth centuries. The new ideal for the representation of nature was found among the landscape painters, especially Poussin, Claude Lorraine, and Salvator Rosa, and the new principles of garden composition were derived from a sympathetic analysis of their works. What the reactionaries favored was really not the direct, first-hand imitation of nature but the reproduction of nature "methodized" — that ideal beauty of landscape such as emerged from the selective processes of the pictorial masters. Claude Lorraine's point of view, as precisely described by Reynolds in his fourth *Discourse*, is exactly that of the sponsors of the natural garden: "Claude Lorrain . . . was convinced, that taking nature as he found it seldom produced beauty. His pictures are a composition of the various draughts which he had previously made from various beautiful scenes and prospects." In other words, since nature in the raw state was imperfect, and since in the canvases of the painters her blemishes had been eliminated and her charms had been culled and combined so as to form a synthesis of her most exquisite beauties, it was the business of the gardener to study pictorial methods of design, adapt them to his medium, create his foreground, middle distances, and background, and arrange for a varied play of light and shade. Shenstone sums up current opinion when he says, "I think the landskip painter is the gardener's best designer."[41]

Indeed, the relationship between gardening and painting was an assumption which the cultivated man of the time never questioned. He felt that to practice one of these arts required as much skill as did the other. When Richard Graves in defence of Shenstone and his garden at the Leasowes protested against Johnson's belittling of his art, he boldly declared that the natural style called into play mental gifts as great "as those which we admire in the descriptive poems of Thomson or in the noble landscapes of Salvator Rosa or the Poussins." [42] The author of *The English Connoisseur* (1766), a book dealing primarily with sculpture and paintings in the houses of the nobility, justified his inclusion of descriptive accounts of the Leasowes and Hagley on the ground that "there is at least as much room for exercising the great arts of design and composition in laying out a garden as in executing a good painting." [43] Obviously in the abandonment of Renaissance formality in gardening there was never the slightest prospect that the new style would either exhibit nature free from human control or exempt the gardener from his exacting task of careful planning.[44]

One fundamental characteristic of pictorial design tended in particular to revolutionize gardening. Now, in any design symmetry is present when the pattern on one side of an axial line dividing an area into two equal parts corresponds with the pattern on the other side; in such a situation the perfect balance is immediately evident to the eye. Conversely, what is sometimes conveniently called "occult balance" is present when the object on one side of the line is not identical with that on the

Fig. 71 — Present View of the Gardens from the House, Stowe

Fig. 72 — Present View of the House from the Gardens, Stowe

other, but is, nevertheless, felt to be in equilibrium. The balance is felt, but cannot be confirmed by mathematical means as in the case of a symmetrical pattern. Obviously in painting the disposition of masses is generally determined by this principle of occult balance as distinguished from symmetry. Consequently, when this pictorial principle became operative in gardening, it inevitably broke up the formal Renaissance plan, banished the monotony of geometric design, and encouraged the variety that arose from the effort — frequently a very self-conscious effort — to balance a hill with a grove or a temple with a hermitage. As Shenstone phrases the idea,

> A landskip, for instance, is always irregular, and to use regularity in painting, or gardening, would make our work unnatural and disagreeable. . . . The eye requires a sort of balance here; but not so as to encroach upon probable nature.[45]

However, I am very far from believing that the gradual disappearance of symmetry from the garden was due solely to the influence of the landscape painters. Other factors were at work. Sheer weariness with an omnipresent uniformity of design made some sort of change a psychological necessity and helped to precipitate a revolt against classicism. This desire for change was evident in other arts that had nothing to do with either gardening or painting. In the field of decoration it led to the development of the asymmetry of *rocaille*, and in poetry it was responsible for the adoption of blank verse and the Spenserian stanza. Moreover, from the early years of the seventeenth century the subtle possibilities of occult balance had been familiar to European eyes in the ornamentation of Chinese lacquers and porcelains. In the eighteenth century the Louis Quinze style also revealed a sense for the beauty of balanced but irregular masses such as the Japanese alone in our own time possess. In view of these contemporary tendencies it may be concluded that, regardless of the landscape painters, a reaction against excessive symmetry, although it might have been delayed for a time, was ultimately inevitable. The formulas of classicism had gone to seed, and a rejuvenating contact with nature was a spiritual need.

This practice of allowing painters to provide the standards by which the beauty of nature or a garden was to be judged represents, in fact, the persistence of a classic habit of mind: the tendency to defer to authority, to respect precedents, and to follow models. When the early romanticist approached nature, he was not apt to rely on his own intuitions and response to its beauty, but he was guided, perhaps shackled, in his appreciation by his knowledge of what aspects of nature, what grouping of trees, hills, lakes, and rivers, and what effects of light and shade had already been approved by Claude or Albani as beautiful. Under such circumstances, the enjoyment of nature was not so much a spontaneous activity as it was the result of a certain degree of esthetic preparation. Just as the appreciation of architecture was dependent upon an acquaintance with Vitruvius and Palladio, so, to taste the quality of a landscape, one had to be familiar with Claude Lorraine and Salvator Rosa. A prospect of plains and distant mountains tremulous in the radiance of a setting sun suggested Claude, and a wild, savage scene of misshapen rocks and blasted trees dusky under swollen storm-clouds recalled Salvator Rosa and automatically was pronounced "sublime." Although the enjoyment of a landscape under the tutelage of Poussin or Lorraine created a romantic mood, this reliance upon an external criterion which would give one's personal impression an objective validity was thoroughly neo-classic.

This need for sanctions which one encounters in eighteenth-century writers usually described as romantic suggests that inbred habits of thought derivative from classicism had developed an inferiority complex which made genuinely subjective appreciations of nature difficult. Indeed, when men like Shenstone and William Mason supported the notion that gardeners should follow humbly in the footsteps of the painters, they were probably betraying unconsciously the effect of their literary training. Brought up in the tradition that the writers of antiquity as supreme examples of human genius were deserving of imitation, they found it hard to emancipate themselves from the doctrine of models even when they theorized about such a subject as gardening. It affords curious evidence of the intellectual tyranny of the classics that Shenstone expresses the hope that his sensible practice of making only English allusions in his elegies "will not be imputed to an *entire* ignorance, or to the *least* disesteem of the ancient learning."[46] In an age in which the herd instinct was strong in literature and the arts, it was wonderfully comforting for a cultivated man to feel that if he liked a poem, a building, or a landscape, he could substantiate his preference by the citation of authorities. When he was certain that a garden scheme made up of temples, wooded hillsides, and winding streams embodied the Claudian spirit, his taste was vindicated, his mind was at rest, and he took a pinch of snuff complacently.

No student of eighteenth-century literature can seriously doubt the influence of the great landscape painters upon the development of interest in wild scenery and the natural garden. Yet, at the same time, several recent writers have erred, I think, in the excessive emphasis which they have placed upon the relation between landscape painting and the enjoyment of nature. Explaining complex phenomena by simple causes, they have made it appear as if the painters were solely responsible for this taste for nature. This is to ignore the very powerful influence of Shaftesbury in molding eighteenth-century thought.[47] His philosophy of harmony in accordance with which he sensed divinity not only in "many bright parts of earth," but also in "obscurer places," led him by an inevitable logic, quite apart from any influence of Salvator Rosa, to admire savage aspects of nature that were completely unappreciated by his contemporaries; the desert "pleases" him, and he prefers "all the horrid graces of the wilderness itself" to the formal garden of the period. It is perfectly conceivable that men who had neither a taste for painting nor an opportunity to see canvases by either Poussin or Salvator Rosa would come in time, through the sympathetic comprehension of Shaftesbury's philosophy and his hymns to nature, to prefer wild scenery and irregular gardens. Much has been made, moreover, of the picturesque quality of Thomson's descriptions. His landscapes in the *Seasons* and more decisively in *The Castle of Indolence* possess the Claudian breadth and love of peaceful lawns, wooded hills, and winding dales; yet far more fundamental than such descriptions is the spiritual interpretation of nature which he learned from Shaftesbury and which inspired him to rhapsody. To put it briefly, Thomson would have had a sympathy with nature even if he had never heard of Claude Lorraine or Poussin. The *Seasons* undoubtedly did much to popularize Shaftesbury's philosophy of optimism and to foster that feeling for untamed nature which even by Joseph Warton was recognized as having its share in creating the vogue of the landscape garden.

On the whole, then, it appears that it was the influence of Shaftesbury, Thomson, Akenside, and a host of minor poetical followers which, combined with the influence of the French and Italian landscape painters, made natural beauty visible where it had not been perceived before. All these influences coming from philosophy, poetry, and painting intermingled, reinforced one another, and brought about what the text-books describe as "the return to nature." Of this "return" the landscape garden was merely one manifestation.

CHAPTER XVIII

THE ARTIFICE OF THE NATURAL GARDEN

As IT ultimately inundated with emotion almost every phase of European thought and feeling in the eighteenth century, it was inevitable that a movement like sentimentalism should affect the garden. As the desire to luxuriate in emotion for its own sake is unfortunately a permanent human tendency, sentimentalism has been a psychological phenomenon present, to a greater or less extent, in every age; but whereas in former periods it was held in check by a dominant rationalism, in the eighteenth century it gained the ascendant, influenced, more than ever before, art, philosophy, and letters, and occasioned the coinage of new words to differentiate it from other recognized modes of feeling. Literary historians have discovered the origin of this European movement in England before the close of the seventeenth century. The word *sentimental* itself did not, however, come into use until the fourth decade of the eighteenth century. When Wesley as late as 1772 observed the term in the title of Sterne's *Journey*, he wrote disgustedly in his *Journal*:

> *Sentimental!* what is that? It is not English; he might as well say, *Continental.* It is not sense. It conveys no determinate idea; yet one fool makes many. And this nonsensical word (who would believe it?) is become a fashionable one! However, the book agrees full well with the title, for one is as queer as the other.[1]

It is an arresting fact that Italian painters, especially those of Bologna, even at the close of the sixteenth and throughout the seventeenth centuries had already run the gamut of emotion. The great religious themes that earlier painters like the Bellinis, Mantegna, Titian, Andrea del Sarto, and Fra Bartolommeo had treated with a grand austerity became at the hands of Carlo Dolci, the Carracci, Guido, Albani, Baroccio, and Guercino merely an excuse for the display of emotion; and as a result a soft, enervating pathos enveloped the Virgin and Child, and sensationalism and melodrama, stimulated by Jesuitism, took the place of tragedy in the depiction of the Passion and the martyrdom of saints. Great as he was, Correggio doted on St. Catharine and the Virgin as maidens of a too exquisitely alluring beauty and melting tenderness, and Guido loved saints praying in rapture or supplication, their delicate hands clasped, their faces trembling with sensibility, and their eyes, turned reproachfully to heaven, dark with the sadness of undeserved suffering. Innumerable painters, moreover, could not resist the temptation to depict Mary Magdalen in repentance, her voluptuous charms only magnified by her tears, her wildly flowing tresses, and her gestures of despair. In the second epistle of the *Moral Essays*, with perfect precision and with obvious contempt, Pope has characterized this sentimental type popularized by such baroque painters:

> Let then the fair one beautifully cry,
> In Magdalen's loose hair and lifted eye,
> Or dress'd in smiles of sweet Cecilia shine,
> With simpering angels, palms, and harps divine.

It is a painful revelation of Wordsworth's taste which even his most ardent disciples must find it difficult to condone that in *The Prelude* he recorded his admiration for the convulsed Magdalen of Lebrun in the Louvre.[2] The Italians also stripped Christ of His dignity, endowed Him with a feminine beauty, and made Him tender, yearning, and wistful.

Much more, indeed, might be said of these predilections of the late Italian painters as a manifestation of sentimentalism prior to its appearance in England. It may be noted, however, that Englishmen on the grand tour in the seventeenth century saw these paintings, admired them, and frequently bought them. Nothing is more surprising than the eulogies which eighteenth-century writers bestow on the Carracci, Guido, and their like — artists who, in spite of their gifts, are to-day frequently distasteful because of their emotionalism. Even though there may be no immediate connection between Italian painting and the rise of sentimentalism in England, it is clear that when Cibber wrote *Love's Last Shift* (1696), said to be the first sentimental comedy, the craving for maudlin emotion was not such a rare phenomenon as literary historians have supposed. One thing is also certain. The failure of the baroque painters to see any necessity for putting a curb upon their tumultuous feelings did not make them any less attractive to the eighteenth-century sentimentalists.

The theory that the garden should as far as possible approximate the ideal Italian landscape of the painters encouraged the sentimental manipulation of nature. In his desire to secure a unity of emotional tone such as characterized the landscapes of the painters — the luminous brightness of Claude's prospects, the serene dignity of Poussin's patriarchal world, and the gloomy romantic wildness of Salvator Rosa's solitudes —, the man of taste conceived the garden as a series of scenes dominated by a single emotional mood and composed, as a picture might be, of natural features that would inspire, for example, cheerfulness, horror, or contemplative melancholy. By such a deliberate endeavor to construct by means of ruins, cypress trees, cataracts, temples, weeping willows, obelisks, grottos, and sunny meadows situations of varied emotional appeal, the designer multiplied opportunities for that inordinate indulgence in feeling for which readers of *Night Thoughts* and *The Pleasures of Melancholy* had a strange craving. The skill of the gardener was exhibited, furthermore, not only in the creation of these individual scenes, but in the art with which he made use of variety and contrast in his transitions from one part of a garden to another. Not only by placing scenes of dissimilar emotional quality in juxtaposition did he seek to give the promenader a more pleasurable thrill, but he sought to increase his gratification by arranging that he should come upon each scene suddenly and unexpectedly. In this way he obeyed the sacred principle of surprise deemed of supreme importance in garden design. Many descriptions of gardens that achieve these emotional effects, such as the Leasowes, Hagley, and Pain's Hill, are written in an appropriate lyrical style — or, at least, in a style that the authors intended should be rhapsodic.

The sentimentalization of the garden was a gradual process to which various authors contributed according to the degree to which they were affected by the tendencies of their time. In his *Lectures on Architecture* (1734) Robert Morris, although an exacting classicist in his judgment of buildings, conceives that a house and its surroundings should be provocative of some pleasing mood in which the owner might be inclined to indulge. In detail he describes a summer-house congenial to meditation where "in the cooler hours of reflection a man might retire to contemplate the important themes of human life"; with unnecessary generosity he gives us platitudinous examples of the "noble and felicitous ideas" which might occupy the mind of an architect, a geographer, or an astronomer under such circumstances. Postulating that landscapes as well as the three classic orders have an individual emotional character, he specifies with what type of landscape each order is in harmony. "The silent streams, the gay, the wanton scene requires the Corinthian order." Under the influence of Morris, John Gwynn in his *Essay upon Harmony* (1739) makes an emotional classification of architectural types as "the grave, the jovial, and the charming," and on this principle he informs us that the Doric would be appropriate to a house on Shooter's Hill and the Corinthian in keeping with a dwelling in the Thames valley near Hampton Court. It is symptomatic of the tide in taste that two practitioners of the most intellectual of the arts should thus juggle with emotional values in accord with a subjective interpretation of the moods of the countryside.

In the sixth decade of the century, when the satire upon Gothicism and *chinoiserie* was fiercest and when, indeed, any phase of artistic appreciation was capable of precipitating a ferment of discussion, works on taste appeared that influenced the development of the garden or were interesting commentaries on its characteristics. Although in 1753, the year in which *The Analysis of Beauty* was published, rococo decoration and the serpentine path and stream had made the curve a familiar element in design, Hogarth, no doubt, did much to strengthen its prestige. To be sure, his attempt to vindicate the undulating line, the S-curve, as the "line of beauty" and as the basis of satisfaction in the arts of form in reality failed because he could not actually define the exact degree of curvature necessary for such a line. To assert that if the curve bulges too much it is "gross and clumsy," and if it straightens too much it is "mean and poor," merely begged the question. Nevertheless, Hogarth's discussion of linear values, and especially his explanation of our pleasure in "winding walks and serpentine rivers" and all forms made up of waving lines as due to our enjoyment of "intricacy" by which the eye is led on "a wanton kind of chase," were arresting and inevitably influential in an age weary of formalism.[3] Indeed, his admission of "intricacy" into the category of the beautiful was in itself a bold advance, because that very quality in Gothic architecture, revealed in its multiplication of buttresses, turrets, and pinnacles, was a source of perpetual irritation to classicists. Then, the great quantity of evidence Hogarth presented to show the frequency of the curve in nature and in various forms popularly regarded as beautiful appeared to give philosophical validity to a preference that had hitherto rested only on an empirical basis. Reynolds quietly laughed in the *Idler* at the connoisseur's foolish insistence upon the "flowing line" as a test of beauty;[4] yet the less shrewd of Hogarth's readers probably felt that he had adequately rationalized their instinctive liking for the curved line which they saw gayly disporting itself in the garden, on the walls and ceilings of their rooms, and on furniture, porcelain, and the very silks of which their clothes were made.

Echoes of Hogarth's phraseology can be heard in contemporary comments on the serpentine. In his *Love of Order* Richard Graves praises Pitt's preservation of "Fair Beauty's waving line" in the pastoral landscape at Hayes, and in *Tewkesbury Park* he describes how

> Cotswold's cliffs and Malvern's heights combine
> To form th' horizon's undulating line,
> That line, tho' few know why, which charms us all,
> And connoisseurs "The Line of Beauty," call.

William Mason stigmatizes as bad taste the excessive curvature of paths that "writhe in convulsive torture"; yet the stilted Muse of *The English Garden* approves

> that peculiar curve,
> Alike averse to crooked and to straight,
> Where sweet Simplicity resides; which Grace
> And Beauty call their own; whose lambent flow
> Charms us at once with symmetry and ease.
> 'Tis Nature's curve, instinctively she bids
> Her tribes of Being trace it.

A visitor at the Leasowes in 1756, charmed by Shenstone's natural garden, was moved to represent even the lovely nymphs that dwelt in its streams and groves as well acquainted with *The Analysis of Beauty*. As they join in

the dance's mystic maze,
"Such is the *waving line*," they cry,
"For ever dear to Fancy's eye!
Yon stream that wanders down the dale,
The spiral wood, the winding vale,
The path which, wrought with hidden skill,
Slow twining scales yon distant hill
With fir invested — all combine
To recommend the *waving line*.

The wreathed rod of Bacchus fair,
The ringlets of Apollo's hair,
The wand by Maïa's offspring born,
The smooth volutes of Ammon's horn,
The structure of the Cyprian dame,
And each fair female's beauteous frame,
Shew, to the pupils of Design,
The triumphs of the *Waving Line*." [5]

These naive lyrical ecstacies are testimony to the impression which Hogarth made upon some of his contemporaries. He certainly did not introduce the serpentine, but he did authenticate it, and by the weight of his name indirectly encouraged its employment in the garden.

Two years later in his *Letters on the English Nation*, in which he ridiculed the craze for Oriental decorations, Shebbeare, dropping for the moment troublesome political questions, stated for the first time fully and definitely the sentimental objective of gardening. What for him is the originality of the English garden is that, abandoning regularity of form, it makes a varied appeal to human moods, or, as he rather clumsily phrases it, the English

have made a garden . . . a sensible consideration, and adapted it to all states which are incident to human minds in general. The gay and airy temper finds the open and chearful spots of light, which are acceptable to that disposition, and the melancholy mood finds the solitary and shady grove, by the side of which slowly creeps along the brook, complaining softly amongst the pebbles.

The planning of such a garden, Shebbeare contends, requires imagination. Having acquainted himself with the lay of the land, the flow of waters, and the woods at his disposal, the designer should employ his materials so as to stir the passions by giving a definite character to each part of the garden. The garden he creates will not, to be sure, be like anything seen in nature, but will represent a combination of objects which, being possible, will strike the person of taste as natural. Just as a musical composition is a union of sounds which affects the feelings, so a garden is, as Shebbeare defines it, a synthesis of "visible objects" which exerts a similar influence upon the heart.[6]

The interest in esthetics did not abate. One year after Shebbeare had thus explained the English garden as the representation of an ideal landscape designed to affect the emotions of a person of sensibility, Burke in his famous *Enquiry*, conceiving beauty as an external reality, defined the various qualities by which objects stir our emotions and impress us as either sublime or beautiful. The importance which he attached to power, terror, obscurity, gloom, and infinity in his discussion of the sublime prepared the way for the appreciation of the developing romantic literature in which those qualities predominate. In effect he accounted for the perturbing appeal of such poems as Ossian, *The Bard*, and *The Fatal Sisters*. The qualities which he undertook to explain are the negation of classical clarity and precision and are not at all concerned with making an intellectual impression; for their influence over the emotions, they depend upon the fear of the unknown or the mysterious. It is very significant of his point of view that whereas Wren had been unable to realize the appropriateness of stained glass windows in an ecclesiastical building, Burke does not hesitate to declare that "darkness is more productive of sublime ideas than light." [7] Moreover, his careful effort to discriminate between the sublime and the beautiful stimulated the gardeners to classify their scenes more precisely and suggested what qualities they should seek to embody in them if they were to make a distinct impression upon the feelings. Undoubtedly Burke reinforced the sentimental tendencies in gardening by revealing, for example, the emotional effect of the horror and gloom that pervaded the landscapes of Salvator Rosa. He strengthened the position of the picturesque gardeners and clarified the vaguely felt, timidly indulged emotions of the early romantics.

Although neither Hogarth nor Burke was interested in the garden, their speculations gave gardening at the time greater esthetic consequence than would have been the case if it had not been possible to link it up with more general principles of beauty. That the garden had points of contact with landscape painting and with esthetic theory dignified it as an art and made it more significant as an expression of contemporary culture. In his *Unconnected Thoughts on Gardening* Shenstone refers to Hutcheson, Gerard, and Burke and patently reveals that he has assimilated the *Enquiry*. He says, "Art should never be allowed to set a foot in the province of nature, otherwise than clandestinely and by night." Yet he is no advocate of the direct imitation of nature, but accepts the landscape painter as the only guide of the garden designer, specifies three types of scene, "the sublime, the beautiful, and the melancholy or pensive," and, to heighten the effect of a lover's walk, suggests as decoration "assignation seats, with proper mottoes — urns to faithful lovers — trophies, garlands, &c." [8] In *The English Garden* (1772–81) William Mason presents the same paradox. He invokes "divine Simplicity" as

> Best arbitress of what is good and fair,

but neither his pseudo-Miltonic style nor his ideas indicate that he had even peeped into the shrine of that goddess. When a poet — God save the mark! — describes an ice-house as

> the structure rude where Winter pounds
> In conic pit his congelations hoar,

there is little likelihood that his conception of a garden will be any more spontaneous. In fact, Mason's apostrophe to Claude, Poussin, and Salvator Rosa, his summary of what these "masters of correct design" can do for the gardener, his detailed directions how to paint a fence so as to make it a boundary of low visibility, his suggestion that, instead of a fence, the children of some poor but worthy cottager, prettily disguised as shepherds, might be employed to keep the sheep from straying, and his description of Alcander's garden retreat where amid willows and cypress trees he bemoaned his beloved in a hermitage of "twisting roots and living moss," all illustrate how the picturesque theory of gardening encouraged a self-conscious, deliberate effort to be natural and imposed dogmas of its own as rigid as those of the repudiated formal garden.[9]

As the result of his excessive precautions against the invasion of art Mason's garden becomes artificial, and one is reminded of all the elaborate tricks and evasions to which Rousseau resorted in order to educate Emile as a child of nature. Frequently preposterous in the theatricalism of its garden scenes — the author claimed that he got his ideas from the Chinese — was Sir William Chambers' *Dissertation on Oriental Gardening* (1772). He favored the picturesque landscape of varied emotional appeal to offset the vogue of "Capability" Brown's tame garden schemes with their clumps of trees, shaven lawns, and all too regular serpentines. Mason ridiculed Chambers in his *Heroic Epistle*, but in reality his own ideas ponderously expounded in *The English Garden* were frequently in their own way only a little less absurd than those in the *Dissertation.*

The studied artlessness that pervades Alcander's ideal garden as conceived by Mason is also present in the anonymous *Essay on the Different Natural Situations of Gardens* (1774), a vivid exposition of the picturesque sentimental theory. Of the four situations with which the author deals — the grand, the romantic, the cheerful, and the flat — his treatment of the second, the romantic, is typical. Given such a situation — a deep, secluded glen, a smoothly flowing river, rocks crowned with trees, and wild birds hovering above —, what must a designer do to emphasize its character and create "a feeling of tranquillity, ever verging into melancholy"? All buildings built here for use should be Gothic, whereas those that are merely decorative should be suggestive "of religion or of grief, as a cloister, a chapel, a spire, a hermitage, or a pyramid." Never in any case should the buildings be white, but always dark and somber in color. To harmonize with the edifices, the trees should be planted thick so that the wind, whistling through them, will produce a melancholy sound such as no open grove can do. Dense woods like these were the dwelling-place of the Druids and the setting of Tasso's scenes of magic and horror. As a solemn silence should brood over the river, all obstacles in its course should be removed so that it can flow in deep, unbroken calm. Over this noiseless stream trees should hang, preferably weeping willows. Willows, we are told, had originally overshadowed Mr. Pelham's serpentine at Esher, but when it was realized that the dominant spirit of his garden was cheerful, they were cut down. In a romantic situation there should be no hint of a lawn. The river may, perhaps, be allowed to flow in a straight line, as such uniformity is soothing to a melancholy temper. It is especially important that cascades should fall in one sheet because the regularity of the sound composes the mind and permits it to pursue its indolent musing. By such devices the designer will intensify the emotional mood that is implicit in the natural situation, and make the garden alluring to a man oppressed by misfortunes.

As Thomas Whately in *Observations on Modern Gardening* (1770) aimed to do for the landscape garden what the unidentified author of *La Théorie du Jardinage* did for the formal garden, his book is a carefully systematic attempt to coordinate the whole subject of the natural garden, and to a degree astonishing to anyone unfamiliar with volumes of this kind abounds in the most minute particulars for the sentimental treatment of woods, water, rocks, and buildings. Yet for such a book there was a demand; within seven years of its first appearance it reached a fourth edition.

Letters on the Beauties of Hagley, Envil, and the Leasowes (1777), by Joseph Heely, is illuminating from a different point of view. Written in a lyrical style, it shows us how the susceptible visitor was expected to react to the various scenes studiously prepared for his delectation by the wily gardener. The sentimental promenader fastidiously culling the "beauties" of the landscape is, indeed, nothing less than an emotional epicure or what Shenstone somewhere calls a "taster" of its charms. Heely delights in the ethical influence of the garden, noting at Hagley that so great was the tranquillity of its secluded bowers that a villain finding himself there would be "disarmed from executing his dark and bloody purposes; and every passion that corrodes the human breast, [would] be lulled into a perfect calm." Even the most ingenious writers of sentimental comedy in the eighteenth century, desperately anxious to reclaim their hero in the fifth act, had never hit upon the garden as an expeditious means of leading him to rectitude. Heely's optimism outdid even their confidence in human nature. Very subtle too in its expressiveness, in Heely's opinion, was the single plank thrown across a tumbling stream at Envil. A bridge in such a wild spot would have been too sophisticated, but a mere plank— how different! — was the inspiration of genius. Although he regards the Priory Walk at the Leasowes as "one of the most distinguished scenes that ever was formed by art," Shenstone's attempt to produce the effect of wild simplicity by permitting the tree-trunks to obtrude into the path Heely thought a most egregious affectation.[10]

Such super-refinements and pedantries of taste inevitably invited the ridicule of the satirists, and moved Johnson on more than one occasion to subject sentimental esthetics to the harsh raillery of an uncompromising utilitarianism. "That was the best garden," he declared, "which produced most roots and fruits; and that water was most to be prized which contained most fish." The report of Shenstone's anger whenever anyone inquired if his beloved streams contained fish always incurred Johnson's laughter. "As if one could fill one's belly with hearing soft murmurs, or looking at rough cascades!" [11] Johnson's attitude, amusing enough in itself, is on a par with the classical belief, universally prevalent before their grandeur was perceived, that utility provided the only possible standard by which either mountains or the ocean could be judged.

But in spite of counter-currents of criticism the tide of sentimentalism flowed on, and people of culture, bitten by what Chesterfield called the *furor hortensis*, continued to rhapsodize over gardens in language that was reminiscent of Hogarth and Burke. Admirers of Salvator Rosa and readers of Ossian had an appetite for the sublime — frequently they discovered it where we should find only melodrama and sensationalism —, and they wrote cheerfully and chatted glibly of its thrills.

CHAPTER XIX

THE SENTIMENTAL VAGARIES OF THE *FUROR HORTENSIS*

THE earliest landscape gardens, the outgrowth of ideas of which the germ is to be found in Addison, Pope, and Switzer, definitely antedate the majority of the various poems, essays, and treatises on gardening mentioned in the last chapters. Kent at Chiswick and Wooburn Farm, Bridgeman at Stowe, and Shenstone at the Leasowes had completed their work before the middle of the century and had inspired others to adopt the new style. The subsequent development of the garden, and especially its appreciation, exhibit theory and practice still in close alliance. But whatever the character of the books written on gardening or esthetics, they were written by men who had no professional interest in their subject. This curious anomaly accounts for the literary atmosphere which pervades the landscape garden. Designed either by men who had received the traditional classical education and who had, perhaps, taken the grand tour, or by gardeners who worked under their direction, the garden reflected the interests of the owner and his friends and abounded — an unkind critic might say was cluttered — with allusions to literature and history, ancient and contemporary. It is these concrete features of the garden that I now wish to consider — features that at once intellectualized and sentimentalized it.

At every possible opportunity inscriptions underscored and labeled the moods that different localities in the garden were intended to convey. Placed on tablets, seats, urns, obelisks, columns, and buildings, quotations from Horace, Virgil, and Milton, and verses that were the composition either of the owner or of his friends crystallized the spirit of a scene and indirectly hinted to the visitor just what emotions it was, at the moment, proper for him to enjoy. Anyone inordinately curious about the nature of these "hortulane" verses can find hosts of examples by simply turning the pages of any substantial anthology of eighteenth-century poetry. A few titles will suffice to satisfy the restless reader: *On a summer-house in my own garden*, *On a dial in my garden*, *An inscription in the cottage of Venus at Middletown Park*, *Inscription for a tree on the terrace*, *Nuneham*, *Father Francis's Prayer written in Lord Westmoreland's hermitage*, *An inscription on the cell*, *An inscription in the cell*, *Inscribed on a beautiful Grotto near the Water*, and *An inscription over a calm and clear spring in Blenheim Gardens*. After reading such effusions one is in a mood to exclaim with Garth:

> What frenzy has of late possessed the brain!
> Though few can write, yet fewer can refrain.

The Leasowes in particular was famous for its inscriptions, as this type of composition gave Shenstone an opportunity to exercise his special gift for writing smooth, graceful verse of delicate refinement. It was, however, a nice question among the critics whether or not the poet had carried to excess this feature of his garden. Heely complained that an inscribed bench was unnecessary in a spot which Shenstone had made so charming that the beholder was spontaneously filled with the appropriate sentiment; "indeed a little enthusiasm, if it hang not about you," Heely added, "should be courted for the more perfect enjoyment of such classic ground." In Heely's own case, we are relieved to be informed, there was no scarcity of susceptibility; he responded to the situation "without the courtship." [1] Whately thought that the style and aptness of the verses compensated "for their length and number," although as a rule such inscriptions, he said, always lost their point after the first visit.[2]

If these matters appear too trivial to deserve consideration, it should be borne in mind as an amusing, but none the less interesting, reflection of the fashionable dilettantism that the eighteenth century regarded them very seriously. Shenstone took the trouble to send his friend Lady Luxborough several versions of a motto he had devised for a garden seat, with a request for her judgment. She, in turn, wrote that a Mr. Hall was anxious that Shenstone should compose a memorial inscription for his deceased father. When Sanderson Miller's Gothic building at Edgehill, commemorative of the battle, was under discussion, she expressed the opinion that the inscriptions, if they were to voice the sentiments of persons susceptible to the historical associations of the locality, would require "a genius somewhat more sublime" than that possessed by a man with a happy knack for Gothic architecture.[3] Even Bolingbroke did not think it beneath his dignity to busy himself with inscriptions for his house and garden. When he was living in exile in France, he sent Swift some mottos of his own composition for correction, and asked him as a special favor to provide him with others "for groves, and streams, and fine prospects, and retreat, and contempt for grandeur, etc." [4] Such inscriptions satisfied the eighteenth-century passion for trite moral sentiment, and often permitted the man of the world to pose as a lover of Arcadian simplicity. Shenstone's own letters reveal how rarely he experienced the contentment he prattles about in his garden verse, and Bolingbroke's personal ambition made a mockery of his mottos.

Someone has said that a platitude makes all the world akin, and this remark probably explains why the inscription enjoyed such a popularity: it neither disturbed thought nor inspired contradiction. The pretty, harmless verses were eagerly collected by tourists. One of the purposes of the guide-book to Stowe, it will be recalled, was to save visitors the trouble of copying the mottos. In the course of her tour with her family — it is described with gentle satire in the *Mirror* (no. 41) — Miss Betsy Blubber visited several gardens, and at one place was at great pains to take down in her notebook "some sweet copies of verses" she discovered in a hermitage and in grottos. In 1797 in the *Philanthrope* (no. 32) the anonymous author of one of the essays contends that the monitory or rural inscription has a sufficiently distinct character of its own to give it the dignity of a special type, and he enumerates as its "captivating graces" perspicuity, brevity, and simplicity. We need not be too complacent; the interest in garden mottos is matched by our own mania for limericks.

As many of the inscriptions were purely commemorative, they made a delicate appeal to sentiment by revealing the owner's affection for his friends and pets and his admiration for some poet, philosopher, or patriot. If he vibrated with some feeling that did him credit, the sentimentalist was delighted to parade it and capitalize it in his garden scenes. To express his gratitude for the immense fortune he had made out of Bath stone, Ralph Allen, the friend of Pope and Fielding, set up in Prior Park a figure of Moses striking a rock from which, with symbolic significance, gushed a cascade. Incidentally the editor of Defoe's *Tour* (1742), evidently one of those pious persons who looked askance at classical sculpture, commended Allen for thus showing his respect for the Christian religion. Philip Thicknesse, the adviser of Gainsborough, scooped out a cave in the side of a dell, and, placing before it a relief of Chatterton, dedicated the spot to that "unfortunate boy." When Thicknesse's daughter died, he enshrined her in Chatterton's tomb "beneath the only monumental stone raised in Britain to the greatest genius Britain, or perhaps any other nation under the sun, has produced." [5]

Dr. Lettsom, the humanitarian, outdid Thicknesse in emotionalism. When his eldest son reached his majority — in itself not a unique achievement —, he signalized the occasion by erecting in his garden at Grove Hill, Camberwell, Surrey, a sculptured group representing the three Fates and Hygeia, the goddess of health. Atropos, armed with her shears, was depicted as eager to cut young Lettsom's thread of life, but Hygeia, seizing her arm, thwarted the execution of her cruel purpose. To enforce the dramatic symbolism of the group, the Doctor planted the vicinity suitably: "savine and deadly nightshade" near Atropos and *arbor vitae* at the feet of Hygeia.[6] Shakespeare enjoyed his share of commemoration. Dr. Lettsom named in his honor a long walk terminated by his statue, and Lord Shaftesbury and Garrick raised garden temples to the glory of the poet. A Mr. Talbot affixed an appropriately worded tablet to his hermitage, in which Cumberland, his guest at the time, had written a few scenes of *The West Indian* — a tribute which the dramatist unctuously described as "a piece of elegant flattery very elegantly expressed."

At Hagley Lord Lyttelton consecrated to Thomson an octagonal seat placed on the brow of a hill which the poet had frequented in his lifetime, and in the midst of a beautiful grove he inscribed to Pope a solitary urn which the latter had chosen as suitable for the spot. This urn, "when shown by a gleam of moonlight through the trees," Whately assures us, "fixes that thoughtfulness and composure, to which the mind is insensibly led by the rest of this elegant scene." [7] The Earl of Buchan as a Scotchman surpassed Lord Lyttelton in the recognition he gave to Thomson. In his garden at Dryburgh he erected an Ionic temple to the author of *The Seasons*, and in 1791 he instituted on Ednam Hill a festival at which the first complete edition of *The Seasons* was formally crowned with a wreath of bays. For this occasion Burns wrote his ode *Address to the Shade of Thomson*. At the Leasowes Shenstone dedicated a grove to Virgil and seats to Thomson, Dodsley, Richard Jago, Joseph Spence, Richard Graves, and Lord Lyttelton — a roll-call, for the most part, of minor men of letters. But it was in his Lover's Walk that Shenstone played most tenderly upon the chords of recollection. There, in the shade of trees and beside a murmuring rivulet, was an ornamental urn to the memory of a Miss Dolman, whom Dodsley graciously identified as "a beautiful and amiable relation of Mr. Shenstone's, who died of the small-pox about twenty-one years of age," and whom the poet more ardently addresses as "Ah Maria, puellarum elegantissima."

As Shenstone's skill in managing these funereal decorations was acknowledged, his advice was in request. When Lady Luxborough contemplated the erection of an urn to Somerville, the author of *The Chase*, Shenstone sketched a design and had it executed in oils, the urn being represented against a background of trees so that its effect might be judged. Lady Luxborough consulted him as to whether the ornament should be in high or low relief, and was "charmed" with the idea that its decorative detail should suggest *The Chase*. But the estimable widow was resolved to be discreet. She insisted that the urn itself should be simple lest beholders should infer that feelings more tender than mere admiration for Somerville as a man and a poet had inspired the memorial. All these delicate questions of taste and propriety were thrashed out, pro and con, in a lengthy correspondence. We finally learn to our great relief that the urn was ornamented with a French horn, "done by the best stone carver in Warwick," and that when it was set up it was visible "from every place, shrubbery, terrace, bowling-green, Long Walk, and the end of the kitchen garden." A year later Lady Luxborough faithfully reported that Somerville's

> urn is now beautifully shaded by its canopy of oak; under which I sat last night agreeably, though alone, looking at the neighbouring hills, hearing my mowers whet their scythes, seeing the troop-horses about my avenue.

When it was fashionable to toy thus delicately with grief, it was natural enough that Lady Luxborough should write to Shenstone that she wished to see his urn dedicated to Thomson, "its shadow trembling in your transparent stream." The memorial, she was certain, gave him "a pensive pleasure." [8]

At Stowe the garden decorations were grander in scale, but similar in spirit to those of the Leasowes. There persons of great consequence in the world of affairs were commemorated: Vanbrugh, Congreve, Wolfe, Nelson, Captain Cook, and the Princess Amelia. At Manilla Hall, Sir William Draper honored Pitt with a triumphal pillar even during the lifetime of the statesman. When the inscription was sent to him for approval, Pitt found it so fulsome that on the strength of his entreaty the last four lines were omitted. But as Pitt himself was famous as an amateur gardener — Bishop Warburton declared that his taste was "inimitable" and "far superior" to that of "Capability" Brown —, he was not exempt from the desire for rhetorical emotion. When in 1765 Sir William Pynsent bequeathed him the noble estate of Burton Pynsent, Somersetshire, Pitt forthwith saw to it that an imposing column was erected to the glory of his benefactor. The more robust sentiments of patriotism were exploited no less than literary admirations and the ties of friendship. In this respect Shenstone envied the good fortune of the Italians, who could do honor to localities immortalized by the classics. But he felt that if an English land-owner possessed an estate which had been the scene of some historic event, it was his duty "to make it more interesting to the imagination. Mottoes should allude to it, columns, &c. record it; verses moralize upon it; and curiosity receive it's share of pleasure." [9]

When the impulses of a humid sentimentalism were thus leading persons apparently sensible to erect memorials of one sort or another in their gardens, it followed inevitably that any object associated with Rousseau, the apostle of natural feeling, should be venerated. Two letters buried in the *Gentleman's Magazine* perfectly exemplify this attitude and constitute a commentary on what has just been said about garden urns and tablets. In September, 1786, an English disciple of Rousseau wrote a letter to the editor in the hope that some foreign reader of the *Magazine* could give him information about the walnut tree which Rousseau, while a young pupil in the home of the Protestant minister M. Lambercier, had planted beside the terrace to shade the family and their lodgers when they sat there in the afternoon. The Englishman phrased his sentimental yearnings in halting French that was cruelly ridiculed in the November issue of the *Magazine*:

> S'il en reste, cet arbre, il faut qu'il ne soit enconnu. Il sera arrosé des larmes des amans; des coeurs inspirés du vrai enthusiasme en tout genre (cet ardeur heroique & bien-faisant.) Des sages, des patriots, des amis du genre humain, sentiront, en soupirant, l'ombre de l'éleve de leur frere. Hereux qui emportera des noix; & dira, en les voyant sortir de la terre — "Voici des fruits de l'enfance du Rousseau."

To this fervid inquiry a Swiss enthusiast, Louis Bridel by name, replied in May, 1787. With that theatrical lyricism which Rousseau's style had popularized, he declared to the unknown Englishman that although their ages, their social position, and their fortunes might be different, nevertheless, as their tastes were the same, they were made to be united in friendship. He was confident that his offer of friendship would be accepted because he wrote to him "avec la confiance des belles ames, comme je le ferois au plus ancien de mes amis." But the tree, alas! no longer lived. If it existed, Bridel asserted that he would have visited it "avec la même dévotion que le pelerin visite les saints lieux," and in its shadows he would have read the immortal works of Homer, Sterne, and his "virtuous master Rousseau." Some "coldly methodic hand," preferring "a tiresome uniformity to a charming relic" of a great man, had cut down the tree because, forsooth, it had destroyed the symmetry of the court in which it stood. Bridel confessed that although he had no fortune, he would have bought that precious walnut tree even at the sacrifice of the little that he possessed. He would not, he explained characteristically, have spoken with such feeling to ordinary men because they would not understand him, but he knew that his English correspondent would sense his meaning because his heart was made to feel, or he would not love the famous citizen of Geneva.

In view of such raptures of hero-worship, it was assuredly in accord with the current mood that beside a colonnade at Nuneham on the Thames an admirer placed a bust of Rousseau,[10] and that at Ermenonville, one of the earliest and greatest of English gardens laid out in France, the Marquis de Girardin dedicated an obelisk to Thomson, an inscribed rock to Shenstone, and an island to Rousseau, where in a tomb encircled by poplars his body reposed for a while.

This relish of feeling for its own sake was typical of an age that prized "exquisite sensibility" and enriched its vocabulary with phrases expressive of its apotheosis of sympathy. Thomson, for example, cannot refrain from moving references to "the flowing heart," "the feeling heart," "the friendly heart," "the comely tear," "the lovely tear," and "the heart-shed tear." As a follower of Shaftesbury setting great store by all the ties that bind the race together, he also freights the adjective *social* with tender significance, alluding to "social friends," "social feeling," "social charm," "social love," "social sweetness," "social passions," "social sleep," the "social sigh," the "social tear," and the "social offspring of the heart."

Indicative of the same tendency is the initial appearance in the language about this time of such words as *philanthropist*, *philanthrope*, and *philanthropic*. This sense of fellowship and the sentimental enjoyment of it flowered in a humanitarianism that extolled sympathy for animals as well as man. The garden did not and could not escape the contagion. Richard Gough, the antiquary, who allowed his aged horses and cows to pass their last years in a luxuriant meadow, was no less mindful of his pets after their death. In different parts of his grounds he set up tablets designed to immortalize a sparrow, a pheasant, a monkey, and a tortoise-shell cat.[11] Implicit in all these epitaphs, even though they hover between whimsicality and seriousness, is the sentimental fallacy of attributing to animals virtues equal, if not actually superior, to those of man. An inscription of this type was not thought beneath the dignity even of Stowe. Placed on the rear of the Temple of British Worthies, it read:

> To the memory of Signor Fido, an Italian of good extraction, who came into England, not to bite us, like most of his countrymen, but to gain an honest livelihood. He hunted not after fame, yet acquir'd it; regardless of the praise of his friends, but most sensible of their love. Tho' he liv'd amongst the great, he neither learn'd nor flatter'd any vice. He was no bigot, tho' he doubted of none of the 39 articles, and, if to follow nature, and to respect the laws of society, be philosophy, he was a perfect philosopher; a faithful friend, an agreeable companion, a loving husband, distinguish'd by a numerous offspring, all which he lived to see take good courses. In his old age he retir'd to the house of a clergyman in the country, where he finish'd his earthly race, and died an honour and an example to the whole species. Reader, this stone is guiltless of flattery, for he to whom it is inscrib'd was not a man, but a grey-hound.

A pervasive ironic humor saves this ingenious epitaph from the maudlin. But so much cannot be said in Shelley's behalf when he undertook to make literary use of this custom of commemorating some beloved animal. In *Rosalind and Helen* a dog, having rescued Lionel's mother from the sea, drops dead from exhaustion. Then Shelley describes how she built

> Amid a bloomless myrtle wood,
> On a green and sea-girt promontory,
> . . . .
> An altar and a temple bright
> Circled by steps, and o'er the gate
> Was sculptured, "To Fidelity."

But this was not enough, in Shelley's opinion, to satisfy the lady's yearning for emotion. At each new moon she resorted to the temple and in gratitude to her dumb benefactor scattered choice flowers on the marble floor and played soft, tender melodies on her harp. Of course the alert architect gladly turned the sorrows of his more sentimental clients to his own advantage. In his *Ferme Orneé or Rural Improvements* (1795), John Plaw gave a design of a paddock house fitted "to commemorate some favorite animal for past services." He suggested that "the skull of a horse [might] be placed over a mural tablet where may be recorded the feats of that noble animal, and the water-trough [might] represent the sarcophagus." Manifestly

Byron's verses to Boatswain, the dog who possessed "all the Virtues of Man without his Vices," were in accord with established custom. When such excesses were possible, it was a happy impulse which prompted waggish persons to hit upon the mimosa, or sensitive plant, as a symbol under which the sentimentalist could be laughed at with malicious consistency.[12]

The frequency of ruins in the landscapes of Claude and Poussin amply sanctioned their presence as a picturesque addition to the beauty of a garden; nevertheless, as the mood of melancholy reflection evoked by fallen columns and shattered walls was irresistibly alluring to the sentimentalist, an obscure desire to create an opportunity to indulge his feelings provided another reason why he welcomed a crumbling castle as an enchanting feature in a garden scene. It was his anxiety to have a ruin at any cost that led him into the absurdity of building one when he was so unfortunate as not to possess any genuine architectural remains on his estate. Whately was very explicit as to how such an artificial ruin might be made to appear of authentic antiquity, pointing out that if ivy and trees were planted judiciously among its scattered fragments it might be expected to awaken the pathos of regret like a real relic of a long vanished past. With the guile characteristic of the landscape gardener laboring to dupe the beholder into believing that what he saw was natural, Whately suggested that if a ruin were put to some modern use obviously different from that for which it was supposed to have been built originally, it would convey the idea that so destructive had been the effects of time and weather that the owner despaired of ever being able to achieve its satisfactory restoration.[13] In other words, if a stable were disguised as a monastery, a beholder realizing the degradation of the ecclesiastical edifice would infer that a great length of time must have elapsed to bring about such a change, and his emotions would be affected accordingly. Lord Anson was also admirably industrious in his effort to create an impression of architectural age. Discovering that his workman had been so deficient in intelligence as to carry to actual completion a building intended for a ruin, his lordship with axes and chisels reduced it to a state of dilapidation such as his own taste for decay approved.[14] In the royal gardens at Kew Sir William Chambers constructed a classic ruin (Fig. 73) that showed him to be a master of the art of premeditated disrepair. A contemporary guide-book refers with approval to the great arch

> confined between rocks overgrown with briars and other wild plants and topped with thickets amongst which are seen several columns and fragments of building. . . . There is a great quantity of cornices and other fragments spread over the ground, seemingly fallen from buildings and in the thickets on each side are seen several remains of piers, brick wall, et cetera.

In his *Elements of Criticism* Lord Kames was careful to specify that a ruin and a parterre should never be placed in juxtaposition, for the cheerful brightness of the flowers would inevitably lessen the pleasurable gloom to which the ruin was conducive. On the other hand, he claimed that if one passed "from an exhilarating object to a ruin" the effect was most ingratiating, "for each of the emotions is the more sensibly felt by being contrasted with each other." By such solicitude the sentimentalist preserved intact the mood of melancholy which he wished to pervade garden scenes consecrated to retirement and contemplation.

Another momentous question agitated the minds of the pundits of garden art. Should a ruin be classic or Gothic? Lord Kames' argument was the quintessence of refined feeling. A classic ruin was, he thought, probably less desirable because it depressed the beholder, reminding him of the tragic circumstance that the barbarians had triumphed over the taste of the ancients. As the condition of the Gothic ruin, on the other hand, represented merely the victory of time over strength, it was on that account to be preferred. It did not convey any painful ideas, but affected the spirit with a melancholy such as was only a source of pleasure to a person of fine sensibility.[15] On more realistic grounds Mason also approved of the crumbling medieval building. A classic ruin in England, he reasonably contended, was

> but a splendid lie
> Which mocks historic credence.

This sound principle — advocated inconsistently in an episode in which the British hero is labeled "Alcander" — led to the

Fig. 73 — Artificial Ruin of a Roman Arch, Kew Gardens

Fig. 74 — A Roman Ruin as a Textile Motive. Linen Manufactured by Collins Woolmers, 1768

wholesale erection of sham medieval buildings in harmony with the relics of England's architectural past. Mason does not shrink from particulars. He directs that round a knoll be built

> in stately Norman mode,
> A wall embattled; and within its guard
> Let every structure needful for a Farm
> Arise in Castle-semblance; the huge Barn
> Shall with a mock Portcullis arm the gate,
> Where Ceres entering, o'er the flail-proof floor
> In golden triumph rides; some Tower rotund
> Shall to the Pigeons and their callow young
> Safe roost afford; and ev'ry buttress broad,
> Whose proud projection seems a mass of stone,
> Give space to stall the heifer, and the steed.
> So shall each part, though turn'd to rural use,
> Deceive the eye with those bold feudal forms
> That Fancy loves to gaze on.

As the humble ice-house and very useful dairy are ugly,

> both to veil,
> He builds of old disjointed moss-grown stone
> A time-struck Abbey. . . .
> . . . .
> The Fane conventual there is dimly seen,
> The mitred Window, and the Cloister pale,
> With many a mouldering Column; Ivy soon
> Round the rude chinks her net of foliage spreads;
> Its verdant meshes seem to prop the wall. [16]

In other words, as the remains of Gothic architecture were familiar objects in England, they were "natural." But paradoxically, in order to achieve the effect of "naturalness," it was necessary to urge the perpetration of elaborate tricks that deceived nobody except such as wished to be deceived. Associated with this sentimental interest in ruins of a native character was the picturesque employment of monuments of pre-Roman Britain. On a hill in his garden the Earl of Pembroke wished to reproduce in miniature, with the aid of the antiquary William Stukeley, the "original glory" of Stonehenge. The editor of Defoe's *Tour* (1748) implies that he actually thinks the manufactured monument will surpass its prototype in grandeur. At Dogmansfield, according to Dr. Pococke, a Mr.

St. John for a distance of half a mile lined an avenue with huge stones set on end in imitation of similar Druid remains.

As was to be expected, when the relics of the Middle Ages were contemplated with sentimental regret, a ruin, whether artificial or genuine, was a cherished possession. In the *Grumbler* (no. 15, 1791) an essayist describes his visit to an estate for the purpose of drawing an ancient edifice. He found the ruin to be "the most picturesque that ever employed the pencil of an artist," but he was exasperated by the owner, a man of taste, who insisted on leading him from point to point so as to exhibit all its "beauties" to most advantage. The light played enchantingly over the edifice, but as the officious importunities of his vain host prevented the visitor from completing his sketch, he returned home in disgust.

The attitude of such a writer is very different from that of Addison, who eighty years before had described Sir Roger's ruined abbey solely for the unromantic purpose of dispelling the illusion that it was haunted. Taste had changed. Ruins were to be found in the most unexpected places. Chippendale designed "a chimney-piece composed of architecture, sculpture, and ruins," and in 1768 Collins Woolmers manufactured English chintz (Fig. 74) decorated with rural motives and a shattered Roman arch that would have been an excellent model for any ruin-builder. Such fragments of classical architecture, a feature of the Claudian landscape, were in competition with medieval remains for the approval of the sentimental man of taste. But whatever type of ruin he preferred, it appealed to him because it was reminiscent of the past, stirred historic memories, and symbolized the pathos of decay and the mutability of all things made by human hands.

The landscape gardener scheming to entrap emotional interest never appeared so much like a stage-manager exploiting the obvious as when he arranged a hermitage in the Protestant environment of eighteenth-century England. Built generally of moss and the roots of trees and set in a lonely situation — Whately insisted that it should never be near a roadside, although it might be placed with impunity on a mountain or in a wood[17] —, the hermitage was supposed to intensify the solitude of a scene by its suggestion of a simple life passed in religious contemplation. The interior was furnished with properties that it was hopefully assumed would confirm the illusion. In Lord Orrery's hermitage, for example, Mrs. Delany noted

> a couch made of matting, and little wooden stools, a table with a manuscript on it, a pair of spectacles, a leathern bottle; and hung up in different parts, an hourglass, a weatherglass and several mathematical instruments, a shelf of books, another of wooden platters and bowls, another of earthen ones, in short everything that you might imagine necessary for a recluse.[18]

Joseph Cradock protested against the presence of a normal, practical dining-table in a hermit's cell on the ground that it was destructive of its solemnity. If it was necessary to be painfully meticulous in the cause of historic verisimilitude, his point was well taken. More callous men, it appears, were in the habit of sinning against propriety; Mr. Hoare of Stourton, one is reluctant to report, was so crass as to give dinners and teas occasionally in his Gothic nunnery, romantically situated in his park at a distance from his mansion.

However, others less prosaic and more ingenious embellished their hermitages with fantastic perversity. The effect of the hermitage at the Thatched Cottage at the foot of Box Hill was enhanced by an adjacent tombstone, a coffin, a pickaxe, and a shovel. The inscription on the coffin reminded the stranger of the eternal *danse macabre*: the nearness of death ready to strike down in the midst of their follies the giddy and the pleasure-loving. The visitor was then invited to pass through a gate into a shady grove, where he was supposed to escape the irritations of life and enjoy the tranquillities of contemplation.[19] At Denbys, the estate of Jonathan Tyers, the proprietor of Vauxhall, similar platitudinous ideas were enforced with even more absurd theatricalism. In a Gothic temple a clock solemnly struck the minutes to remind man of the flight of time and his consequent duty to think of eternity. A label held in the beak of a raven and inscriptions on the panels of the wall iterated the same admonition. In the middle of the room Young's *Night Thoughts* and Blair's *The Grave* bound in black lay on a desk. Another temple called "Il Penseroso" housed a monument representing a corpse rising from a tomb as an angel blew the last trump, and in yet another paintings by Hayman displayed the contrast between the death of an unbeliever and that of a good Christian. One may suspect that Tyers was not so naive as he appeared. As an astute business man, he surmised that it would be to his commercial advantage if he could persuade his more sanctimonious contemporaries that he "had religion" in spite of the damning evidence of Vauxhall to the contrary.

Be that as it may, it was on such commonplaces, plucked, as it were, from Shallow's threadbare philosophy, that the sentimentalist nourished his emotions. If these calculated appeals to feeling leave us cold, they did not, at any rate, impress the eighteenth century as merely empty gestures. A susceptible person gave an admiring description of Tyers' garden in a long letter to the *Gentleman's Magazine* (March, 1781), and the editor thought it deserving of publication. The worldly and sophisticated society that was duped by sham reminders of death also paid its "tribute of tears" to the shroud made by Clarissa with her own hands. How completely a house and garden advertised in the *St. James's Chronicle* in 1785 met the needs of the age!

> To be let and entered upon at midsummer. St. Catherine's Hermitage, most delightfully situated on the side of Lansdown Hill, about a thousand yards from the back of the Royal Crescent of Bath. There is a lawn in front of the house, and a small wood on the east side ornamented with stately trees, shrubs, and serpentine walks in which is the Hermit's Hut, a comfortable room, a grotesque monument erected to the memory of Chatterton, a large cave, a small stable and thatched chaise-house.[20]

The English garden represented the strange, disconcerting mixture of tastes that lasted throughout the century. The mania for hermitages and Gothic ruins did not oust classicism from favor so much as the text-books might lead one to suppose. As long as classical training remained the basis of education and a knowledge of Greek and Latin was regarded as the indispensable equipment of a man of culture, the ancient world exercised an incalculable influence over the imagination that no subsequent interest in the Middle Ages could displace completely. In the garden, if the hermitage and the chapel were deemed appropriate to seclusion and retirement under the auspices of Claude and Poussin, room was found elsewhere in different situations for temples dedicated to Roman deities and to abstractions conceived in a sentimental spirit. At Kew temples consecrated to Victory and Peace and at Stowe temples inscribed to Friendship, Ancient Virtue, Concord and Victory, and British Worthies were testimonies of the continued allegiance to classicism. Although the impulse that inspired such buildings was not, perhaps, so cold as the personifications which, like inert sculpture, chilled the pages of neo-classic poetry, neither depth of feeling nor imagination was responsible for these edifices in honor of Fidelity, Contemplation, or what-not. Pedantry and a desire to evoke a pleasant emotion sufficiently account for their presence; the beholder enjoyed these reminders of virtues which he admired even if he did not practice them. Such temples were designed to touch the feelings, like those vases described by Mason as an embellishment of the garden of the matchless Alcander:

> Many an urn
> There too had place, with votive lay inscribed
> To Freedom, Friendship, Solitude, or Love.

The moral delight with which one was supposed to respond to such classical symbolism was exemplified by Mrs. Montagu, who was too rich and too fashionable not to obey the precepts of the sentimental code. In 1744, after her visit to Stowe, she sent the Duchess of Portland a rapturous letter:

> The first of August we went to Stowe, which is beyond description, it gives the best idea of Paradise that can be; even Milton's images and descriptions fall short of it, and indeed a Paradise it must be to every mind in a state of innocence. . . . The buildings are indeed in themselves disagreeably crowded, but being dedicated to Patriots, Heroes, Lawgivers and Poets, men of ingenuity and invention, they receive a dignity from the persons to whom they are consecrated. Others that are sacred to imaginary powers, raise pleasing enthusiasm in the mind. What different ideas arise in a walk in Kensington Gardens, or the Mall, where almost every face wears impertinence, the greater part of them unknown, and those whom we are acquainted with, only discover to us that they are idle, foolish, vain and proud. At Stowe you walk amidst Heroes and Deities, powers and persons whom we have been taught to honour, who have embellished the world with arts, or instructed it in Science, defended their country and improved it. The

Temples that pleased me most for the design to which they were consecrated, were those to "Ancient Virtue," to "Friendship," and to "Liberty." [21]

But classic garden buildings were not always devoted to the refining of the sensibilities; fortunately on occasion they were the scene of more real experiences. In Dr. Lettsom's Temple of the Sibyls, modeled after that at Tivoli, Boswell often entertained his friends with singing when, in the words of Nichols, he was "exhilarated by moderate potations from a bowl either of delicious syllabub, or generous Tortola punch." [22]

That the words *allegro* and *penseroso*, borrowed from Milton's pair of poems, acquired a sentimental connotation and became current colloquially to signify two sharply contrasted modes of feeling is evidence of contemporary vagaries. The word *penseroso* seems, indeed, to have been employed as a synonym of *sentimentalist.* In Frances Brooke's *The History of Lady Julia Mandeville* (1763) Miss Wilmot declares "*il divino Enrico* is a little in the *penseroso,*" [23] and in *The Contrast* (1787), the American comedy by Royall Tyler, Charlotte, the worldly young lady of fashion, ridicules the angelic Maria and her no less perfect admirer, Colonel Manly, as "that pair of pensorosos . . . looking as grave as two sailors' wives of a stormy night, with a flow of sentiment meandering through their conversation like purling streams in modern poetry." [24]

Much more pertinent to our discussion, however, was the practice of employing the two words when the writer had in mind the mood of garden scenes. As early as 1743, at the beginning of the renewed interest in Milton's minor poems, Mrs. Montagu, asserting that she chose to live with Mirth, congratulated herself that the prospect of her charming garden at Sandleford was "allegro." Again in 1780, when she had been consulting with Wyatt about the design of two rooms in her new house on Portman Square, she assured her correspondent that the south windows of the larger apartment

will command a very rich and gay prospect, and will give me all the splendours of a Summer when I am inclined to the allegro; when I am more disposed to the penseroso, those windows may be shut against the garish day and a large gothick window be thrown open.[25]

In *The Spiritual Quixote* (1772) Richard Graves describes Mr. Rivers' garden as

> laid out in a romantic taste, with a proper mixture of the allegro and the penseroso, the chearful and the gloomy: tufts of roses, jasmines, and the most fragrant flowering shrubs, with a serpentine walk of cypresses and laurels, here and there an urn, with suitable inscriptions, and terminated by a rough arch of rock-work that covered a dripping fountain, were its principal beauties.

Mrs. Rivers, I am glad to say, evidently partook of the *allegro*: her smile, "like the sunshine so much admired in the landscapes of Claude Lorraine, diffused an additional chearfulness over every other object." [26]

Hermitages, Gothic ruins, and classic temples did not complete the architectural medley of the "natural" garden. China, having embellished domestic interiors with porcelain, lacquer, furniture, and wallpaper, also influenced the decoration of the landscape. Walpole thought that the "paltry" Chinese buildings and bridges at Wroxton were the first, or at any rate among the very first, of their kind, but unfortunately he did not attempt to date them.[27] At all events, they had a numerous and flourishing progeny of one sort or another. At Woburn Abbey, on an island in a lake surrounded by finely wooded hills, the Duke of Bedford erected a Chinese edifice where in summer he was able to entertain at dinner as many as thirty guests. In 1757 at Rose Hill, belonging to Governor Hart, Mr. Montagu saw an elaborately decorated Chinese house of which he estimated the cost to have been more than £3000, but in his opinion it was only "a whim" and represented "so much money flung away." [28] At Wentworth House, Yorkshire, the Marquis of Rockingham possessed an aviary in the Chinese style, and the Duke of Cumberland embellished Virginia Water with a Chinese ship equipped with a luxurious cabin. These fantastic buildings, brightly painted, gilded, japanned, and decorated with bells and grotesque dragons, decked every English garden of any pretensions, to judge by the innumerable references to them in contemporary guide-books.

But the great pagoda built in 1761 by Chambers at Kew probably surpassed them all in splendor. The various roofs were adorned at the angles with a total of eighty dragons covered with a thin, colored, glass-like veneer that shone with dazzling brilliance in the sunshine. Chambers also provided the royal garden with a House of Confucius, the small salon in the second story being painted with incidents from the lives of the philosopher and the Christian missionaries in China. In addition to temples dedicated to Pan, Arethusa, and Bellona, Kew possessed a Gothic church, a mosque, and a Moorish building called the Alhambra. This last structure Walpole sneered at, and probably justly, as "ill-imagined, and I dare say like the buildings of no country." Mason and Richard Graves protested against the grotesque mingling of architectural styles borrowed from other countries and other ages. The impeccable Alcander, it will be recalled, admitted no outlandish buildings into his garden, but satisfied himself with the erection of medieval edifices such as he felt to be in keeping with England's historic past.

Of course such decorations became all the more absurd when they were crowded together on a small estate, as frequently seems to have been the case. Dr. Francis Wise, one-time Librarian of Radcliffe, for example, at Ellesfield near Oxford managed to get into his garden of a few acres "ponds, cascades, seats, a triumphal arch, the tower of Babel, a Druid temple, and an Egyptian pyramid."[29] At Reigate a gentleman put into his garden of limited area so many features common to a great country estate that the townspeople called it "the world in one acre of land." [30] The public gardens exhibited the same taste for incongruous variety. At Ranelagh in the middle of the canal was a Chinese temple (Fig. 75) which was illuminated at night with twenty-eight lamps. At Vauxhall the dining-pavilions were in an ornate pseudo-Gothic style, but the railings that surrounded the wilderness were Chinese. In the Sidney Gardens in Bath "a grotto of antique appearance," a sham castle equipped with some cannon, and two cast-iron Chinese bridges were attractions which, if we can believe an old guide-book, had "an effect that commands admiration and gratifies curiosity."

The pattern-books that flooded the market with designs for those who wished to follow the fashion of embellishing their garden scenes with appropriate buildings reflect the instability

Fig. 75 — Chinese Rotunda in the Canal at Ranelagh

FIG. 76 — PORTIA'S GARDEN, CONCEIVED NATURALISTICALLY BY THE PAINTER, W. HODGES

of contemporary taste. Eclecticism was in the saddle. The classic, Gothic, and Chinese styles competed for popular favor on an equal footing. Yet in one point the classic style did wield an authority not enjoyed by the others. So great was the respect for its traditions that it managed, often to an amusing degree, to impose its symmetry upon its brethren. As a result hermitages and Oriental summer-houses frequently acquired a strange rigidity and regularity of design. In most instances Chinese and Gothic ornament was merely applied with a gay irresponsibility to structures of classic form. Amazing hybrids emerged from the ludicrous indifference to racial and often geographic facts. Wrighte gives the design of what he calls an Oriental hermitage; it is built around a tree-trunk, over the door is an Arabic inscription, and the roof is thatched "in the Chinese taste." The titles of some of these books will be sufficient to illustrate their general character:

Rural Architecture in the Gothick Taste, being twenty new designs for temples, garden-seats, summer-houses, lodges, terminies, piers etc. . . . by William and John Halfpenny. 1752.

Ornamental Architecture in the Gothic, Chinese, and Modern Taste, being above fifty entire new designs . . . (Many of which may be executed with roots of trees) for gardens, parks, forests, woods, canals, etc. containing paling of several sorts, gates, garden-seats both close and open, umbrellos, alcoves, grottoes, and grotesque seats, hermitages, triumphal arches, temples, banqueting houses and rooms, rotundos, observatories, ice-houses, bridges, boats, and cascades . . . from the designs of Charles Over. 1758.

The Carpenter's Complete Guide to the Whole System of Gothic Railing, consisting of twenty-six entire new designs for paling, and gates of different kinds . . . by Robert Manwaring. 1765.

The Temple Builder's Most Useful Companion, being fifty entire new original designs for pleasure and recreation . . . in the Greek, Roman, and Gothic taste . . . by Thomas Overton. 1766.

Grotesque Architecture, or Rural Amusement, consisting of plans . . . for huts, retreats, summer and winter hermitages, terminaries, Chinese, Gothic, and natural grottoes, cascades, baths, mosques, moresque pavilions, grotesque and rustic seats, green houses etc. many of which may be executed with flints, irregular stones, rude branches, and roots of trees . . . by William Wrighte. 1767.

The Carpenter's Companion for Chinese Railing and Gates, containing thirty-three entire new and beautiful designs, very proper to be executed at the entrance or round Chinese temples, summer houses, rotundo, alcove, and umbrelloed seats, parks, grottoes, hermitages, ice-houses, islands, cascades, ha! ha's!, gardens, courts, yards, etc.... from the original designs of J. H. Morris, carpenter, and J. Cruden. 1770.

Flimsy as were the structures for which these pattern-books provided the designs, they yet served their purpose in satisfying the romantic desire for variety and picturesque detail. In dramatic criticism the classic demand for singleness of mood was still so strong as to banish from the stage the comic scenes in Shakespearian tragedy, but in garden planning, at any rate, no such strict interpretation of unity prevailed. Emotional contrast between adjacent parts of a garden was sought for as an effect which kept curiosity alive and entertained the imagination. As hermitages, classic temples, pagodas, and Chinese boats and bridges called up different associations, they gave character to a garden scene and provided an element of whimsical piquancy as one encountered them in a wood, by the side of a lake, or at the bend of the serpentine path.

Such a description of the features of the landscape garden as I have attempted may appear to have concerned itself with matters too unimportant for lengthy discussion. With possibly a few exceptions, the architectural value of the hermitages and temples was nil, and a recent writer has hinted at the absurdity of taking pseudo-ruins "very seriously." But the point is that the eighteenth century did take these garden embellishments seriously, and if we pass by them with amusement, there is a likelihood of our missing their significance. The vogue of the inscription, the urn, the ruin, and the temple is associated with the admiration for the pictures of Claude and Poussin, the enthusiasm for medieval architecture, and the craving for emotion that marked the reaction against the too hard rationalism of the classicists. Because of its connection with these interests, vital at the time, gardening secured a place in eighteenth-century culture that at present seems out of proportion to its intrinsic importance.

Only on such grounds can we understand the ardor with

which a man like Pitt, for example, carried on his garden schemes. He took great care in centering his vistas and in imparting to his rivers the fashionable serpentine, and at South Lodge, Enfield Chase, he erected a Temple of Pan that won the praise of Whately. Lord Rosebery cites an incident that illustrates the impetuosity with which Pitt pursued his hobby. At Burton Pynsent, when he observed a hill that offended his taste, he peremptorily instructed his gardener to plant it with cedars and cypresses to moderate its harsh outline. The gardener protested that the necessary number could not be found. "No matter: send for them from London." The command was fulfilled, and in due time, after great expense for their purchase and transportation, the trees arrived. Although his income was large, it was not, in fact, equal to the drains Pitt made upon it to indulge his taste for building and gardening, and as a result during his last years he was bogged in debts. Moreover, he was indefatigable in assisting his friends in laying out their gardens. He planned a walk at West Wickham for Gilbert West; beautified the water at Wotton, Buckinghamshire, for George Grenville; designed a garden scene in imitation of Milton's Bower of Bliss for another friend; generously but in vain offered Shenstone £200 to carry out improvements at the Leasowes that the poet himself could not afford; and provided Sanderson Miller, whom he frequently visited at Radway, with means to lay out there the Laurel Walk and Strawberry Bank. On one occasion, when Pitt intended to help a friend in designing his grounds, he received during the night an urgent message to return to London. Not to be thwarted, after ordering his carriage to be made ready, by the light of lanterns he superintended the staking out of the grounds according to his plan.[31]

When so much artistic importance was attached to gardens, owners were anxious that their estates should be seen and admired. The Lytteltons were notoriously jealous of the reputation of the Leasowes. When Joseph Spence was at Hagley, two weeks passed before they suggested a visit to Shenstone's garden, which was adjacent to their own and dimmed its glory.[32] Shenstone himself was piqued when he heard that Lord Lyttelton planned to build a sham castle and a rotunda, and refused to call upon a Mr. M—— because he had been twice in the neighborhood and "never deemed my place worth seeing." In his *Letters* Shenstone registers the hopes and fears of an owner of a show-place. He congratulates Richard Graves on the increasing popularity of the latter's garden near Bath; he expresses the hope that Lady Luxborough will make a visit to the Leasowes, as the visit of a person of social importance will bring it into repute; he is grateful to Mr. Miller for bringing "the genteelest company" to see his walks; he reports that his place has taken with "the mob" and that he has "multitudes" of visitors every Sunday evening, and confesses that on one such occasion, when he received as many as a hundred and fifty people, he exhibited himself "with no less state and vanity than a Turk in his seraglio." Eager as he was for visitors, Shenstone must have been distressed at the necessity of closing his grounds to the general public when he came to realize that his guests were imposing upon his hospitality and wantonly damaging his property. Indeed, as Shenstone's enjoyment of his garden was always largely dependent upon his success in getting people to visit it, his discontent ebbed and flowed accordingly, and his *Letters* are a rather naive record of his elations and petty mortifications.

He had no reason to complain of lack of appreciation. Dodsley wrote a rhapsodic poem on the Leasowes and a guide-book to the grounds; Jago extolled Shenstone's skill in the making of cascades in a clever fable in verse, *Labor and Genius*; and after the poet's death Graves drew a whimsical but affectionate portrait of Shenstone in his novels *Columella* (1779) and *The Spiritual Quixote* (1772). Could Shenstone have read John Wesley's *Journal*, he would have been gratified beyond measure by his eulogy of the Leasowes:

> I have seen nothing in all England to be compared with it. It is beautiful and elegant all over. There is nothing grand, nothing costly; no temples, so called; no statues (except two or three, which had better have been spared); but such walks, such shades, such hills and dales, such lawns, such artless cascades, such waving woods, with water intermixed, as exceed all imagination! On the upper side, from the openings of a shady walk, is a most beautiful and extensive prospect. And all this is comprised in the compass of three miles! I doubt if it be exceeded by anything in Europe.[33]

But the vanity of the owners of famous gardens was encouraged by the curiosity to see them. Rather than miss the Leasowes, Johnson and the Thrales inspected its cascades in a rainstorm;[34] and even such a staid, busy man as Wesley, who generally took occasion to deplore that their ostentatious owners were now mingled with the dust like common beggars, visited and described in his *Journal* not only the Leasowes but Stowe, Stourhead, Cobham, Hagley, King's Weston, Castle Barnard, and Wentworth House.

The interest in gardens led even to the decoration of snuff-boxes and candlesticks of Battersea enamel with views of such famous places as Wooburn Farm and Pain's Hill.[35] As one could not fail to realize at the recent London exhibition of English conversation-pieces of the eighteenth century, the natural garden as an outdoor background in paintings of family groups enjoyed the greatest popularity. In one instance only was there a hint of a formal garden: in the picture of *Miss Mary Warden* by Arthur Devis a rectangular canal and a classic summer-house are visible in the distance behind the young girl standing on the terrace. In other pictures the human figures, father, mother, and children of all ages and sizes, are placed in landscapes planted irregularly with flourishing trees and frequently embellished with boldly serpentine rivers. When a fundamental revolution in taste is under way, its ramifications are surprising. The preference for natural gardens modified even the type of table decoration suitable for formal occasions. Here, too, such a preference had to compete with classicism and the deep-rooted liking for a pompous parade of mythology. Walpole describes a dessert which appeared at a state dinner given by the French ambassador, the Duc de Mirepoix; it represented the story of Perseus and Andromeda, the sea being "silver tissue covered with barley-sugar." At the coronation banquet of George III in Westminster Hall the decoration of the royal table, according to Gray, consisted of a Mount Parnassus and numerous figures of Muses, the Arts, and other symbolic personages.[36] However, the favor with which such traditional ornaments were received existed by the side of a taste for greater naturalism. In an essay (no. 6) in the *World* Walpole mentions table decorations that employed "whole meadows" of china cattle, and cottages and temples in sugar. An unfortunate man who had married a woman of fashion was amazed to see on his table "gravel walks, rivers, groves, and temples." [37] In *The London Art of Cookery* (1783) John Farley, discussing "elegant ornaments for a grand entertainment," gives careful directions how to make a delicate pastry with which to cover tin molds in the form of a Chinese temple: "If you cut it neatly, and the paste be rolled very thin, it will be a beautiful corner for a large table." For a dessert called "Desert Island," Farley conscientiously explains how to "make gravel walks of shot comfits" and border them with Chinese railings of baked paste.[38] These culinary marvels were designed not to whet the appetite, but to feast the eyes of the fashionable victims of the *furor hortensis.*

In the decades when the symmetrical garden was held in contempt and the desire to be natural was veering toward fanaticism, it is no wonder that the stiff, elaborate style of men's hairdressing which the Augustans had approved began to be affected by the change in taste. Clipped trees and wigs were obviously modes of an age that was determined to disguise nature in the interests of an ideal of formal dignity. As it was desirable in a society governed by class distinctions and a code of ceremonious etiquette that the individual should be externally impressive, he patiently accepted the wig in the realization that a great quantity of false hair could be dressed with a stately regularity not achievable by his own unruly locks. But with the development of a greater respect for nature the mode changed. In 1765 the master peruke-makers found it necessary to petition George III to assist them, on the ground that as men of all ranks were adopting the habit of wearing their own hair, their trade had fallen off to an incredible extent and distress was widespread among their dependents. But even the King was not powerful enough to check the tide of the new fashion, and he could do nothing but benevolently assure the petitioners that he would always have their welfare at heart.[39] Indeed, the barbers got little but ridicule for their pains. Walpole laughed at them in his letters,[40] and an anonymous hack poet published *The Wig* (1765), "a burlesque-satirical poem." It closed with an exhortation to the "sons of Art who weave the flowing curl":

Arise—be vigorous in your own defence,
Maintain your title to pre-eminence.
Arise—and to the fight undaunted go,
Nor doubt a glorious conquest o'er the foe.

. . . .

Arise—exert your fortitude of heart,
And shew that Nature must submit to Art.

But the exhortation was in vain. That nature should be bridled by art was a principle the validity of which was everywhere under suspicion, and the wig was doomed to follow the clipped tree into oblivion.

CHAPTER XX

LITERARY ALLUSIONS TO THE GARDEN

As THE popularity of the landscape garden increased, the reputation of Versailles suffered a progressive decline. An anonymous letter-writer in the *Guardian* (no. 101) seems to have been the first to voice the heresy that Versailles was not the final expression of beauty. He preferred Fontainebleau because the hand of art had there meddled less with nature, and remarked that he took as much pleasure in "a river winding through woods and meadows" as in water tossed up into the air in the form of bottles, arches, and pyramids. In spite of his desire for greater naturalism in the garden, Switzer admired Versailles, and in his epistle to Burlington Pope actually linked together Le Nôtre and Inigo Jones as craftsmen possessed of the inner light of common sense as a guarantee against the commission of egregious artistic folly. This incidental judgment indicates in what a moderate spirit Pope's plea for a return to nature should be interpreted. His theory of gardening was not, after all, so radical as to hinder him from appreciating the French master of formalism. But by 1740, when Joseph Warton wrote *The Enthusiast*, taste had changed, or at any rate the younger generation was impatient and more uncompromising. With a positive exultation Warton lauded the superiority of nature over art, and scorned without compunction the statues, the parterres, and "the tortur'd water" of the fountains of Versailles. Heely stigmatized Le Nôtre as "that celebrated, but cruel spoiler" who "mangled the sighing earth."[1] Lord Kames did not hesitate to declare in sober prose that the gardens of Versailles were "a lasting monument of a taste the most vicious and depraved";[2] and with some such thought in his mind Bishop Berkeley rapturously exclaimed, when he viewed the natural beauty of Muckross Gardens near the Lakes of Killarney, "Another Louis Quatorze may make another Versailles, but the hand of the Deity only can make another Mucruss."[3] Miss Burney's Evelina was taking only the current attitude toward formalism when she complained that, although "very pretty," Vauxhall Gardens were too regular and would have pleased her more had straight walks and symmetrically balanced groves been less in evidence.[4] Yet even at Vauxhall a gesture was made in the direction of naturalism. By means of a ha-ha a view of the neighboring meadows had been made available, so that jaded visitors yearning for pastoralism might see, in the words of a guide-book, "haycocks and haymakers sporting during the mowing season."

It is illustrative of the vicissitudes of taste that as the prejudice against the symmetrical Renaissance garden developed, similarities were discovered between its formalism and a common spiritual phenomenon: the discipline of man's natural forces or talents by external authority imposed by habit, custom, or convention. Men of letters perceived that in so far as the clipping of trees and the subjection of water to the mechanical contrivances of a fountain were a departure from the purposes of nature, such a treatment was analogous to the regulation of human impulses by social or traditional influences. Whether this regulation was regarded as good or bad was dependent upon the extent to which one was classical or romantic in his sympathies. As was natural for a man who was the nephew of Sir Richard Temple of Stowe and the friend of such famous amateur gardeners as Lyttelton and Pitt, Gilbert West looked upon the features of a formal garden as a perversion of nature. In his poem *Education* (1751), in which he employed the style and allegorical method of Spenser's *The Faerie Queene* to make his didacticism more palatable, he tells the story of a gentle knight who, guided by a "Palmer sage" (Locke), undertakes to conduct his son and heir to the abode of Paedia (Education). In the course of their journey they come to a forked mountain, appearing from a distance like Parnassus but in reality the stronghold of the nine virgins who preside over false or traditional education.

> Thereto, the more to captivate the sight,
> It like a garden fair most curiously was dight.

Appropriately enough, this garden, the abode of wrong ideas of education imposed upon youth by the power of custom, was excessively regular and planted with trees the natural forms of which had been mangled by clipping:

In figur'd plots with leafy walls inclos'd,
By measure and by rule it was out-lay'd;
With symmetry so regular dispos'd,
That plot to plot still answer'd, shade to shade;
. . . .
There likewise mote be seen on every side
The yew obedient to the planter's will,
And shapely box of all their branching pride
Ungently shorne, and with preposterous skill
To various beasts and birds of sundry quill
Transform'd, and human shapes of monstrous size;
Huge as that giant-race, who, hill on hill
High-heaping, sought with impious vain emprize,
Despight of thund'ring Jove, to scale the steepy skies.

Near by, fed by the torrent that roared from the mountain, was the Lake of Philology, into whose bitter, swirling waters helpless, crying, protesting children were driven by nurses, guardians, and fathers.

Right piteous was the spectacle, I ween,
Of tender striplings, stain'd with tears and blood,
Perforce conflicting with the bitter flood.

From this dreadful fate our noble knight was able to rescue "his blooming son" only after a fierce Spenserian combat with the giant Custom, the usurping lord of this domain who had subjected nature to his sway. What is significant is that by 1751 the formal garden was in such ill-repute that West regarded its features as likely to contribute to his picture of an imaginary world of intellectual folly. He had, in a sense, anticipated Rousseau, who in the famous opening paragraph of *Émile* cited the tree trimmed in conformity with its owner's taste as an example of the injury which man habitually does to God's handiwork.

The obvious contrast between the formal garden and wild scenery which epitomized the difference between art and nature suggested, moreover, to the literary critic in particular a parallel between the genius developed by culture and training and the genius unhampered by control and left to the happy accidents of spontaneous intuition. The analogy was helpful, as it strengthened and clarified the thought of the more liberal even among the neo-classicists, who felt called upon to defend individualistic poets like Homer, Pindar, and Shakespeare against the cavils of the pedants. In an age when criticism was permeated with self-complacent and often stupid dogmatism, it was a benefaction to show that ignorance of the "rules" and exemption from their discipline did not necessarily involve a poet in disaster. In other words, more sagacious readers were conscious that something was to be said in behalf of untrammeled nature, whether typified by a poet or a landscape.

Addison, while noting in the *Spectator* (nos. 160, 417) the distinction between the natural and the cultivated genius, appeared as a neutral, refraining from the allocation of absolute superiority to one type or the other. To him the former was "a rich soil" that produced a luxuriant vegetation of which the growth revealed neither "order" nor "regularity." The latter was the same territory "laid out in walks and parterres and cut into shape and beauty by the skill of the gardener." The *Iliad* was a country of wild, awe-inspiring scenery. The *Aeneid* was a "well-ordered garden" beautified with loveliest flowers. Tolerance such as Addison's disappeared, however, before the growing individualism of the mid-century, and hereafter the dice were loaded in favor of nature. In complaining of the insincerity and false sentiment of his own day, Goldsmith inveighed against the warping of native talent:

> The genius, instead of growing like a vigorous tree, extending its branches on every side, and bearing delicious fruit, resembles a stunted yew, tortured into some wretched form, projecting no shade, displaying no flower, diffusing no fragrance, yielding no fruit, and affording nothing but a barren conceit for the amusement of the idle spectator.[5]

In the revolt against formalism the tree, indeed, the shape of which had been determined by the shears almost automatically became the symbol of an artificially limited, if not an actually distorted, personality. When someone praised Corneille to the detriment of Shakespeare, Johnson retorted, "Corneille is to Shakespeare as a clipped hedge is to a forest." [6] A similar note was struck by an alert writer in the *Mirror* (no. 100) in a protest against the omission of the grave-digger's scene from Garrick's *Hamlet.* An attempt to "improve" Shakespeare and to force him into conformity with the classic rules was, he thought, bound to prove abortive. It meant the sacrifice of the dramatist's most individual qualities, and was as absurd and impracticable as "to apply the minute labors of the roller and the pruning-knife to the nobler irregularity of trackless mountains and impenetrable forests." As long as the defenders of Shakespeare had the mountains and forests on their side, they felt that they could safely justify his audacities and inequalities. Voltaire, while he acknowledged the "irregular beauties" of Shakespeare and the insipidity of English plays on the classic model, nevertheless concluded that the poetical genius of the English was like a tree which flourished as long as it was left alone, but which died as soon as one undertook to lop it in imitation of the avenues of Marly. When Southey weighed the merits of *The Task* and other moral poems of the same general character, he phrased his estimate in a familiar simile: "The best didactic poems, when compared with the Task, are like formal gardens in comparison with woodland scenery." [7]

Implied in all these passages is the thought that nature was something grander and more magnificent than art, and that beside it the Renaissance garden was a rather contemptible object. When the critics — Voltaire should be excepted — discovered, to their own satisfaction, at any rate, points of spiritual identity between a poet and a wild landscape, they felt that he was ennobled immeasurably. That they employed this analogy as frequently as they did testifies to the place which the garden occupied in the consciousness of the eighteenth century. In any age the sources or phases of experience from which men of letters draw the material of their analogies are generally an index of what, at the time, is familiar and a matter of common knowledge. Homer's memorable similes referring to the vicissitudes of pastoral life reflect the state of society that produced them. Similarly the allusions of eighteenth-century critics to gardening reveal the interest of the educated upper classes, who amused themselves with "rural elegance" and appreciated the beauty of untamed nature.

In his *Letters on Chivalry and Romance* (1762) Richard Hurd also relied on the current knowledge of garden art to elucidate his theory of the unity of *The Faerie Queene*. It is true, he admits, that Spenser's romantic epic does not possess the unity demanded by the classicists, that is, unity of action, but it does possess a unity of its own imposed upon it by the nature of its medieval subject. The adventures of the various knights, he points out, are bound together by the fact that each is engaged in the execution of a common purpose, the injunction laid upon him by the Faery Queen, the instigating cause of their activity. Hurd then proceeds to set forth his idea more clearly by an ingenious analogy drawn from gardening. The unity of *The Faerie Queene* is like that of the old-fashioned garden of Renaissance origin. The separate avenues through a wood were entirely independent of one another and each had its own termination; yet they were related by the circumstance that they all radiated from a "common and concurrent center." Just as this "Gothic method" of garden design — the epithet seems a strange one to apply to a type of design that did not appear in England until the reign of Charles II — has its characteristic unity, so Spenser's epic is held together by a similar principle, the Queen being, so to speak, the "concurrent center" of the whole action. When Hurd adds that "you and I are, perhaps, agreed that this sort of gardening is not of so true a taste as that which Kent and Nature have brought us acquainted with," he leaves us to infer that the unity of *The Faerie Queene* was of a somewhat inferior kind because its plan was like that of the now discredited formal garden, and that the unity of the epic on the classic model had greater merit because it resembled the design of the landscape or natural garden.

In effect, Hurd says that the romantic garden popular in his own day was more classic in its unity than the garden that was the product of Renaissance formalism! But such a startling inconsistency troubled neither Hurd nor his contemporaries. The point is that when he was vindicating the unity of *The Faerie Queene* by references to types of gardening, Hurd was confident that his readers would get the full value of his comparison, because he knew that he was addressing a generation of garden lovers.

Followers of Shaftesbury also made some interesting allusions to gardening. In a paper (no. 67) in the *World* John Tilson was concerned with the familiar formula of his teacher: that taste and morality are identical. After drawing a portrait of Philalethes, a man whose judgment of painting and sculpture is as delicate as his sense of ethical values, Tilson contrasts him with Micio. The latter imagines himself to be a man of taste, but, as is unhappily often the case with mere mortals, his impression of his own character is quite erroneous. The same corrupt tendencies that in conduct are responsible for his gambling and his libertinism are equally accountable for his barbarous artistic preferences. On a par with his vicious habits are "his trimmed trees, his unnatural terrasses, his French *treillage*, his Dutch parterres, his Chinese bells, and his tawdry equipage." Clearly to such a low estate had the formal garden sunk by 1754 that Tilson, assuming, as a matter of course, the agreement of his readers, felt at liberty to cite, on Shaftesburian principles, a liking for it as the artistic equivalent of immorality.

Illustrative also of the discredit which had overtaken formalism is the apology which Richard Graves felt called upon to make in the preface of his poem on Shaftesbury's philosophy, *The Love of Order* (1773). Fearful lest "an attempt in this age, to recommend regularity and uniformity" may offend men of taste, Graves explains that he is concerned primarily with order as "a principle of virtue" rather than as an element of design. The extent to which he has made Shaftesbury's point of view his own is plain from his motto, a quotation from Shenstone: "An obvious connexion may be traced between moral and physical beauty, the love of symmetry and the love of virtue." Shaftesbury's doctrine, one may remark in passing, was attractive to men who were interested in art, because in enhancing the importance of their hobby by attaching to it ethical as well as esthetic values it pleasantly flattered their egotism and lulled them into complacency. Everyone is ready to enroll himself as the disciple of the philosopher who can make him think better of himself than he suspects he deserves.

But Graves' sympathy with Shaftesbury got him into a logical difficulty which he himself was quick to recognize. After having extolled the order which "pervades the schemes of Providence" and which is patently revealed in the physical universe in the movement of the planets and in the mutual dependence of animals and plants, Graves realizes that it follows from his premise that he should praise the symmetrical and condemn the natural garden. He somewhat hedges on the issue. On the one hand, he opposes the irregularity of the contemporary small garden in the natural style on the ground that it is only confusing; on the other hand, he approves of the irregularity in the layout of great estates because, as he comforts himself, that irregularity is apparent rather than real, and is, indeed, by no means out of harmony with his principle of order:

When Mason seems in every line,
My principle to countermine,
And, planting more extensive glades,
Promiscuous blends his sylvan shades,
Did we his system truly scan,
He works but on a larger plan.

. . . .

We soon should trace a secret art
That regulates each different part,
That corresponding groups supply
The want of uniformity;
See distant objects harmonize,
And order from disorder rise.
The painter thus, to gain his end,
His various tincts with art must blend.

. . . .

From well-rang'd lights one mass compose,
Till with full strength the landskip glows.[8]

That is to say, Graves contends that, notwithstanding the fact that the prevalent passion for variety has multiplied the number of features in a garden, they are skilfully, although not obviously, related to one another by occult balance and not by symmetry. Thus unity is assured for the whole plan of the garden by the employment of the principles of pictorial composition. Such unity is not that of the old formal garden of Le Nôtre, with its emphasis on the architectural elements of design, but that of a carefully balanced landscape by Claude or Poussin. In view of the date of *The Love of Order* Graves' conclusion is most correctly orthodox, but before he arrives at it, we see him struggling to extricate himself from the necessity of sanctioning, in defiance of contemporary taste, such an unpopular thing as the formal garden.

But as time went by and as terraces and fine old avenues were swept away at the behest of fashion, frequently to make room for "Capability" Brown's lawns, belts and clumps of trees, and monotonous serpentine walks and rivers, it was realized with regret, when it was too late, that the loss was perhaps greater than the gain and that a formal beauty had been destroyed that it had taken years to create. At all events, persons more sensible than fashionable began to look with tenderness upon the old-style garden as a quaint relic of the past. Cowper's lament for the "fallen avenues" and his praise of John Throckmorton for the preservation of the lime walk at Weston Underwood are familiar.[9] Among writers of fiction arose the habit of attributing this regard for the formal garden to whimsical old gentlemen who, like Sir Roger de Coverley, cherished with lovable obstinacy the customs and fashions of their youth. Mr. Umphraville, around whose eccentric personality are written some of the most persuasive papers (nos. 61, 68) in the *Mirror*, is an old man of this type. He prefers to the modern improvements the narrow Gothic windows of his ancient mansion, the poorly lighted rooms, and the old tapestries which he refuses to replace with imported Oriental wallpaper. In spite of the ridicule of his frivolous visitor Sir Bobby Button, who wishes him to cut down "those damned hedges and trees," Umphraville is loyal to his

> stiff, rectangular walks and straight, narrow avenues. In his garden the yews and hollies still retain their primeval figures; lions and unicorns guard the corners of his parterres, and a spread-eagle, of a remarkable growth, has his wings clipped and his talons pared the first Monday of every month during spring and summer.

In Henry Pye's *The Aristocrat* (1799) Mr. Aldworth is also in the tradition of Sir Roger. Upon his return from the Orient after many years' absence he follows the mode of life that was in vogue at the time of his departure, and preserves the old parterre and long, straight avenue that form the approach to his house.

Other novels, although they lie well beyond the limits of this study, can be mentioned here. As Scott lamented like Cowper the decline of the old style of gardening, he sympathetically represents Jonathan Oldbuck, the antiquary, as looking with a tolerant eye upon his "tall clipped hedges of yew and holly."

Oldbuck realized also that if he disturbed the quaint arboreal figures he would break the heart of his ancient gardener, who was proud of his ability to cut trees into fantastic shapes. *Tremaine, or, The Man of Refinement*, by the jurist Robert Plumer Ward, was published in 1825, but to an extraordinary degree its characters, situations, and interpretation of experience belong to the eighteenth century. Its hero is a belated man of feeling and the twin brother of Harley, Werther, and William Godwin's Fleetwood. Inheriting a great fortune and dissatisfied with the rewards of an active life, Tremaine retires to a splendid country estate. The novel is concerned with his spiritual redemption under the influence of the virtuous Dr. Evelyn and his daughter, who is lovely as only eighteenth-century heroines knew how to be. Tremaine is too sophisticated and fastidious to appreciate the charm of Evelyn Hall, where the kindly old Doctor maintains an ancient simplicity of life. His garden is, of course, out of date. His house is approached by a double row of elms, and although there were no figures in yew in his garden, the arrangement of the flowers was objectionably symmetrical. It was, however, rumored that at one time Evelyn had conspired with his gardener to restore a yew tree to its former shape, that of a peacock, but that the gardener had lacked the necessary skill. Desirous of improving one of his own estates after the newer fashion, Tremaine contemplates the destruction of a group of cottages occupied by some of his tenants, but offensive to a person of taste. When Evelyn hears that in their place Tremaine plans to erect a temple, he sharply reproves him for his lack of feeling. Tremaine, he says, has no use for a temple in an English park — a temple of Jupiter of which the altar never smokes or a temple of Diana or of Flora, the names perhaps of the very dogs scampering by his side. A picturesque hamlet visible among the trees should give Tremaine more pleasurable emotions because of its human associations. The impressionable Tremaine forthwith decides against the temple in favor of the village.

His decision was entirely in accord with current taste, because, as the principles of the picturesque became familiar, persons of sensibility regarded a church, a cluster of cottages, and blue smoke rising above the tree-tops from lowly chimneys as a distinct asset in a landscape. In various pictures George Morland had, for example, exploited the peasant's thatched hut and its ragged occupants for the gratification of those who luxuriated in their sympathy for the poor. In depicting Umphraville, Aldworth, Jonathan Oldbuck, and Dr. Evelyn as lovers of the garden of their youth, writers were registering their protest against the violent dislike for formality such as Warton, West, Tilson, and Kames had voiced a few decades before. The force of the initial reaction had now spent itself, and it was possible to take a more reasonable view and see some merit where Lord Kames had discovered only a depraved taste.

But it must not be supposed that the novelists neglected the natural garden. Indeed, in Robert Ward's novel it is such a garden, functioning as a *deus ex machina*, that must receive the credit for precipitating Tremaine's conversion. In a secluded part of his estate Tremaine's uncle had a retreat devoted to contemplation where beside a quiet pool he had set up a series of busts of such worthies as Bacon, Milton, Locke, and Cudworth. Tremaine, disillusioned by Voltaire and Bolingbroke, gazes upon the faces of the believers enviously: "How then can I refuse to yield to such authority? Why is my soul so stiff? . . . Oh! God, enlighten me and touch my heart!" His prayer is answered. Evelyn opportunely enters the retreat for an hour or two of meditation, as is his wont. He talks to Tremaine of religion, awakens his conscience, and restores his faith in Christianity. With religion and a wife — he marries Evelyn's matchless daughter — Tremaine at last finds happiness.

In 1798 Thomas Skinner Surr, inspired by Mrs. Siddons' interpretation of Millwood, turned Lillo's famous bourgeois tragedy, *The London Merchant*, into a substantial novel. Stripping the plot of its democratic significance, he elevated George Barnwell's social position and made the humble apprentice the son of an educated clergyman and the nephew of a knight with £10,000 per annum. Surr also achieved the miracle of depicting George as even more maudlin than in Lillo's play — a miracle of which the reading public approved, for the novel was published in America and in 1834 reached its sixth English edition. Young Barnwell weeps over Dr. Gregory's life of Chatterton, writes a sonnet on the neglect of men of genius, sheds tears at the simple pathetic ballads by which Millwood artfully appeals to his sensibility, and finally falls from virtue to the soft languorous music of her harp. But what is more to the purpose, a natural garden enriched with homiletic inscriptions and replete with tender memories provides Surr with one of his most sentimental incidents, designed to reveal the vibrant, sympathetic heart of his youthful hero. The occasion is George's departure from the rectory after his father's death. The lachrymose passage must be quoted in full:

To quit forever his native home — cost his young heart — which was the shrine of sensibility — some struggles. Among the various objects that called reflection to its pleasing painful task, there stood in the centre of the garden a small temple, built in the Gothic style, and dedicated to retirement. This was constructed under the direction of George himself, and was the favourite retreat of the rector. To this place young Barnwell would frequently retire, where memory would rehearse to him those lessons, to which he had often listened with reverent attention — and, aided by fancy, would place his father's countenance and form before him. — As he strolled round the grounds, in one place a plant, in another some little monument with classical quotation, would remind him of the pleasing employment of his past hours.

"Days of happiness! — hours of hope! — farewell!" exclaimed the youth: "and you, sweet home, where first the light of heaven beamed upon these eyes — farewell! Oh, you have cheated me, false Hope! How often has my sainted father, too, added false prophecies to my delusive tales! How often has he said, 'When I am gone, my George, this plant shall speak to you of me — this tablet shall remind my son — that he must also die!' and now, alas! some stranger's eye shall gaze indifferent upon these plants — some fool, perhaps, shall scoff at Wisdom's lesson — whilst those for whom they were designed, like the wanderers from Paradise, are even to explore an unknown world!"

Such really were the reflections of a youth of sixteen, incredible as they may appear to those who judge of human nature, and it's faculties, by the same calculations as a surveyor values timber, its size and growth. Such persons would deny the existence of Chatterton.[10]

With this comic scorn for the doubts of the cynical — doubts in which most modern readers will share — and with great satisfaction to himself, Surr brings to a close Barnwell's farewell. Such a scene was unfortunately part of the stock in trade of sentimental literature. Madame de Staël's Corinne bids adieu to Rome in a fervid apostrophe, and in *Sense and Sensibility* the satirized Marianne on the eve of her departure addresses a lament to Norland and its beloved trees. But George, with epicurean enjoyment culling emotional pleasures among the inscriptions and tablets, is no more refined in his sensibility than Alcander bemoaning his Nerina or Lionel's mother strewing fragrant flowers in the temple dedicated to her canine rescuer. The creators of these characters relished the delicious melancholy which it was the province of the sentimental garden to create.

In the representation of the garden the stage, like the novel, reflected contemporary taste, just as had been the case with the gorgeous court masque of the seventeenth century. A scene in Bickerstaffe's *The Maid of the Mill* (1765) disclosed "a view of Lord Aimworth's house, and improvements; a seat under a tree; and part of the garden wall, with a Chinese pavilion over it." [11] A garden setting for Reynolds' comedy *The Rage* included "a Temple surrounded with Weeping Willows." [12] The opening act of Cherry's light opera *The Travellers* (1806) was laid in China and revealed "A beautiful garden in the Chinese style — with many bridges — intersecting canals, etc." Over these bridges a chorus of Chinese gardeners, "lads and lasses," made their entrance. In *Who Wants a Guinea?* George Colman the younger also capitalized the garden mania. John Torrent, weary of London and effervescing with benevolence, retires to his country estate and among other changes decides to improve it in the natural style — with the proviso that no Chinese bridges be built to span dry ditches. When the eccentric Jonathan Oldskirt arrives at the manor house, Torrent mistakes him for the new gardener, and to the bewilderment of both a discussion ensues as to whether the goddess of nature should be habited with much or little adornment. That a scene of comic misunderstanding about the style of laying out a garden should "carry" before an audience of the year 1805 is proof of general familiarity with the topic and of the dramatist's confidence that it could be utilized as the source of innocent merriment.

As we saw, illustrations in early eighteenth-century editions of Shakespeare displayed amusing anachronisms that were confirmation, if any were needed, of the vogue of classical architecture and the rococo style. At the end of the century the landscape garden was responsible for a similar situation. In 1787, stimulated by the reproach of foreigners that the English could paint only portraits, John Boydell conceived an ambitious plan of establishing an English school of historical painting. For this purpose he enlisted a host of artists to paint pictures — his catalogue itemizes fifty-six — in illustration of scenes in Shakespearian drama. Boydell not only exhibited these pictures in a great gallery built on the site of Dodsley's house in Pall Mall, but subsequently issued large expensive engravings of them.[13] In two of the paintings historical accuracy has been frankly sacrificed to the contemporary taste in gardening. In the work of the Reverend Dr. Peters it is in a natural garden that Beatrice overhears the conspiring Hero and Ursula report Benedick's passion for the eavesdropper. We have here reproduced Hodges' conception (Fig. 76) of the setting appropriate for the first scene of the fifth act of *The Merchant of Venice*. Not in an architecturally formal garden of the Italian Renaissance but in a romantic English garden of the eighteenth century Lorenzo and Jessica breathe the perfumes of that lovely night. The steps of Portia's villa lead from the columned portico down to the riverside, and the lovers sit on the bank of a winding stream that glimmers in the moonlight as it glides from beneath the shadow of overhanging trees. The serpentine river, the varied shape and varied foliage of trees that have not felt the insolence of shears, the tombstone, the urn, the circular classic temple, and in general the studied absence of symmetry constitute a natural garden that has been refined by the influence of Claudian design.

Literary criticism, didactic poems like those of West and Graves, fiction, and the drama all bear the impress of this interest in gardening. In other words, ideas about gardens phrased in one form or another entered into the substance of literature, and are a minor note which helps us to identify the spirit of the eighteenth century.

CHAPTER XXI

THE EMERGENCE OF THE TOURIST

As HAS been repeatedly pointed out by previous writers, especially by Professor Myra Reynolds and more recently by Mr. Christopher Hussey,[1] the interest in the English garden was merely a phase of that wider appreciation of nature which embraced the enjoyment of even the wildest scenery. To-day when amateur climbers are scaling every local peak, when mountaineering clubs are exploring the Sierra Nevadas of California, the Canadian Rockies, the Lake District, the Alps, and the Himalayas, and when thousands of ordinary tourists bent on viewing mountain grandeur are the sole support of whole districts, it requires a positive effort of the mind to conceive of a time when mountains were viewed with a dislike often amounting to horror. Yet a general taste for wild scenery is really very young. In the first half of the eighteenth century the taste was in its infancy. With the exception of John Dennis' enthusiastic account of a trip across the Alps which he made in 1688, Shaftesbury's "hymns" in which he voiced his spiritual consciousness of the Divine amid the remote wild scenes of nature, a few scattered passages in *The Seasons*, and the letters of Gray and Dr. Thomas Herring, books antedating the middle of the century are not concerned about the grandeur or mystery of mountainous localities. In 1691 in *The New State of England* Guy Miege described Westmorland, the heart of the Lake District, as "one of the worst Counties in England," and explained that he admired England because it was

> generally a flat and open Country, not overgrown with wild and unwholsom Forests, nor dreadful high Mountains. What *Hills* it has are generally very gentle and pleasant, and raised as it were to give a charming Prospect to the Eye; as its *Forests* seem only contrived for Variety, and the pleasure of Hunting.[2]

Spectacle de la Nature, a compendium of knowledge, compiled by Pluche for the use of children, translated in 1733 and blessed with eight editions within twenty years, transmitted to the younger generation the orthodox idea of mountains that had been current for centuries and was soon to become antiquated. The book justified their existence on the basis of their utility as storage-places for the water that supplied the rivers and sustained the life of animals and plants, and as a means of fostering gratitude to God by reminding us "what uncomfortable quarters might have been allotted us" had it not been for Divine goodness. In Lillo's *Fatal Curiosity* (1736), when young Wilmot, returning to England after a long absence, apostrophizes his native land, the only comment he has to make upon her "lofty mountains" is that they are "rich with useful ore." [3] In his *Reflections on a Flower Garden* (1745–46) Hervey is no less materialistic in his judgment of the "mighty hills": "Bare and deformed as their surface may appear, their bowels are fraught with inward treasures! Treasures, lodged fast in the *quarries*, or sunk deep in the *mines*."[4]

In his *Tour* Defoe's attitude is equally limited. He is repelled by the Welsh mountains, scorns the Peak district in Derbyshire, is amazed that Chatsworth should have been built in such a spot, and finds that Westmorland is a county "eminent only for being the wildest, most barren and frightful of any that I have passed over in *England*." Resolutely applying the utilitarian standard, he notes that the hills of Lancashire are much worse off than other mountainous regions. There are

> no rich pleasant Valleys between them, as among the *Alps*; no Lead Mines and Veins of rich Oar, as in the *Peak*; no Coal Pits, as in the Hills about *Hallifax*, much less Gold, as in the *Andes*, but all barren and wild, of no use or advantage either to Man or Beast.[5]

No doubt such utilitarian arguments in defence of mountains had been forced to the front by Burnet's inability to see in them anything but proof of the confusion that fell upon the world in consequence of man's sinfulness. His *Theory of the Earth* had been widely read, and its doctrines were familiar. It was not until 1778, the date of the eighth edition of Defoe's *Tour*, that the editor, confessing that hitherto the northern counties of England had been regarded merely as inhospitable wastes, stressed that in the present edition special attention had been given at last to their "natural beauties." The result of this change of policy was that an amazing amount of space was devoted to the pure description of wild landscapes, gloomy forests, plunging cataracts, and crumbling ruins.

But this attitude toward the Lake District was no longer a novelty in 1778. Between 1748 and 1760 Dr. Brown and John Dalton, and about the same time Thomas Amory, had described the glories of the region, and between 1760 and 1770 Arthur Young and Thomas Gray had toured the District. In 1770 Joseph Cradock published his *Letters from Snowdon*, which Professor Reynolds specifies as the earliest "record" of "travels in Wales for the special purpose of enjoying the scenery"; and in 1779 Young gave to the press his *Tour in Ireland*, in which he expatiates on the enchantment of the Lakes of Killarney. Thus gradually men of imagination were discovering the beauty of the more remote, wilder regions in the British Isles, and in their published accounts of their tours were communicating their enthusiasm to others.

It is, however, possible to supplement this familiar list of early appreciations of mountain scenery by the letters of some other travelers whose feeling for untamed nature deserves to be remembered. In 1756 George, Lord Lyttelton, anticipating Cradock by many years, made a tour of Wales which he described in a series of letters to his friend Mr. Bower, who had intended to accompany him. Though these letters show that Lyttelton was evidently repelled by the more barren, forbidding aspects of the mountains, he did, nevertheless, feel their magnificence. Bad weather alone prevented him from climbing Snowdon, and he was so completely emancipated from the utilitarian point of view that he was able to write of one wild locality that "the grandeur of the ocean, corresponding with that of the mountain, formed a majestick and solemn scene; ideas of immensity swelled and exalted our minds at the sight; all lesser objects appeared mean and trifling . . ." [6]

In 1775 Henry Penruddocke Wyndham published *A Gentleman's Tour through Monmouthshire and Wales in . . . 1774* in order to induce British travelers to visit a country of such romantic beauty. He confesses that hitherto Wales had been "strangely neglected," and that in the course of his journey of six weeks he did not meet a single party of tourists. His book evidently met a need, for there were editions of it in 1794, 1798, and 1809. Indeed, the editor of *The British Tourists* (1798) gives Wyndham the credit for making the Welsh tour "fashionable." Previous to his journey "many of the grand scenes of Wales were little known, and travelers for pleasure in that country were few. How is the case now altered!"

The beauty of Ireland was recognized long before Arthur Young's well known tour in 1779. As early as 1750, when Mrs. Delany was a guest of Lord Grandison she met the sister of Lord Kenmare, who described to her so vividly the charm of her brother's estate on the Lakes of Killarney that, had it not been entirely out her way, Mrs. Delany admits that she would have visited "this *enchanted place*"[7] — a characterization that denotes sensibility to its romantic appeal. The year 1760 is important, for it witnessed the visits of two travelers who have left records of their impressions. Mr. William Ockenden made a special journey to see the Lakes of Killarney, which he significantly remarks the Irish regard as "one of the capital ornaments of their country." He found that so numerous had been Lord Kenmare's visitors that on the island of Innisfallen he had restored a ruin as a shelter for sightseers and had laid out a path along the borders of the isle to enable them to view the surrounding scenery to advantage. As Mr. Ockenden and his party approached the southern shore by boat, they

> were quite transported with a marvellous scene of pure nature . . . more exquisite than any I had ever seen, either in France, Italy, or England: . . . We rested upon our oars within the bowery bosom of this sublime theatre . . . and remained there some time enraptured with the beauties we beheld.[8]

The second traveler of the year 1760 was Samuel Derrick, at one time Master of Ceremonies at Bath. Unexpectedly we discover that this leader of worldly, sophisticated society, induced by a Mr. Willoughby to change his itinerary for the specific purpose of visiting the district, was profoundly impressed by his experience. Even though a driving wind swept the mists in their faces, Derrick enjoyed the dancing rainbows and "the showers posting round the borders of the mountains, upborn by the wings of the wind." The impetuous cataracts and the mountains, "in some places bald, white, and naked . . . in others, crowned with flourishing trees," awakened his religious emotions to such a pitch that he was justified in describing one of his letters as "a travelling rhapsody." [9] Although not published until 1767, seven years after the tours of which they give an account, Ockenden's and Derrick's letters antedate the narratives of Young, Gray, Pennant, Gilpin, and others whom Professor Reynolds lists as ushering in "the great period of English travels." As 1767 was also the year in which appeared "Estimate" Brown's famous letter to Lyttelton on the Lake District, written possibly as early as 1748, the date may be regarded as a turning-point in English travel literature which expressed enthusiasm for mountain scenery.

Every new phase of experience develops a vocabulary to describe it. As the feeling for the beauty of Scotland, the English Lakes, Wales, and Ireland became more common, and as the number of persons who visited those regions of enchantment annually increased, the word *tourist* was coined to designate the traveler who went hither and yon in search of scenery. The *New English Dictionary* finds the first occurrence of the word at the very outset of the nineteenth century, but I have encountered earlier and conspicuous instances of its use. In June, 1789, the *Gentleman's Magazine* announced among the obituary notices the death of Mrs. Boswell, "wife of the celebrated tourist." As the term is employed here without comment, it is evident that at that date it was already current and familiar. In 1798 G. Thompson used the word several times in his *Sentimental Tour . . . from Newbiggin . . . to London*, and in the same year William Mavor entitled his collection of English travels *The British Tourists.* In 1800 Mrs. Piozzi, referring to her romantic Welsh estate, wrote to Penelope Pennington, "Brynbella is the fashion. We have people coming to take views from it, and travellers out of number, — *Tourists*, as the silly word is." Mrs. Piozzi herself was very evidently out of sympathy with the travel mania which infected the younger generation and especially her daughters by Mr. Thrale, with whom her relations since her second marriage had been somewhat strained. To her former remarks she adds with a touch of sarcasm: "Miss Thrales are among the Lakes, I believe these are modish places now for summer, as for winter modish streets. Comical enough!" Two years later the Misses Thrale ventured even farther afield, to their mother's disgust. Mrs. Piozzi refused to be convinced

that rural pleasure is really to be found where deformity is sought. Miss Thrales have been looking for both, as I understand, among the Western Islands, described by every traveller as barren, bleak, and dangerous. Had Mr. Piozzi and I known that they were navigating the stormy Sound of Mull when we heard the wind roar so a fortnight ago . . . we should have been in pain for them, not for the furniture expected from Mayhew and Ince to decorate pretty Brynbella.[10]

During the last twenty years of the century, as Mr. Hussey has clearly shown, the taste for travel was nourished by that wider interest in the esthetics of the picturesque which Gilpin's narratives of his tours in search of picturesque beauty and Sir Uvedale Price's essays on the same subject occasioned and stimulated. Indeed, the picturesque tourist became a recognized figure — the traveller who sought to find in nature scenes which realized his ideal of landscape derived from a study of Claude Lorraine, Poussin, and Salvator Rosa. Although his chance of achieving his quest was slight just because it was an ideal one, the hope of doing so constantly urged him to go on. This type of touring, which Isaac D'Israeli satirically described in *Flim-Flams!* as belonging to "the more *sentimental* department of travelling" and requiring a pair of "stout shoes," [11] encouraged pedestrianism, or what Americans — may sensitive English ears forgive me! — more forcibly call "hiking." Walking for pleasure was a novelty, and it brought the tourist into closer contact with nature than if he traveled by coach or on horseback. In *Letters from England* (1807) Southey, writing under the name of Don Manuel Espriella, describes the imaginary Spanish gentleman as eagerly undertaking a tour in the English style. The passage is really an excellent summary of this new taste for outdoor life:

Within the last thirty years a taste for the picturesque has sprung up; — and a course of summer travelling is now looked upon to be as essential as ever a course of spring physic was in old times. While one of the flocks of fashion migrates to the sea-coast, another flies off to the mountains of Wales, to the lakes in the northern provinces, or to

Scotland; some to mineralogize, some to botanize, some to take views of the country, — all to study the picturesque, a new science for which a new language has been formed, and for which the English have discovered a new sense in themselves, which assuredly was not possessed by their fathers. This is one of the customs to which it suits a stranger to conform. My business is to see the country, — and, to confess the truth, I have myself caught something of this passion for the picturesque, from conversation, from books, and still more from the beautiful landscapes in water colours, in which the English excel all other nations.

To the lakes then I am preparing to set out. . . . We go by way of Oxford, Birmingham, and Liverpool . . . designing to travel by stage over the less interesting provinces, and, when we reach the land of lakes, to go on foot, in true picturesque costume, with a knapsack slung over the shoulder. . . . Even so: — it is the custom in England. Young Englishmen have discovered that they can walk as well as the well-girt Greeks in the days of old, and they have taught me the use of my legs.[12]

So great was the number of visitors in the Lake District that Espriella is represented by Southey as unable to secure accommodations in the inns at Ambleside and Keswick.

No doubt this popularity of picturesque travel had much to do with the decline of Bath and Tunbridge Wells. Developed and organized as resorts, they were prepared to provide entertainment for people whose tastes were primarily urban. With their crowded program of balls and cards they satisfied the social needs of an age that was indifferent to the country. But the days of their glory were past when it became "modish" to go to the Lakes, and to Scotland and Wales. An advertisement which in 1785 appeared in the *St. James's Chronicle* (no. 3783) would certainly have had no appeal to readers who were in the habit of making an annual sojourn in either of the great English watering places: "To be sold or let furnished or unfurnished Abbott Hall . . . most desirably situated in the vicinity of the different lakes of Westmoreland and Cumberland." The location of an estate in the northwest counties, which in the first half of the century would have been an almost insurmountable obstacle in the way of its sale or rental, was now a positive asset in its favor. Fiction, always a mirror of passing tastes, also reflected the new attraction of the remoter parts of England. The Lake District or Wales became the setting of many a contemporary novel: Samuel Pratt's *Shenstone Green*, Lloyd's *Edmund Oliver*, Mudford's *Nubilia in Search of a Husband* and *Augustus and Mary, or, The Maid of Buttermere*, and Peacock's *Headlong Hall* and *Melincourt*.

A regatta, a form of outdoor amusement for which Venice was famous, was undertaken for the first time in England on the Thames on June 23, 1775. The novelty of the affair stirred high society. Dr. Johnson expressed his gratification that Mrs. Thrale was able to witness the event, and in a vivacious letter Horace Walpole described the river as "covered with boats, barges, and streamers, and every window and house-top loaded with spectators." The regatta was introduced for the entertainment of people of fashion on Bassenthwaite Lake in 1780 and on Derwentwater in 1781. The *Cumberland Pacquet* was moved to employ its most rhetorical flourishes: "no breast, however unsusceptible of pleasure, can be indifferent to that display of every beauty which decks the ancient Vale of Keswick on a regatta day." But it is to the credit of the contemporary feeling for nature that within a few years, according to a popular eighteenth-century guide to the Lake District, the regatta was discontinued. The reason was noteworthy. It was felt that the regatta "resembled too much the busy scenes from which the opulent wish to retire to the enjoyment of rural delights." Persons of sense recognized that "the assistance of art" was not needed to "heighten the most exalted charms of nature." Is it not a painful commentary on our own taste that to-day golf courses have to be maintained in the Engadine, at Banff in the Canadian Rockies, at Glacier Park, and even within the purlieus of the Yosemite Valley?

CHAPTER XXII

HOSTILE CRITICISM OF THE NATURAL GARDEN

In the eighteenth century the spirit of ridicule remained ever alert and indefatigable, even though the enervating influence of sentimentalism tended to check its acerbity. The privilege of whipping folly into conformity with common sense was a liberty which a generation soaked in the traditions of Juvenal, Horace, and Persius was disinclined to relinquish. So it came about that almost as soon as the character of the natural garden had declared itself, it became an object of laughter. The satirists did not as a rule make their attack upon it as defenders of the symmetrical formal garden who sought to halt the progress of the new style, but they struck at the excesses of irregularity of which the new style soon became guilty. They jeered at the pretenders to taste who, nervously anxious to be in the vanguard of the race after fashion, leaped from the folly of extreme formality to that of extreme irregularity. The earliest criticism of this sort that I have encountered occurs in 1739 in a paper (no. 150) of the periodical journal *Common Sense*. The anonymous satirist mocks the man who squanders a fortune in building and gardening. In the fashionable jargon of the day, every man is "doing something at his place," and generally after the first ceremonious greetings are over he hastens to explain to a guest that he is "in mortar" and is engaged in the "moving of earth." To maintain his self-respect, even if his income is only moderate, he regards as indispensable "a serpentine river and a wood." Having disguised "an old decaying mansion" with Venetian windows and a Greek portico, he elongates at great expense "a dirty ditch" into a meandering river. In the latter, according to the satirist, "the spacious windings of the serpent are burlesqued by the ridiculous wriggles of the worm."

An interval of more than ten years elapsed. Then the essayists in the *World* directed the artillery of light laughter at the perversity of the natural cult. Walpole (no. 6) complained that with the fanaticism of a reformer even Kent had carried his naturalism too far when he planted dead trees and undertook to reproduce mole-hills in his gardens. Coventry (no. 15) blamed the successors of Kent for their endeavor to improve upon him by distorting "their ground into irregularities the most offensive that can be imagined." He was convinced that "all our professors of horticulture" agreed with the doctrine of Hogarth's forthcoming book "that the line of beauty is an S" because "for that crooked letter at the tail of the alphabet" they appear to have "the most idolatrous veneration." Ironically Coventry raised the question whether any modern gardener could be persuaded to ascend to heaven by a path that was not serpentine: "there is reason to believe that paradise itself would have no charms for one of these gentlemen, unless its walks be disposed into labyrinth and maeander."

Cambridge (no. 65), who had been the first to ridicule the mania for Gothicism in his *Scribleriad*, also put on record what a poor opinion he had of the contemporary garden. He deplored — and his regret became a common one in the later years of the century, when the enthusiasm for naturalism had somewhat cooled — that the straight avenue of trees which formerly had admirably kept the eyes focused on the principal front of the mansion was now superseded by a "round-about serpentine" and by new plantations of which the purpose was to shut off the view of the house so that one might suddenly come upon it. At the core of Cambridge's criticism is a recognition that there is sound logic in a design that concentrates the attention upon the house as the chief object of interest and as the center with which all other features should be correlated, and that utilizes the straight avenue as obviously the most direct route by which a visitor can reach his destination. These considerations, esthetic and practical, Cambridge saw sacrificed to the desire for surprise and for the variety of views of different parts of the estate which a serpentine afforded.

The upshot was that many a traveler in the future was to complain of his weariness in following the all too long windings of roads that led from the entrance of a seat to the mansion. In the *Observer* (no. 4) Cumberland frets at "the nonsensical zigzaggery" of Sir Theodore Thimble's serpentine; and in the

Lounger (no. 62) Marjory Mushroom protests that the walk to her brother's Temple of Venus is "so artfully twisted" that although it is barely two hundred yards from the house it is "a good half mile off by the serpentine." The imitation of the waywardness of nature was not without its penalties. The curving line of the new style became as inflexible a convention as had been the straight line of Renaissance design.

The rejection of the canal, the basin, and the jet hurling water into the air in defiance of gravity put a premium upon water flowing over rocks in the more natural form of a cascade. Shenstone was praised for the cascades at the Leasowes. And when the owner of a country-seat was not the fortunate possessor of a river or a lake as a source of supply but was nevertheless determined to have a cataract in his garden, he often resorted to mechanical devices that invited the ridicule of satirists. Some, if we can believe Heely, made cascades of tin to produce an illusion of shimmering water.[1] More frequently others kept water stored in small reservoirs, and upon the arrival of visitors proudly turned a spigot which permitted a thin stream of water to flow until the tank was empty. The cascade at Vauxhall, which enraptured thousands, appears to have been thus mechanically manipulated. A bell announced when the water was about to flow, and as it functioned for only a few minutes, there was always a rush of expectant visitors to secure a point of vantage. Evelina marveled at this cascade,[2] and in *The Prelude* even Wordsworth refers to the glamour enveloping the "fairy cataracts" of Vauxhall.[3] At Chiswick Burlington had hoped to have a noble cascade falling into his river, but the engine which he had installed to raise the water proved defective. As a result the cascade played only occasionally and even then for only a limited time.[4] Whenever Johnson was touring with his friends, he followed, though with qualified enthusiasm, the custom of visiting cascades. At Bodryddan he "trudged unwillingly" to see the waterfall and confessed his satisfaction upon finding that it was dry. But he had to admit that when the water was turned on the effect was fine. At Chatsworth, although he felt "complimented" because the cascade was made to flow for his enjoyment, he ventured to agree with a friend's opinion that "when one has seen the ocean cascades are but little things." [5]

Such man-made cascades operating for only a brief period repeatedly excited the ridicule of Richard Graves:

> Curio, ambitious of a taste,
> Having his little garden grac'd
> With every object for the eye
> Which Art or Fancy could supply:
> To crown the whole, at length had made,
> *Without water*, a cascade.
> Behind his artificial rock,
> A cistern plac'd, he turn'd a cock,
> And lo! the little Naiads spout
> And sputter — till the tub ran out.
> Not with more rapture Israel spied
> The streams by Moses' rod supplied.[6]

In *Columella* Graves thrust into the scene an enthusiastic servant who describes his master's garden near Hammersmith, where a cascade of "real water" adorned with shells and bits of looking-glass and encircled with flower-pots is capable of the astonishing feat of performing for a half-hour.[7] In *The Spiritual Quixote* Graves mingled with a pleasant eulogy of his dear friend Shenstone harmless satire upon Methodism and gardening. Geoffry Wildgoose, the religious fanatic, discovers that "the now celebrated Mr. Shenstone" is an old college acquaintance, and is accordingly welcomed at the Leasowes. The poet is in his garden, inspecting his cisterns and keeping his laborers at work beyond the usual hour in order to complete a cataract in preparation for the visit of some titled guests he expects on the morrow. Like everyone else Wildgoose admired the garden, but he expressed the fear that the poet's attachment to the inanimate beauties of nature might alienate his love from God. When Shenstone arises in the morning, he is surprised to find that his guest has already departed, leaving an explanatory note:

> I must own, that, like the good Publius, you have received and lodged us courteously, and my bowels yearn for your salvation. But, my dear friend, I am afraid you have set up idols in your heart. You seem to pay a greater regard to Pan and Sylvanus, than to Paul or Silas. You have forsaken the fountains of the living Lord, and hewn you out cisterns, broken cisterns, that will hold no water: but my conscience beareth testimony against this idolatry. . . . I have delivered my own soul, and will pray for your conversion.

To his dismay, Shenstone discovers that to hasten his regeneration Wildgoose, before his departure, has overthrown the statue of a piping faun, opened the sluices, and drained the reservoirs so that there is no possibility of repairing the damage in time for the arrival of the people of quality.[8] So much for the esthetic sympathy of a Methodist for a natural garden and its indispensable adjunct, a cascade! Graves has, indeed, admirably parodied here the attitude of a man like Wesley, who in the midst of his enjoyment of famous gardens that he visited deplored that the owners, forgetful of their eternal destiny, had based their happiness on the things of this world.

Satire was amply justified in its derisive treatment of these paltry manipulations of water. In fact, sham cascades — and here might be included serpentine paths and rivers of exaggerated curvature — were all the more censurable because they were travesties of objects which they were supposed to imitate; they were generally deceptions that did not deceive. The formal gardeners were far more sincere; they never pretended that the contrivances of their magnificent fountains were anything but works of art in which the designer frankly and without apology had imposed his will upon water to create novel and frequently splendid effects. In any absolute sense the imitation of nature was and is an unattainable ideal, and, such being the case, the landscape gardeners of the eighteenth century and of our own time have been compelled to resort to various tricks to produce an illusion of reality which persuades only those who wish to be persuaded. Strictly speaking, if he were consistent, the natural gardener would leave nature completely untouched. The moment he begins to tamper with the materials of woods and water with which she provides him, he is introducing the very art which in theory, if not in practice, he abhors.

The eighteenth-century gardener, grouping his trees, leveling his hills, digging his "ha-has," laying out his serpentines, constructing his cascades, and building his ruins to create "natural" scenes which would play upon the emotions, was an ingenious stage-manager who carefully studied and painstakingly arranged his effects. On that account it is not too much to say that the landscape garden was shot through with artistic insincerity and was, indeed, in its own way as artificial as the most formal garden condemned by the apostles of the new cult. The satirists attacked the extravagances of the natural garden, but they did not perceive that its principles were tainted with fallacy.

Ridicule did not spare the fantastic buildings that thickly dotted the gardens of wealthy vulgarians. Such an uncultivated upstart, satirized in the *Mirror* (no. 106), "stuck full of statues" every walk and crowded every field with temples, and whenever he showed his grounds to a chance visitor, he never failed to announce the price of his statues and the cost of his temples. Lord Grubwell, for example, disfigured a noble hill with "a vile Gothic tower" from which he discharged a half a dozen little cannon on holidays, on birthdays, and whenever some person of consequence took tea there. He spanned a serpentine river with a Chinese bridge, and offended the eye of every man of taste by temples and statues of "white plaster and paint." In self-protection his neighbor, Colonel Caustic, was forced to plant a hedge to shut out all these "impertinencies." [9] Such small unsubstantial buildings were not worth looking at and were useless to their owners; yet every Tom, Dick, and Harry insisted on erecting them. Graves derides the hermitage of "our honest country mouse" who built a "little house" as

A place — for holy meditation,
For solitude, and contemplation;
Yet what himself will rarely use,
Unless to conn his weekly news;
Or with some jovial friends to sit in,
To take his glass, and smoke, and *spit* in.[10]

An essayist in the *World* (no. 88) recounts the woes of a man whose wife and daughters, always in pursuit of the latest fashionable folly, made their garden the victim of their capricious taste. One summer they erected a Chinese temple, but found it too cold for occupancy. The following winter they appropriated wood, set aside for Christmas, to build a hermitage which was frequented upon completion only by the girls of the family and "the female hermits of taste." In the spring they resolved to put up a ruin in the park, but workmen, lopping some trees, by chance fortunately disclosed to view "my lord Killdollar's house, the noblest, perhaps, and most natural ruin extant." In *The Spiritual Quixote* a virtuoso complains of modern ruins as "deceptions, which must necessarily mislead future antiquaries, and introduce great confusion into English history." [11] In her delicious mock *History of England*, written in her girlhood, Jane Austen solemnly opines that Henry VIII abolished the monasteries and left them "to the ruinous depredations of time" principally for the purpose of improving the English landscape.[12]

The passion for garden decorations in the Chinese style met the ridicule of James Cawthorn. Master of Tunbridge School, he evidently thought it well to inculcate his charges with dislike for the absurdities of Orientalism, and accordingly composed a sprightly satire for recital by one of his pupils on the anniversary visitation in 1756. He derides the Englishman who takes the mandarin as his model in all matters of taste, and,

> whimsically great, designs
> Without the shackles or of rules or lines.
> Form'd on his plans, our farms and seats begin
> To match the boasted villas of Pekin.
> On every hill a spire-crown'd temple swells,
> Hung round with serpents, and a fringe of bells:
> Junks and balons along our waters sail,
> With each a gilded cock-boat at his tail;
> Our choice exotics to the breeze exhale
> Within th' enclosure of a zig-zag rail;
> In Tartar huts our cows and horses lie,
> Our hogs are fatted in an Indian stye.[13]

When proper allowance is made for the distortions of satire, there unquestionably remains in such criticisms of contemporary taste altogether too much truth. The mania for Gothic and Oriental buildings was responsible for the multiplication of flimsy structures that courted the contempt of men of sense. But as long as fashion approved of these grotesque garden decorations, it is doubtful if even persistent satire was successful in bringing them into a disrepute such as they deserved.

Other features of the landscape garden secured a due share of slighting comment. The owner of temples erected to the gods and goddesses who troop through the poetry of Homer and Ovid is represented in the *Connoisseur* (no. 113) as amazed at his own knowledge of the classics as he reads all the apt inscriptions which he chose for their adornment. Never before did he suspect the extent of his own learning. The composers of mottos were not, indeed, always taken as seriously by others as by themselves. William Hayley delineated in his comedy *The Happy Prescription* (1784) an absurd poetaster, Sapphic by name, who hopes to ingratiate himself with Sir Nicholas Oddfish by his verses for the Temple of Pan which Sir Nicholas is building in his garden. A writer in the *Sentimental Magazine* (October, 1773) evaluated correctly these dabblers in polite verse when he disdainfully asserted that "in the trade of wit" they were the "haberdashers of small wares." Nothing can escape their inscribing hand: houses, porticos, temples, arbors, and every possible movable. In the house of one of these versifiers, or "demi-geniuses," as the essayist dubs them, every object was decorated with a motto: the carving knife, the bellows, the snuff-box, and even the *pot de chambre*. Over the door of his wife's dressing-room was painted "Procul este profani." Above the entrance to a winding walk was the announcement "Regular Confusion," and on a card attached to a sensitive plant was the phrase "Noli me tangere." Such ridicule had its point, for the social prestige conferred by wit in the eighteenth century encouraged persons with more leisure than brains to perpetrate incredible insipidities. The garden suffered the more from this craze because the composition of the brief inscription appropriate for a bench or an urn appealed to the blue-stocking or the worthy clergyman whose muse was exhausted by the demands of anything longer than a motto.

In his *Modern Novel Writing, or The Elegant Enthusiast* (1796) William Beckford entitled one of the chapters "Captivating Scenery." Here at length and with delightful relish Beckford satirized the accounts of sentimental gardens to which pages were devoted in contemporary letters, guide-books, and narratives of tours. He reveled in his mock description of Mahogany Castle and its gardens: the lawn, the shrubbery, the flowers, the views, and the "temples designed after the best ancient models." But his burlesque touched the superlative when he depicted the enchanting spot in the vicinity of the cave where all was silent except for the murmurs of a rill:

Round this cave no gaudy flowers were ever permitted to bloom; this spot was sacred to pale lilies and violets. . . . Here stretched supinely on a bed of moss, the late Lord Mahogany would frequently pass the sultry hours of the day, and here its present worthy possessor Lord Charles Oakley would sometimes also indulge himself. . . . Here he formed schemes of delusive joys, stiffled the rising sigh, stopped the flowing tear, and in social converse with his dear friend Henry Lambert would oftentimes smoke a comfortable pipe, when the soft radiance of the moon played upon the pearly bosom of the adjacent waters.

Absurd though it is, Beckford's parody does not much exaggerate the style of such a work as Heely's *Letters on the Beauties of Hagley, Envil, and the Leasowes*.

What Samuel Johnson thought of the garden of his time was only a corollary of his estimate of the country. Although scores of his contemporaries gained consequence in their own eyes as well as in the opinion of their friends and the public by the laying out of gardens, he refused to rate such achievements any higher than he thought they were actually worth. As always, his standard of values was a purely intellectual one. Endowed with slight esthetic feeling, Johnson cared for neither painting nor music. The country starved the mind, and excessive preoccupation with garden design was, in his judgment, a trivial employment for a rational being. Habitually he laughed at Shenstone's pride in the Leasowes, and without ceremony he punctured the complacency of any unfortunate individual whom he detected taking undue satisfaction in showing the beauties of an estate. It was the garden lover's lack of a sense of proportion that irritated Johnson beyond measure. When Mrs. Piozzi reproved him for his harsh treatment of a man who had lectured to them on gardening, Johnson retorted that there was "no harm in a fellow's rattling a rattle-box; only don't let him think that he thunders."

Although grotto-building with fancy shells and minerals was one of the recognized amusements of ladies of fashion — John Buncle expatiates with enthusiasm on the artistic handiwork of several elegant females of his acquaintance[14]—, Johnson, to judge by his reply to a Lincolnshire lady, could not be led to admire them. He rebuffed her with the comment that her cool grotto probably would be satisfactory in summer — "for a toad."

When his friend Mr. Wickins of Lichfield showed him his garden, Johnson did not handle him any more tenderly. He suggested that the Venus de Medici standing by a cold bath be pitched into the pond "to hide her nakedness and to cool her lasciviousness"; and he abruptly declared that a walk twisted into windings so as to appear longer than it was in reality was more than a "deception; a lie, Sir, is a lie, whether it be a lie to the eye or a lie to the ear." In obedience to the sentimental mood of the day Mr. Wickins had erected and dedicated an urn to a deceased friend. Johnson would have none of it. "Sir, I hate urns; they *are* nothing, they *mean* nothing, convey no ideas but ideas of horror — would they were beaten to pieces to pave our streets!" Always subject to unseemly agitation at the very thought of death, Johnson would have, no doubt, swept away without compunction all the commemorative garden ornaments which played delightfully upon the feelings of visitors at Stowe, Hagley, and the Leasowes, and in every garden in the fashionable taste.

In spite of his personal repugnance for this mark of admiration, Johnson was too big a lion to escape the honor of a commemorative urn even in his lifetime. In 1774, when in the course of his tour of Wales he visited Colonel Myddleton near Denbigh, Johnson took great satisfaction in reciting poetry as he stood on the bank of a rivulet in the park. Forthwith the locality became consecrated, and the Colonel, who was evidently not without his sentimental leanings, placed there an urn inscribed as follows: "This spot was often dignified by the presence of Samuel Johnson, LL.D. Whose moral writings, exactly conformable to the precepts of Christianity, Gave ardour to Virtue and confidence to Truth." Johnson was far from gratified at what impressed him as "an intention to bury me alive." He wished his admirer would hit upon "some more acceptable memorial." Nor was he any more pleased when Boswell told him, as they strolled through the woods of his ancestral estate, that if he survived his famous friend, he planned to erect a monument to him at Auchinleck. Johnson snapped, "Sir, I hope to see your grand-children." His ridicule of the vanity of garden owners, and his sharp comment on the grotto, the serpentine, and the urn, declare his lack of sympathy with one of the dominant enthusiasms of his day. He was exasperated when people talked about taste in gardening, and indirectly hinted his own opinion when he said that an ungracious person might regard Shenstone's exploits at the Leasowes rather as "the sport than the business of human reason." As there was never any likelihood that Johnson with his strong intellectual bias would be tempted by the trivialities of a passing fashion, it was in the nature of things that he should thus take his stand beside the satirists of the garden mania.[15]

According to the *New English Dictionary*, Shaftesbury in 1711 was the first to employ the word *villa* as descriptive of an English house. Earlier instances of this noun had reference only to Roman or modern Italian edifices. In the sense of a small country house, the word *box* first occurred in 1714. The dates are significant: the suburban villa, or country-box, was distinctly a development of the eighteenth century. It met the need of the tradesman who, having prospered, wished to own some place where he and his family might pass the week-end and enjoy a bit of rural life. But these villas — there were hordes of them in the neighborhood of London — did not escape criticism. They impressed the satirists of contemporary taste as the epitome of folly and ugliness. The serpentines, the temples, and the Gothic and Chinese buildings, for which the satirists had no particular liking, were all the more ridiculous in their eyes when they were crowded together in the cramped grounds of the "cit's" country-box. Although his house was small and his property limited to an acre or two, the pompous, vulgar owner of the typical villa was unwilling to omit any of the fashionable ornaments. Walpole, in the sixth number of the *World*, was apparently the first to poke fun at the citizen who took as much "pains to torture his acre and a half into irregularities" as "he formerly would have employed to make it as formal as his cravat." Coventry (*World*, no. 15) derided Squire Mushroom's achievements: his house in a mixed Gothic and Italian style, his stagnant, murky serpentine river winding in "a beautiful valley" nearly sixty feet in length, and spanned by a bridge "partly in the Chinese manner," his grove cut by "crooked walks," his hermitage ostentatiously called "St. Austin's Cave," and his "clumsy, and gilded" temple dedicated to Venus, because, as the writer surmises, the Squire sometimes reveled there with orange girls.

Other periodicals took their cue from their predecessor. The *Connoisseur* (no. 33) laughed at the "tin cascades" of shoemakers and tailors, and a place of convenience disguised by "an alderman of great taste" as a Gothic temple with "some battlements and spires of painted wood." Chatterton in *A Hunter of Oddities*, probably one of his satiric contributions to the *Town and Country Magazine*, took a passing shot at a drysalter of Thames Street whose serpentine stream was not even two feet wide and whose ruins were "not in the most perfect condition." [16] These various garden embellishments, all the more absurd because they were on a Lilliputian scale and were exposed to the heat and dust of the London highways upon which the villas invariably abutted, were likewise burlesqued in verse. Robert Lloyd hilariously described them in *The Cit's Country-Box*. The Chinese bridge,

> With angles, curves, and zigzag lines,
> From Halfpenny's exact designs,

the

> sly Ha-Ha;
> By whose miraculous assistance
> You gain a prospect two fields distance,

the "squabby Cupids" and "clumsy Graces" from Hyde Park Corner, the mart of garden sculpture, make

> All own, that Thrifty has a taste:
> And Madam's female friends and cousins,
> With Common-Councilmen by dozens,
> Flock every Sunday to the seat
> To stare about them, and to eat.[17]

The same type of bourgeois elegance forms the substance of the satire in Garrick and Colman's spirited comedy *The Clandestine Marriage* (1766). Mr. Sterling, the Babbitt of the play, is puffed up with the pride of possession and, bent only on the satisfaction of his coarse vanity, he insists on exhibiting to Lord Ogleby all the grotesque attractions of his garden until that rheumatic old beau is well-nigh ready to collapse from fatigue. When his lordship ironically praises the serpentine as "a perfect maze" with windings "like a true lover's knot," Sterling, not detecting the sarcasm, obtusely agrees: "Ay, here's none of your strait lines here — but all taste — zig-zag — crinkum-crankum — in and out — right and left — to and again — twisting and turning like a worm, my lord!" With no less complacency Sterling contemplates his ruins, which have just cost him one hundred and fifty pounds to put "in thorough repair," his spire "built against a tree, a field or two off, to terminate the prospect," and his "little gothick dairy," where his sister wishes Lord Ogleby to take "a dish of tea" or "a sullabub warm from the cow."[18] The satiric prints which enjoyed such extraordinary popularity in the eighteenth century and seized avidly on current follies did not, of course, overlook the "cit" and his suburban villa. The most telling thrust of ridicule in the print entitled *The Delights of Islington* is directed against the flimsiness and diminutive size of the "cit's" garden decorations. A signboard reads as follows:

> Whereas my new Pagoda has been clandestinely carried off and a new pair of Dolphins taken from the top of the Gazebo by some bloodthirsty Villains, & whereas a great deal of Timber has been cut down & carried away from the Old Grove that was planted last Spring & Pluto & Proserpine thrown into my Bason, from henceforth Steel-Traps & Spring Guns will be constantly set for the better extirpation of such a nest of Villains by me Jeremiah Sago.[19]

Rather surprisingly this kind of satire turns up in France. When in his comedy *L'Anglomane* (1772) Bernard Saurin undertook to ridicule the pro-English sympathies of his fellow-countrymen, he represented Eraste, the Anglomaniac, as eager to possess just such a crowded small garden as made the London tradesman ridiculous.

The contempt with which the periodical essay, the drama, and the print treated the country-box was justly earned, and impatience with flagrant bad taste no doubt inspired the bulk of this satire. At the same time, one detects another note less acceptable to modern ears: the selfish protest of an entrenched ruling class against the extension of a weekly holiday and the opportunity for recreation to those who were engaged in trade. Duty demanded that they should labor without intermission. An essayist in the *Connoisseur* (no. 33) evidently thought it positively comic that "shop-keepers, artificers, and other plebeians" should own country-seats, no matter how successful in business. He deplored that tradesmen should be absent from their work two days a week, and he expressed the hope that the mercantile classes would not resort more and more to the country as the wealth of England increased. This was but another form of the familiar outcry against luxury and its evil effect on the middle and lower classes. Undemocratic feeling as well as amusement at the incongruities of the suburban villa accounts for the sharp and abundant satire of which it was the object.

Garden buildings in outlandish architectural styles, having historically no relation to either time or place, rightly incurred the ridicule of those who felt how absurdly inappropriate were such decorations in an English environment. These buildings were not only bad in themselves and offensive because they were frequently made of cheap, utterly unsubstantial materials, but were the more grotesque because employed altogether too often for purposes totally alien to their character. Dairies, stables, wood-houses, and all the necessary appendages of a country estate were rarely allowed to hint their real nature, but were systematically disguised in classic, medieval, or Oriental dress. The royal garden at Kew, laid out by Chambers, as well as the suburban villa, rejoiced in these architectural monstrosities. Few of these buildings have survived, but what they were like one can judge from the pattern-books. The long, flamboyant titles of the latter and the fantastic taste to which they catered were burlesqued by Robert Morris in *The Architectural Remembrancer* (1751). An admirer of Inigo Jones and Kent, he himself strove for classical simplicity and succeeded in producing façades that are barren and hard. A man with such a bias had little mercy on the purveyors of a mixed architecture. In his postscript to his introductory remarks (with perhaps Halfpenny's designs in mind) he drops into an ironic key:

I beg leave to make an observation or two on the peculiar fondness for novelty which reigns at present. I mean the affectation of the (improperly called) Chinese taste. As it consists in mere whim and chimera, without rules or order, it requires no fertility of genius to put in execution; the principals are a good choice of chains and bells, and different colors of paint. As to the serpents, dragons, and monkeys, etc. they, like the rest of the beauties, may be cut in paper, and pasted on anywhere, or in any manner. A few laths, nailed across each other, and made black, red, blue, yellow, or any other color, or mixed with any sort of chequer work, or impropriety of ornament, completes the whole. But as this far-fetched fashion has lately been introduced, I am prevailed upon by a friend to give him a place for the following:

"Advertisement. There are now in the press and speedily will be published, A Treatise on Country Five Barred Gates, Stiles, and Wickets, elegant Pig-styes, beautiful Henhouses, and delightful Cow-cribs, superb Cart Houses, magnificent Barn Doors, variegated Barn Racks, and admirable Sheep-folds, according to the Turkish and Persian Manner; a work never (till now) attempted. To which are added some designs of Fly-traps, Bees' Palaces, and Emmet Houses in the Muscovite and Arabian Architecture; all adapted to the latitude and genius of England. The whole entirely new and inimitably designed in two parts on forty pewter plates under the immediate inspection of Don Gulielmus De Demi Je ne scai Quoi, Chief Architect to the Grand Signior. Originally printed in the seraglio at Constantinople, and now translated into English by Jemmy Gymp. To be sold (only by Ebenezer Sly) at the Brazen Head near Temple Bar."

But in spite of Morris' excellent parody of the pompous claims of many a pattern-book, he himself was not above paltry tricks. Among his own designs was one of

an eye-trap [20] or wall, only to represent a building terminating a walk, or to hide some disagreeable object. . . . An erection of this kind requires a wood behind it and an avenue to the approach, the better to conceal the deception.

This momentary lapse into inconsistency notwithstanding, Morris' satire was decidedly apposite. It was aimed against dishonest architecture and pretentious "gingerbread-work." But his criticism had no effect. The next twenty years witnessed the stream of fantastic pattern-books still flowing from the press without interruption.

In his *Critical Observations* (1771) "Athenian" Stuart protested against what he regarded as an extreme example of the mania for naturalism. He attacked the ideal of *rus in urbe* — the attempt to introduce into the congestion and bustle of a city the charms of the country. He ridiculed the perverted logic by which nature was made to appear where she was entirely out of place. In his review of London squares, Stuart approved only of St. James's Square. All the others were dominated by false principles and accordingly were, not formal squares appropriate to a city, but gardens, parks, or sheep-walks. Especially absurd, in Stuart's opinion, was Cavendish Square, in the center of which were cooped

> a few frightened sheep within a wooden pailing which, were it not for their sooty fleeces and meagre carcasses, would be more apt to give the idea of a butcher's pen. . . . To see the poor things starting at every coach and hurrying round and round their narrow bounds requires a warm imagination, indeed, to convert the scene into that of flocks ranging the fields, with all the concomitant ideas of innocence and a pastoral life.

Sarcastically he suggests that with Luneville, the park of the King of Poland, as a model, any future adherent of *rus in urbe* should have all his sheep painted. "And I think if a pasteboard mill and tin cascade were to be added, it would complete the rural scene."

In his judgment Stuart was guided by the classic conviction that the formal architectural character of a city square required that its surroundings should be equally regular. This sound principle an assertive naturalism had driven out of favor and replaced by the too frequent irrelevance of unsymmetrical gardening. Just how great was this irrelevance Americans can realize by two examples in their own country, where the naturalistic school has perpetrated numerous ineptitudes. The pretentious public buildings that line the Mall in Washington and the winding paths and irregularly planted trees in the parkway in the center are completely uncoordinated and illustrate the painful discrepancies of an ununified plan. By contrast the Lincoln Memorial and its formal setting in the French style indicate what impressive dignity can be secured by the correlation of a building and its surroundings. Central Park in New York City is another case in point. The natural style in which it was originally laid out was, at the time, absolutely fitting, because the Park was in the country on the outskirts of the city. But since the city has grown up around the Park and the towering skyscrapers that gird it are everywhere visible, the rural illusion has been destroyed. The roar of traffic and the odor of gasoline, constant reminders of the city, mock the wooded hills, cascades tumbling among the rocks, and paths serpentining through would-be glades.

What Stuart would have thought of Central Park it is easy to imagine. But his objection to the *rus in urbe* was not in tune with the spirit of his day. Naturalism was having a disintegrating influence even upon ideas of town planning inherited from the Italian Renaissance. Reynolds, classical in his taste in painting, nevertheless admired the irregularity by which the picturesque cult set such great store. Whereas Stuart congratulated the citizens of Bath upon the beautiful symmetry of their architecture and the harmony of their public squares, Reynolds in one of his later *Discourses* (the thirteenth) noted that "the turnings of the streets of London and other old towns" give them a commensurable attraction. He even ventures the opinion that had London after the fire been rebuilt in accordance with Wren's regular plan, the result might have been "rather unpleasing; the uniformity might have produced weariness, and a slight degree of disgust." In other words, Reynolds liked the irregularities that were the consequence of "accident"; they were natural, and imparted that variety of design which was the fetish of the modernists of his day. Travelers of our own time who sentimentally dote upon "quaint" villages and their "old-world" atmosphere will sympathize more with Reynolds' than with Stuart's classic point of view.

As the touring of country-seats became a fashionable mode of passing the summer months, the satirists pilloried people who journeyed in pursuit of taste to satisfy their vanity or craving for excitement. Indeed, in their restlessness and unintelligent curiosity these eighteenth-century travelers seem to have anticipated tourists of our own day who would, if they could, undertake to see Versailles, Fontainebleau, and Chantilly all in one day. Incapable of appreciating the gardens that they inspected, they turned their visits into picnics or hurried on from estate to estate, never remaining long enough at any one to relish the scenes that they had traveled far to see. They were in too great haste to enjoy the shade of the trees which they admired or to rest in the temples which they had reached by crossing a scorching lawn. All this fatigue and constant agitation they endured for what they fondly imagined was improvement.[21] When Sam Softly, a sugar-baker, inherited a fortune and decided to play the gentleman, he bought an elegant chaise and pair of geldings and proceeded to visit every summer "the most eminent seats of the nobility and gentry in different parts of the kingdom, with his wife and some select friends." He was delighted with this opportunity to exhibit both his chaise and his skill as a driver and to parade his knowledge of the intermarriages of noble families. Whenever his party arrived at a seat, he had a genius for finding "some shady bench in the Park, where the company may most commodiously refresh themselves with cold tongue, chicken, and French rolls," or for selecting the "cool temple in the garden . . . best adapted for drinking tea, brought for this purpose, in the afternoon." It was within the mansion, however, that Sam was most successful in the display of his vulgarity. He examined the furniture, inquired the cost, scrutinized the family portraits, and, affecting taste, found fault with the decoration of the apartments. In short, the satirist concludes that it would have been better if Sam Softly had kept to his sugar-baking, for, as it was, his vanity and pretension now made him appear a fool.[22] But as Richard Graves remarks, whoever the tourists might be, the inn-keeper in the neighborhood of a show-place always profited during the season for traveling and, as well he might in England, prayed "God to send fine weather." [23]

The pompous owner of a show-place as well as the empty-headed tourist came in for his share of satire. The reign of taste had developed a new type of proprietor — the man who as an active, restless individual was incessantly engaged in alterations and wished to be regarded as an "improver." Whenever he had a visitor, immediately after breakfast he inveigled him into taking a short walk. But invariably it proved a long one as he led his guest "from the Palladian portico to the Gothic tower; from the Lapland to the Chinese house; or from the Temple of Venus to the hermitage." Forced to make a tour of numerous "temples, pagodas, pyramids, grottoes, bridges, hermitages, caves, towers, hot-houses, etc.," and overcome with fatigue and the heat, the soured and unwilling guest was too exasperated to flatter the owner with the compliments on his taste which he was expectantly waiting to hear. In revenge for his discomfort the visitor deliberately made himself unpleasant. He

absolutely denies the existence of hermits, mandarins, and the whole heathen system of divinities. He disputes the antiquity of your ruin, and the genuineness of your hermitage: nay, he will descend to cavil at the bell with which the hermit is supposed to ring himself to prayers. . . . If he suspects a building to be new-fronted, he finds out a private way to the decayed side of it.

What is worse, he spreads in the countryside unfavorable accounts of the estate:

He either describes it as a bog that will not bear a horse, or as a sand that cannot produce a blade of grass. . . . If your principal object be a lake, he will strain a point to report it green and stagnated; or else take the advantage of a thunder-storm to pronounce it white or yellow. If you have a stream, he laments the frequency of floods; if a tide-river, the smell of mud at low-water. He detects your painted cascade, misconstrues your inscriptions, and puns upon your mottoes.

Richard Cambridge, the author of this excellent satiric essay in the *World* (no. 76), advises the owner, if he would avoid these humiliations and the pains of wounded vanity, to ply his guests with champagne. Then, when they tour his estate, "they never see a fault in his improvements." The same type of persistent ostentation masquerading as hospitality until the visitor was in a ferment of impatience was satirized by Cumberland in the *Observer* (no. 58) and by Garrick and Colman in *The Clandestine Marriage*.

The seeker of picturesque natural beauty, a type of traveler for whom the works of Sir Uvedale Price and William Gilpin were responsible and for whom the term *tourist* had been primarily coined, was subjected to ridicule as sharp as that to which the frequenters of gardens were exposed. Journeys through the more remote, wilder parts of Great Britain to indulge in raptures over the grand irregularity of mountains were a fad of the romantic era deemed as deserving of satire as had been the china mania of the earlier decades of the century.

In *Love and Freindship* Jane Austen, whose incorrigible sense of humor made her perceive, even in her girlhood, amusing aberrations of folly, depicts Augusta, who had a "considerable taste for the Beauties of Nature," as lured to Scotland after reading Gilpin's account of his tour in the Highlands.[24] In the same witty spirit Miss Austen wrote the altogether too brief *Tour through Wales in a Letter from a Young Lady*. Like all picturesque tourists, Fanny was indefatigable in making sketches of views that had thrilled her, but unfortunately, although they were "very beautiful," they did not closely resemble the original scenes, as they were drawn under somewhat difficult circumstances. As Fanny was on foot, and as her mother was on horseback and in the habit of pressing her steed into a gallop, the girl had to do all her sketching while she ran along the road in an effort to keep up with her mother's horse. This is Miss Austen's burlesque explanation of the pathetic inexactitude of drawings such as probably shoals of young amateurs displayed to their friends as proof of their taste and their touring. Such ardent pedestrianism also kept Fanny and her sister "in a fine perspiration"; they not only wore out two pairs of shoes, but had to borrow from their mother "a pair of blue Sattin Slippers, of which we each took one and hopped home from Hereford delightfully." [25] Even in her later work Miss Austen did not neglect to make a thrust at the picturesque. But in *Northanger Abbey*, as in all the novels of her maturity, the characters are less eccentric and the satire is tempered by a due respect for actuality. Nevertheless, although the laughter that there plays over the picturesque is never hilarious, it penetrates the shams of the current pose.

When Isaac D'Israeli resorted to satire, he preferred the burlesque mood. His *Flim-Flams! or, The Life and Errors of my Uncle and the Amours of my Aunt!* (1805) also ridicules pedestrianism as one of the absurdities of the day, and parodies the ecstasies of the susceptible traveler:

> Romantic delights were mine when I went a castle-hunting in Wales — exclaimed a picturesque tourist. Ah! ye golden hours of venerable antiquity and pictorial nature! The sun, all the while I was in Wales, was a sun no Welchman ever saw! it had always a golden effulgence, shining over varied hills, gleaming on nodding groves, gilding over the valley, and, at the same time, the valley was obscured in grandly-projected shadows! Ah! what things we picturesquists see! I ascended a rock crowned with the frowning ruin of a castle, with a tempestuous cloud breaking against it!

Stop! interrupted my Uncle — did you always find the tempestuous cloud upon the frowning ruin?

Sir, observed the picturesque tourist — would you insinuate I am flim-flamming?

My Uncle apologized; the picturesquist proceeded. — Ah! how sublimely have I wandered among Druidical remains! I have eaten my bread and cheese in a Cromlech; and when I could not get a bed, I walked by the side of a Welch river, and apostrophized it! Ah! did you never hear my Address to the river Llandovery? "Farewell, thou limpid current! — Flow on, thou sweet stream! My feeble pen is far beneath thy merits!"

Ah! what language! what ideas! exclaimed the sentimental Russian, "striking his forehead, stamping his feet," — you would have been a worthy companion of Lavater. This great man loved "AHS! and OHS!" He had a little Ejaculating and Epitheting Society about him.[26]

A by-product of the mania for traveling which also fell under the bane of satire was the passion for writing and publishing accounts of tours regardless of their triviality or the would-be author's inexperience as a writer. D'Israeli hits at the inanity of these volumes. His imaginary uncle urges him to undertake some form of "tourification" with a view to the subsequent publication of a book as the only means by which he might acquire literary fame. While the uncle admits that his nephew has no ideas of his own, he thinks that he could at least write down what he "saw and heard." An essayist in the *Looker-On* (no. 73) likewise condemns "the rage for tour-writing," and deplores that in contrast to a serious book of travels a "Tour" is only an account of unrelated incidents and frivolous observations. Ironically he advises ladies to refrain from writing for a year after returning from their travels. Then, having forgotten the insignificant details of their experience, they will discover that the residuum of their information is so small in quantity that they will have not enough material to make a book.

The most ludicrous satire on travel for the sake of wild scenery probably was *The Tour of Doctor Syntax in Search of the Picturesque*.[27] Written by William Combe at the request of the publisher of the *Poetical Magazine* in order to provide a suitable text for Rowlandson's drawings of a comical schoolmaster who imagined he was the possessor of taste, it depicted Syntax as smitten with the idea of touring the Lake District to replenish his empty purse:

> I'll make a *Tour* — and then I'll *write it.*
> You well know what my pen can do,
> And I'll employ my pencil too: —
> I'll ride and write, and sketch and print,
> And thus create a real mint;
> I'll prose it here, I'll verse it there,
> And picturesque it everywhere.

In his account of the adventures of Syntax and his horse Grizzle, Combe obviously took his cues from Cervantes and the host of burlesque-writers who adopted his narrative method. Combe scored the most points when he ridiculed the artistic fanaticism of the Doctor. Syntax refuses an invitation to join in a hunt for these characteristic reasons:

> Your sport, my Lord, I cannot take,
> For I must go and hunt a lake;
> And while you chace the flying deer,
> I must fly off to Windermere,
> 'Stead of hallooing to a fox,
> I must catch echoes from the rocks;
> With curious eye and active scent,
> I on the picturesque am bent;
> This is my game, I must pursue it,
> And make it where I cannot view it.

Combe also scored effectively when in his facile rimes he described the Doctor's inclination for whatever was irregular and misshapen. Having under the guidance of painters like Morland and Gainsborough and a theorist like Price swung far away from the symmetry and the refined, carefully proportioned forms of classicism, the picturesque cult reserved its raptures for ruins, dilapidated cottages, ungroomed horses, hairy goats and asses, untidy peasants, and ragged children, beggars, and gypsies. Although Syntax, who is not an extremist, balks at pigs, "straggling brambles," and "a decay'd and rotten tree" as necessary elements in a picturesque landscape, he can enunciate the dogmas of the cult with glib proficiency:

> What, though the blackbird and the thrush
> Make vocal ev'ry verdant bush;

Not one among the winged kind
Presents an object to my mind.
Their grace and beauty's nought to me;
In all their vast variety
The picturesque I cannot see.
A carrion fowl tied to a stake
Will a far better picture make,
When as a scarecrow 'tis display'd
To make all thievish birds afraid,
Than the white swan, in all its pride,
Sailing upon the crystal tide.

With an eye to their picturesque values Syntax compares a rector and a curate:

A rector, on whose face so sleek
In vain you for a wrinkle seek;
In whose fair form, so fat and round,
No obtuse angle's to be found,
On such a shape no man of taste
Would his fine tints or canvas waste;
But take a curate who's so thin,
His bones seem peeping through his skin,
Make him to stand, or walk, or sit,
In any posture you think fit,
And, with all these nice points about him,
No well-taught painter e'er would scout him;
For with his air, and look, and mien,
He'd give effect to any scene.[28]

At the end of his long, good-natured satire Combe fittingly rounds out his narrative of Doctor Syntax as a picturesque tourist by rewarding him with a vicarage in Cumberland near Keswick. But the Doctor's career was not yet ended. His grotesque figure amused the contemporary imagination. The account of his adventures was not only imitated and parodied in other books, but incidents from his whimsical experience were incorporated in decorative patterns now to be seen on early nineteenth-century chintz and on Staffordshire plates and platters.

CHAPTER XXIII

THE RESURGENCE OF THE CLASSIC

A CONSIDERATION of an arresting contrast may properly complete this account of the noteworthy fluctuations in English taste between the days of Inigo Jones and the appearance of Gilpin's studies of the picturesque. Beginning in the year 1760 — the date is approximate — the history of literature and the history of architecture, furniture, and decorative design did not follow exclusively parallel lines of development as had been the case in the preceding period that we have discussed, but for the most part letters and the arts pursued separate ways in independence of one another. They continued to exhibit only one phenomenon in common: interest in the Middle Ages. *The Rowley Poems*, *The Borderers*, *Christabel*, *The Eve of St. Agnes*, *The Lay of the Last Minstrel*, and the Waverley novels were akin in spirit to Strawberry Hill, Fonthill Abbey, Ashridge, Abbotsford, the Tudor cottages of early nineteenth-century architects, and Pugin and Barry's new Houses of Parliament in the late Gothic style.

But aside from this single yet important point of contact, literature and architecture (the latter in association with allied arts) progressed divergently in the second half of the eighteenth century and expressed dissimilar enthusiasms. Whereas in literature romantic impulses found freer and freer play and more vivid and more intense embodiment, in architecture and the allied arts those impulses were not permitted unimpeded growth, but encountered continued opposition from a revitalized classicism. Medievalism had to contend with its ancient foe, rendered, for the time being at any rate, somewhat more threatening because of a sudden increase of strength. Thus it came about that while the prose writer and the poet, moved by an impatient individualism, were exploring fresh fields of emotional experience, the student of artistic form, more conservative, was with invigorated confidence putting his faith in inherited modes of design.

The sources of that new strength are not far to seek. Toward the middle of the eighteenth century, when the classicism that had been inspired by the Italian Renaissance was rapidly going to seed and creative energy was dangerously content with obedience to the dry formulas of an excessive intellectualism, the discovery of Herculaneum and Pompeii checked the impending decline, excited a multitude of new interests, and made thrillingly concrete countless ideas about the customs and habits of the Roman world.

Under the patronage of Charles VII, King of Naples, the excavation of Herculaneum began in 1738 and that of Pompeii in 1748. Seven years later the Accademia Ercolanese was founded and undertook to publish on a magnificent scale *Le Antichità di Ercolano*, containing plates of many of the treasures that had been unearthed — pictures, bronzes, and lamps. The first volume of this epochal work appeared in 1757 and was followed at intervals by seven others. Before the middle of the century Piranesi commenced to issue from the press his remarkable etchings of the remains of ancient civilization. Urns, statues, shattered columns, overturned altars, and ruined temples, baths, palaces, and amphitheaters overgrown with vegetation, beset in their recesses by black shadows and haunted by beggars and thieves, were delineated, to be sure, not with exact archeological truth but with an imaginative vehemence and a feeling for the grand and the tragic that satisfied the craving of the age for sublimity, intensified the glamour with which Poussin and Claude Lorraine had already enveloped the ruins of ancient buildings, and made Piranesi famous throughout Europe. In 1755, while Piranesi was feverishly depicting the crumbling splendors of classic architecture, Winckelmann came to Rome, devoted himself to the study of ancient marbles, and finally in 1764 published his *History of Ancient Art* — a work which revealed, as had never been done before, the serenity and majesty of Greek sculpture. Two years later in the *Laokoön* Lessing supplemented Winckelmann's study of the actual materials of ancient art by his famous discussion of the essential differentiating characteristics of poetry, painting, and sculpture. Thus interest in the increasing first-hand knowledge of classic art was in turn stimulated by a new and enlightening esthetic theory.

In the meantime, Englishmen were not inactive. They followed with enthusiasm what was taking place in Italy and contributed their own share to the revival of Hellenistic culture. Two years after the King of Naples began his excavations, Walpole, who was taking the grand tour, visited Herculaneum and was evidently so impressed by what he saw that in his letter to Richard West he involuntarily restrained the flippancy that was natural to him:

> One hates writing descriptions that are to be found in every book of travels; but we have seen something to-day that I am sure you never read of, and perhaps never heard of. Have you ever heard of a subterraneous town? a whole Roman town, with all its edifices, remaining underground? . . . This underground city is perhaps one of the noblest curiosities that ever has been discovered. . . . There is nothing of the kind known in the world; I mean a Roman city entire of that age, and that has not been corrupted with modern repairs. Besides scrutinising this very carefully, I should be inclined to search for the remains of the other towns that were partners with this in the general ruin. 'Tis certainly an advantage to the learned world, that this has been laid up so long.[1]

In 1751 Lady Featherstonhaugh, who seems to have been an adventurous person — she was the first woman to climb Mont Cenis — examined Herculaneum, and her account of her experience was subsequently read before the Royal Society by her brother and afterwards published in its *Transactions*.[2] To satisfy the curiosity that had been excited by the excavations, Wickes Skurray translated from Italian in 1750 Venuti's description of the "finds," and in 1753 (?) and 1756 appeared English versions of Bellicard's *Observations sur les antiquités d'Herculanum*.

The foundation of the Society of Dilettanti in 1732 was another symbol of the continued loyalty of many Englishmen of taste to classic art.[3] Its members were young men of wealth and position who, having made the grand tour, met at various London taverns to enjoy a social evening and to keep alive the artistic interests which individuals among them had, no doubt, cultivated on the Continent. Although the primary purpose of these gatherings was convivial to a bibulous degree, the Society did not neglect "the cause of Vertù." Indeed, its established toasts were "Viva la Vertù" and "Grecian taste and Roman spirit." In 1741 it was decided, moreover, that the President of the Society should wear a Roman toga of scarlet cloth while he occupied the chair. The draping of the folds of this official robe was delegated to the Painter of the Society, who was at one time Sir Joshua Reynolds. The figures of Minerva and Apollo constituted the decorative device on the great seal of the Society, and the figure of Bacchus very appropriately ornamented the box in which the books were kept. Later these dashing young bloods, anticipating their Victorian progeny, agreed in solemn conclave that "as Bacchus' backside appeared bare, there should be some covering provided for it." When from time to time the question of having a permanent home for their organization was considered, the Dilettanti approved, as might be expected, a classic model, especially the Temple of Pola, of which Stuart and Revett had made drawings. In these various ways, superficial in themselves, the Society bore witness to its allegiance to antiquity. The social prominence of its members undoubtedly helped to crystallize opinion in favor of classicism and gave direction to the current of taste. This was likely to be the result, particularly when, as time went by, the Society made a practice of giving financial support to enterprises which promised an increase of contemporary knowledge of ancient civilizations. Such activities served to check the popularity of medievalism.

In the middle of the century, in a series of almost epoch-making works, several Englishmen who had been both adventurous and scholarly in their enthusiasm for learning gave accounts of their archeological explorations and discoveries in seats of ancient civilization with which the West had little first-hand acquaintance. As these remote localities were under the control of non-Christian peoples and as travel there had always been attended with hardship and even danger, they had remained virtually unvisited for centuries. Ignorant, as a result, of the monuments of Greek civilization surviving in Greece, Asia Minor, and the Archipelago, the Western European had confined his attention to the relics of Roman culture in Italy, and on the basis of that limited material had formulated his conception of antiquity. Now that conception was to be modified and enriched by a growing familiarity with the remains of

Fig. 77 — Silk with Stripes Characteristic of the Period of Louis XVI

Fig. 78 — Ceiling in the Adam Style

Greek sculpture and architecture. In 1753 Robert Wood, who had traveled as far as Syria, published *The Ruins of Palmyra* and four years later *The Ruins of Balbec.* Although periodical essayists recognized immediately the value of the books, they feared that the craze for Chinese and Gothic art would prevent them from receiving the appreciation that they deserved:

Thus the Greek and Roman architecture are discarded for the novelties of China; the *Ruins of Palmyra* and copies of the capital pictures of Correggio are neglected for Gothic designs and burlesque political prints. — *Adventurer* (no. 139).

Yet many there are, and men of taste too, . . . who through a shameful neglect of their minds, have little or no relish of the fine arts; and I doubt whether, in our most splendid assemblies, the Royal Game of Goose would not have as many eyes fixed upon it, as the lately published curiosity of the ruins of Palmyra. — *World* (no. 63).

The latter contributor was confident, however, that those who "do not labour under a total loss of appetite for liberal amusements" would find the book "a sumptuous entertainment." The critic in the *Monthly Review* was a little more optimistic. He ventured to believe that Wood's informing volume on Balbec (Heliopolis) might accomplish some good in the correction of taste:

But it is with peculiar pleasure we observe such a work as this produced at a time when war seemed to have engrossed the attention of mankind. The drawn sword has not yet frightened the muses from their seat; they have more dangerous enemies in the Chinese and Goths, than in the sons of Mars. Such specimens of architecture as have already been communicated to the public, by the learned and ingenious Editor of the Ruins of Balbec, with others which are expected of Athens, &c. will, we hope, improve the taste of our countrymen, and expel the littleness and ugliness of the Chinese, and the barbarity of the Goths, that we may see no more useless and expensive trifles; no more dungeons instead of summer-houses. — Vol. XVIII (1758), p. 59.

But while some anti-medievalists were thus envisaging a brighter future for English art, the practical and energetic proprietor of Vauxhall was turning to financial profit the public interest in the recent archeological discoveries. On July 9, 1754, Mrs. Montagu mentions that she and a party of friends were going to Vauxhall, "where Mr. Tyers has had the ruins of Palmyra painted in the manner of the scenes so as to deceive the eye and appear buildings." [4]

The seeds of a saner culture which Wood had scattered in what seemed to the orthodox the polluted soil of English taste were multiplied immeasurably in 1762 when Stuart and Revett published *The Antiquities of Athens.* In preparation for this work the collaborators had visited Greece — then under Turkish rule —, where they had painstakingly examined the remains of Greek civilization, of which Christian Europe had no precise knowledge. Their book is recognized today "as containing the earliest accurate reproductions of the monuments of Athens," and Stuart and Revett are described as "pioneers of classical archaeology." In their own time they were welcomed and substantially rewarded by the Society of Dilettanti.

Encouraged by the results of such investigations in foreign lands, the Society a few years later commissioned Richard Chandler, author of *Marmora Oxoniensia* (1763), a valuable work on the famous Arundel marbles, to head a small party of experts who were, at the expense of the Dilettanti, to explore Greece and Asia Minor, copy inscriptions, and make measurements of buildings and drawings of bas-reliefs. Upon his return from his travels Chandler published by means of the funds supplied by his aristocratic patrons *Ionian Antiquities, or, Ruins of Magnificent and Famous Buildings in Ionia* (1769). Moreover, the classicists made an effort to inculcate sound traditional ideals in students of artistic promise. In 1774 the Society of Dilettanti decided to send two such students to either Italy or Greece for a sojourn of three years. In 1762 the Society for the Encouragement of Arts, Manufactures, and Commerce had already offered prizes

(1) For the best design of a London house and offices for a person of quality . . . the designs to be regular, the parts well proportioned, and decorated in the Palladian style.

(2) For the best drawings of the Banqueting House built by Inigo Jones . . . by youths under the age of eighteen.[5]

In the meantime, as was inevitable, this fresh and enlightened study of art and archeology invested the classic tradition with new authority and conspicuously influenced architecture and interior decoration in the second half of the century. In France the taste for the antique was responsible for the Louis Seize style, exquisitely exemplified, as every tourist will recall, in the apartments of Marie Antoinette at Fontainebleau. The new feeling affected even textile design, and in the patterns of French silk (Fig. 77) the waving floral sprays of the rococo (Fig. 60) were stabilized by the introduction of straight lines at regular intervals. In England the style, inspired by similar ideals and possessing corresponding decorative qualities, was the achievement of Robert Adam. His work was the fruit of his own archeological studies and his association with the apostles of the new enthusiasm for antiquity. During his three years' sojourn in Italy and Dalmatia (1754–57) he made the acquaintance of Winckelmann, became one of the cherished friends of Piranesi, who dedicated to him some of the plates of his *Campus Martius* (1762), and visited Spalato in company with Clérisseau, the French archeologist, for the purpose of examining the palace of Diocletian so as to supplement his knowledge of the public buildings of the Romans through an acquaintance with an imperial private residence. Upon his return to England he published the results of his research, and, soon becoming the fashionable architect of the hour, disclosed in Syon House (1761–62), Lansdowne House (1765), and other noble mansions his characteristic treatment of the antique.

Adam recognized that contemporary Palladian architects erred in their practice of employing in English interiors without discrimination heavy constructional features that were found only in the interior of a Roman temple or basilica. His studies in Italy had made it plain to him that the Romans themselves, guided by a nice sense of scale, had carefully distinguished between the internal decoration of a public edifice and that appropriate to moderate-sized rooms and domestic apartments. He protested as a result against the weight and depth of compartment ceilings (Fig. 10) designed without regard for the proportions of a room; he condemned the ponderous cornices and complete entablatures that crowned the walls of apartments; and he objected to the formal tabernacle frames, that is, the columns or pilasters supporting a pediment, that usually encased the doors and windows of the orthodox English interior in the classic style.

Profiting by his observation of the practice of the Romans and of the sixteenth-century Italians, who had themselves been inspired by the ancient decorations in the Baths of Titus, Adam challenged the tradition of massive dignity in interior ornament. He favored decorative patterns that were "light," "gay," "elegant," "whimsical," and even "bizarre." What influenced him most in the development of his own style was antique stucco-work in low, delicate relief and Raphael's playful painted arabesques in the loggia of the Vatican. He declared that "this classical style of ornament [was] by far the most perfect that has ever appeared for inside decorations," and when employed with skill was "capable of inimitable beauties." His own mural designs, utilizing as motives the sphinx, the griffin, the ram's head, the fan, the oval medallions, the oblong plaque or tablet, and festoons of drapery, were executed in low relief of great refinement and generally colored, the background frequently being a delicate green or pink and the small inserted plaques or panels a turquoise blue. George Richardson's *A Book of Ceilings* (1776), from which our illustration (Fig. 78) is taken, embodies the characteristic features of Adam's style. The unknown designer of the fan (Fig. 79) shows that he has been influenced by the same taste except that he has filled his medallions not with classic subjects but with incidents from Sterne's *A Sentimental Journey*. The contrast between the stucco decoration of an Adam ceiling and the massive compartments (Fig. 10) approved by Inigo Jones and Isaac Ware needs no comment. They represent a different conception of classic ornament.

Adam secured, moreover, an effect of absolute unity in his rooms by designing not only the decoration of the walls and ceiling but all the furnishings: chairs, tables, carpets, mirrors, grates, and candlesticks. As a result, whereas his work as an architect is mediocre and marked even in the famous Adelphi Buildings in the Strand by insipidity, Adam's reputation as an interior decorator of distinction is deserved. But the grace and the delicate scale of his ornament displeased classicists who hankered for the massiveness and sobriety of the style that he replaced. In two screeds, quoted by Mr. Bolton, Adam is

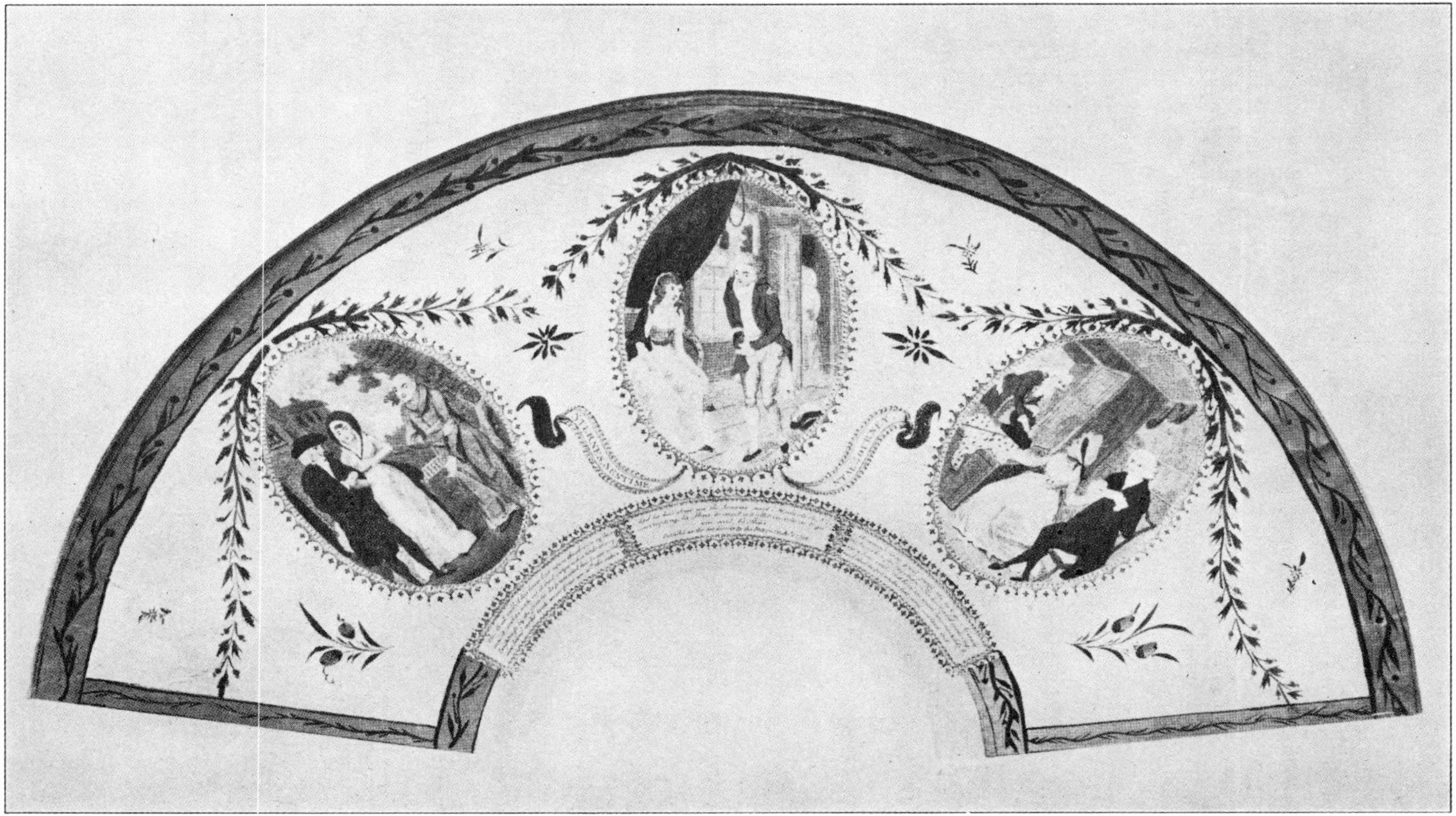

Fig. 79 — Fan with Decorative Motives in the Adam Style. Pictures in the Panels Represent Incidents from *A Sentimental Journey*

Fig. 80 — Two Armchairs, Sheraton Style

treated with contempt. A Robert Smirke relieved himself in this fashion: "Most of the white walls, with which Mr. Adam has speckled this city, are no better than models for the Twelfth-Night Decoration of a Pastry Cook." A person calling himself Jose Mac Packe wrote in mockery that in rooms

> the nicknackery of the Cabinet maker, Toyman and Pastry cook, preside with impunity. Here let the light and elegant ordonnance of the bed post triumph over the clumsy orders of old Greece. Here let Pilasters rival the substance and ornaments of figured ribbons, and the rampant foliage of antiquity, give place to the exquisite prettinesses of casts from the cabinet, the medal case, or the seal engraver's show glass.[6]

Walpole also sneered at the "Adamitic mode," its filigree, and its "gingerbread and sippets of embroidery." [7] But undoubtedly Mrs. Montagu expressed the prevailing opinion of Adam when in 1767 she wrote to Lord Kames that if his wife

> would have anything *en meubles* extremely beautiful, she must employ my friend Mr. Adam here. He has made me a cieling and chimney-piece, and doors, which are pretty enough to make me a thousand enemies: Envy turns livid at the first glimpse of them.[8]

Lecturing in the early decades of the nineteenth century as Professor of Architecture at the Royal Academy, Sir John Soane rejoiced that Adam had broken the "talismanic charm" of the rococo by his ornament derived from antiquity and admirably adapted to domestic interiors.

Classicism did not, however, enjoy an absolute monopoly of favor. It had to share popularity with Gothic architecture, which was destined to score a triumph when it was decided that the new Houses of Parliament should be in the medieval style. In 1786 an essayist in the *Lounger* (no. 79) still deemed it necessary to satirize the mania for Chinese porcelain, and in 1814 at the celebration of the peace a Chinese bridge on the center of which was erected a seven-storied pagoda formed one of the chief attractions.[9] Yet Archibald Alison was, in the main, correct when in 1790 he declared in his *Essay on the Nature and Principles of Taste* that "the Taste which now reigns is that of the Antique. Every thing we now use, is made in imitation of those models which have been lately discovered in Italy." [10]

As Alison's remark indicates, workers in various arts were to a greater or less degree cooperating with Adam in establishing the supremacy of the classic. In furniture design Hepplewhite and Sheraton (Fig. 80) preferred the straight line more often than did Chippendale (Fig. 58); they favored chair-legs that were reminiscent of the classic pedestal or column; they imparted a very definite axial emphasis to their chair-backs, frequently employing for this purpose a tall, slender antique vase-form as a splat; and they differentiated carefully between table-tops and chair-seats and the legs that functioned as their support. In the arrangement of a room they advocated, furthermore, as their plans show, an uncompromising symmetry in the distribution of the furniture.

At the same time the famous woman painter, Angelica Kauffmann, who had sojourned in Rome and absorbed its traditions, exploited classic material and filled many of Adam's small oval and oblong panels on walls and ceilings with nymphs, *amorini*, and mythological incidents, conceived in spite of their subject-matter in a sentimental style. Wedgwood likewise followed classic models in the form and decoration of his much sought-after blue and green jasper ware, keeping in his service in Rome various craftsmen to make plaster casts and to copy reliefs on engraved gems and the ornament on vases. John Flaxman, the sculptor, who was one of his ablest assistants, drew illustrations for Homer and other Greek poets as well as designs for the antique plaques of Wedgwood ware with which furniture and mantel-pieces were often embellished. In the meantime Gavin Hamilton, who had been industriously excavating in Rome and its neighborhood for years, furnished the homes of English art-lovers with many fine examples of ancient sculpture from Hadrian's Villa, the Via Appia, the villa of Antoninus Pius, and other sites that his spade had ravaged.

Nor was this all. The admiration for the antique affected even women's dress. In *The Pharos* (1787), a collection of essays, a writer who described himself as "a Friend to Female Beauty" deplored, with his tongue in his cheek, that the hoop, a creation of Queen Anne's day, had been discarded in favor of the "Grecian mode." The new fashion requiring clinging gowns of soft material exhibited the feminine figure to a most indecorous degree and was suggested, as the essayist opined, "by the sight of wet drapery." Obviously unnatural, the hoop was, nevertheless, something no modest female should have cast aside, as it was the rampart that protected her virtue. Although the writer unctuously insisted that woman was "sacred," it is unfortunately only too clear that he thought that she should not place too great confidence in man's respect for her sanctity. Hence the plea for the hoop and the indictment of the "Grecian mode."

It is not difficult to see why English literature and art did not follow entirely similar lines of development in the last quarter of the eighteenth century. They moved in different directions because the forces that rejuvenated classicism were not of a kind to have a corresponding influence upon literature. The discovery of Herculaneum and Pompeii, thrilling though it was as an historic incident, disclosed no new material such as would stir the man of letters. The greater knowledge of antiquity that accompanied more systematic archeological research and the excavation of seats of ancient culture, as well as the measured drawings and study of buildings that hitherto had been little more than a name, stimulated the sense of beauty and invigorated architecture, interior decoration, and other formal arts. But such activities were not likely to affect literature as would undoubtedly have been the case if, as in the Italian Renaissance, precious Greek and Roman manuscripts had come to light and amazed mankind. Indeed, Keats' *Ode on a Grecian Urn* is one of the few and rare literary flowers that the new enthusiasm for the antique contributed to English literature.

NOTES

NOTES

Chapter XIII

1. James M. Holzman, *The Nabobs in England: a Study of the Returned Anglo-Indian, 1760–1785* (New York, 1926), p. 97.
2. Act III.
3. Act I, sc. iii.
4. Vol. III, 28–30, 69–70.
5. Holzman (*The Nabobs in England*, p. 34) quotes an item from the *Public Advertizer* (Dec. 25, 1783) that throws light on *Serim*: "A gentleman charging one of our nabobs at Brooks's with being concerned in the monopoly of rice, which destroyed half a million of people, was answered by the great man, that his calculation was entirely erroneous, as the whole number, upon a fair enquiry, did not exceed *one hundred and fifty thousand, men, women, and children included.*"
6. Act V, sc. i.
7. Act I, sc. iii. In his *British Drama* (New York, 1925, p. 298) Allardyce Nicoll states that *Fatal Curiosity* "deals with an ordinary peasant couple led by poverty to commit a terrible crime." This is far from being the case; Wilmot and Agnes clearly belong to the propertied, educated classes and have known wealth and luxury. Had he been a mere peasant, Wilmot would not have possessed a copy of Seneca to sell in order to relieve his distress (Act II, sc. iii). Agnes reproaches her husband because he had squandered her own "fortune" and "ruined our estate" by his "wasteful riots" (Act III, sc. i). When young Wilmot arrives, he refers to his father as "the gentleman," and exclaims,

> "What wild neglect, the token of despair,
> What indigence, what misery appears
> In each disorder'd, or disfurnished room
> Of this once gorgeous house!" (Act II, sc. iii.)

Mr. Nicoll's mistake is the more serious because the significance of *Fatal Curiosity* as a domestic tragedy depends largely upon the social position of the characters. Had the Wilmot family been peasants, Lillo would have been departing more widely than he did from the classical dogma that tragic characters should be of high rank.

8. Charles W. Wilkins, *The Bhagvat-geeta, or Dialogues of Kreeshna and Arjoon . . .* (London, 1785). Hastings' letter, dated at Banaris, Oct. 4, 1784, occupies pp. 5–15.
9. *Memoirs and Observations*, 3rd ed., pp. 126–127.
10. John Nichols, *Literary Anecdotes of the Eighteenth Century* (London, 1812–15), IX, 604.
11. John Nichols, *Illustrations of the Literary History of the Eighteenth Century* (London, 1828), V, 318.
12. *Ibid.*, V, 318–319; *Gentleman's Magazine*, 1771, p. 237. The third Duke of Dorset (d. 1799) had as servant a Chinese boy whom he had educated in the Grammar School of Seavenoaks. His picture, painted by Reynolds, is still at Knole. V. Sackville-West, *Knole and the Sackvilles* (London, 1922), p. 192.
13. Louis Wann, "The Oriental in Elizabethan Drama," in *Modern Philology*, XII (1914–15), 423–447. Of the forty-seven plays considered by the author, Moors appeared in eighteen and Turks in thirty-one. India as well as China was ignored by the Elizabethans.
14. *Les Masques Anglais* (Paris, 1909), p. 519.
15. Enid Welsford, *The Court Masque* (Cambridge, England, 1927), p. 170.

16. George C. D. Odell, *Shakespeare from Betterton to Irving* (New York, 1920), I, 192–195.
17. Frank A. Hedgcock, *David Garrick and his French Friends* (London, 1912), Part II, chap. IV.
18. Cf. J. Kenney, *The Illustrious Stranger*, an operatic farce produced in 1827.
19. *Chinese Letters . . .* (London, 1741), pp. 161–164.
20. I have not seen *The Orphan of China* (London, 1756) by Dr. Thomas Francklin.
21. *Critical Review*, May, 1759.
22. Feb., 1770, pp. 68–69.
23. The Marquis d'Argens was also the author of *Lettres Juives*, published in 1738 and translated into English the following year. To the same *genre* belongs Madame de Graffigny's *Lettres d'une Péruvienne* (Paris, 1747), of which translations appeared in 1748, 1771, 1774, 1782, 1805, and 1818.
24. *Citizen of the World*, nos. XIV, XLI.
25. Vol. VI, Letters XXV and XXVI.
26. June, 1773.
27. *The Spiritual Quixote*, ed. Charles Whibley (London, 1926), I, 149.
28. Vol. IV, Book I, chap. XV.
29. *Journal*, Feb. 17, 1787.
30. Cf. Wallace Irwin, *Letters of a Japanese Schoolboy* (New York, 1909); Ernest Bramah [Smith], *The Mirror of Kong Ho* (New York, 1930).
31. See also Edmond Pery, *Letters from an Armenian in Ireland to his Friends in Trebisond* (London, 1757); "Athenian Letters, or, The Epistolary Correspondence of an Agent of the King of Persia, residing at Athens during the Peloponnesian War," in the *Gentleman's Magazine*, April, 1784. Employing the method of "spy" literature, but lacking some of its point and much of its humor, are books in which a Continental European is represented as passing judgment upon England. See John Shebbeare, *Letters on the English Nation by Batista Angeloni, a Jesuit . . . Translated from the Original Italian* (London, 1755); Robert Southey, *Letters from England by Don Manuel Alvarez Espriella. Translated from the Spanish* (London, 1807). Walpole's pretences in regard to the authorship of *The Castle of Otranto* and Chatterton's forgeries were phases of this current literary habit of concealing one's identity in this masquerade.
32. *Spectator*, no. 511.
33. *Ibid.*, nos. 584–585.
34. *Ibid.*, no. 545.
35. *Fog's Journal*, no. 377 (1736).
36. *Robinson Crusoe* (Oxford, 1927), III, 151–156.
37. *Works*, ed. Henley (Westminster, 1901), XII, 237, 233.
38. *Athenaeum*, Aug. 8, 1904.
39. *The Oeconomy of Female Life* (London, 1751).
40. P. 9, sects. V–VIII, X.
41. *Some Observations on Dr. Brown's Dissertation . . .* (London, 1764), p. 4.

Chapter XIV

1. A. O. Lovejoy, "On the Discrimination of Romanticisms," in *Publications* of the Modern Language Association of America, XXXIX (1924), 241.
2. *A History of the Gothic Revival* (London, 1872), p. 42.
3. *A History of English Romanticism in the Eighteenth Century* (London, 1898), p. 234. The last sentence is quoted from Sir Leslie Stephen's article on Walpole in *Hours in a Library*, Second Series (London, 1876).
4. *The Gothic Revival* (New York, 1929), p. 13.
5. *Ibid.*, pp. 20–21; Evelyn, *Diary*, 1654. In this year, for example, Evelyn recorded favorable opinions of Christ Church (Oxford), King's College (Cambridge), Newstead Abbey, and the Cathedrals of Salisbury, Gloucester, and York.

6. *An Account of Architects and Architecture* (London, 1706), pp. 9–15, following *A Parallel of the Antient Architecture with the Modern*, 2nd ed. (London, 1707).
7. Letter IX.
8. Letter VII.
9. Christopher Wren, *Parentalia*, p. 282.
10. Andrew Clark, *The Life and Times of Anthony Wood . . .* (Oxford, 1891–1900), I, 209. To save space, I group here all references to this work: I, 225, 228–229, 268–270, 309; II, 410; III, 436.
11. Anthony à Wood, *Survey of the Antiquities of the City of Oxford*, ed. Andrew Clark (Oxford, 1889–99), I, 256, 276.
12. *Ibid.*, II, 218–224.
13. *London Spy* (London, 1699), Parts VIII, IX.
14. *Archaeologia*, I (1770). For the history of the antiquarian societies, see also Nichols, *Literary Anecdotes*, VI, 4–5, 136–162.
15. *The Remains of Thomas Hearne. . . .* Collected with a few notes by Philip Bliss, 2nd ed. (London, 1869), II, 63–77.
16. *The Family Memoirs of the Rev. William Stukeley, M.D., and the Antiquarian and other Correspondence of William Stukeley, Roger and Samuel Gale, etc.*, in *Publications* of the Surtees Society (1882–87), I, 18, 32, 45.
17. *Ibid.*, II, 324–329.
18. *Letters*, ed. Toynbee, III, 151.
19. *The Antient and Modern History of the Loyal Town of Ripon . . .* (York, 1733), p. 26 (second pagination).
20. Part I, pp. 136, 199, 244–245.
21. II, 498–499.
22. *Tour*, ed. Cole, II, 491, 479–481 (Letter VII).
23. *Ibid.*, II, 440 (Letter VI).
24. *Ibid.*, II, 638 (Letter IX).
25. Thomas Herring undoubtedly had the medieval cathedral in mind when, in 1728, he praised the buttress, one of its most characteristic structural features: "And virtue, thus secured and guarded, may, perhaps, not unfitly be compared to those buildings of a Gothic taste, which, though they have a good foundation, are furnished nevertheless (against all accidents) with many outward supports and buttresses, but so contrived and adjusted by the architect, that they do not detract from, but even add to the beauty and grandeur of the building." *Letters to William Duncombe* (London, 1777), p. 6.
26. Pp. viii, 50–51.
27. Was Gray making an oblique punning reference to Thomas Gent and his topographical works when he sent to Wharton from the Continent his mock *Proposals for printing by Subscription, in This Large Letter, The Travels of T: G: Gent:*? This title is followed by a prospectus of fifteen chapters in which Gray burlesques his own journey. *Letters of Thomas Gray*, ed. Duncan C. Tovey (London, 1900), I, 52.
28. *Archaeologia*, Vol. IV, *Some Observations on Lincoln Cathedral.*
29. *Letters*, ed. D. C. Tovey, 2nd ed. (London, 1909), I, 17.
30. *Ibid.*, I, 58.
31. See his article on Walpole in *Hours in a Library*, Second Series (London, 1876).
32. Letter IV.
33. *Family Memoirs*, I, 317.
34. Letter VIII.
35. Defoe, *Tour* (London, 1748), I, 231.
36. *Family Memoirs*, III, 70. In view of the recent agitation in behalf of the Roman Wall in Northumbria it is interesting to note that in 1754, when Stukeley was presented to the Princess of Wales at Carlton House, he expressed his concern "at the havoc now making of this most noble antiquity by the surveyors of the new road." A few days later he wrote to the Princess, urging her to interfere and prevent the destruction of the Wall. *Ibid.*, III, 140–143.

37. *The Gothic Revival*, p. 102.

38. "Romantic Aspects of the Age of Pope," in *Publications* of the Modern Language Association of America, XXVII (1912), 297–324.

39. *The Gothic Revival*, p. 54.

40. *Correspondence of Jonathan Swift*, ed. F. Elrington Ball (London, 1913), V, 34–35.

41. *Letters to William Duncombe* (London, 1777), pp. 39–40.

42. *Family Memoirs*, I, 367.

43. *Letters*, ed. Toynbee, III, 186.

44. *An Eighteenth-Century Correspondence*, ed. Lilian Dickins and Mary Stanton (London, 1910).

45. *Correspondence*, II, 35–37.

46. Maud Wyndham, *Chronicles of the Eighteenth Century* (London, 1924), II, 132.

47. Climenson, *Elizabeth Montagu*, II, 139.

48. Part II, Letter I.

49. Nichols, *Illustrations*, III, 454. That the anonymous letter-writer reveals a sentimental attachment to old hangings (frequently a product of domestic industry crudely depicting some Scriptural incident) suggests that ancient heirlooms were now prized by those who deplored current tastes. Sir Roger also valued these relics of other days: "I love to see your Abrahams, your Isaacs, and your Jacobs, as we have them in old pieces of tapestry, with beards below their girdles that cover half the hangings" (*Spectator*, no. 331). An elderly female correspondent of the *Spectator* sharply disapproved of the decline of needlework and expressed her disgust at seeing "a couple of proud idle flirts sipping their tea, for a whole afternoon, in a room hung round with the industry of their great-grandmother" (no. 606). But sophisticated people scoffed at these quaint wall decorations. A husband wrote in distress to the *Spectator* that the demands of his wife whenever she was in pregnancy were becoming more exorbitant. On one occasion she longed for "as much china as would have furnished an India shop," and on another occasion she insisted that the furnishing of her room be changed lest "she should mark the child with some of the frightful figures in the old-fashioned tapestry" (no. 326). In *The Way of the World* Millamant, laughing at Mirabell's excessive gravity, exclaims: "Prithee, don't look with that violent and inflexible wise face like Solomon at the dividing of the child in an old tapestry hanging" (Act II, sc. vi). In *The Tender Husband*, in a ridiculous enumeration of articles inherited by Sir Harry Gubbin's niece Bridget, is listed "a suit of tapestry hangings, with the story of Judith and Holofernes, torn only where the head should have been off" (Act V, sc. ii).

50. *Letters*, ed. Toynbee, II, 423; III, 150, 167, 119.

51. *Ibid.*, V, 369.

52. *Ibid.*, II, 433–434.

53. *Family Memoirs*, I, 114.

54. Nichols, *Illustrations*, II, 769 *et seq.*

55. *A Sketch of the Spring-Gardens, Vaux-Hall, in a Letter to a Noble Lord* (London, n.d.).

56. *The Gothic Revival*, p. 61.

57. L. S. Benjamin, *The Life and Letters of William Beckford* (London, 1910), pp. 221, 240; see also pp. 217, 222, 299.

58. *The Gothic Revival*, p. 108.

59. Avray Tipping, *English Homes, Period VI, Late Georgian, 1760–1820* (London, 1926), I, 339–346.

60. *Cambridge History of English Literature*, X, 217–218 (246 in American reprint).

Chapter XV

1. Character IX, first complete edition (London, 1633).

2. *Characters*, ed. A. R. Waller (Cambridge, England, 1908), pp. 42–43.

3. *The Lives of Those Eminent Antiquaries John Leland, Thomas Hearne, and Anthony à Wood* (Oxford, 1772), II, 253–254.

4. This passage is also interesting from another point of view. Whereas cabinet-makers had made furniture of oak in the Middle Ages and in the Tudor period and of walnut in the reigns of the last Stuart kings and of William and Mary, they did not employ mahogany, a new wood imported from the tropics, before the eighteenth century, when its possibilities were exploited by Chippendale in particular. Bramston's comment indicates to what an extent the wood was regarded as the latest fashionable taste. In Thomas Warton's satire *On Luxury* (1748) is a passage of similar import. The fastidious man of mode, who, refusing to wear British wool, clothes himself only in imported silk and fetches his cups, bowls, and urns from China, likewise scorns such native woods as oak, yew, beech, ash, and poplar:

"My Lord contemptuous of his country's groves,
As foreign fashions foreign trees too loves;
'Odious! upon a walnut-plank to dine!
No — the red-vein'd mohoggony be mine!
Each chest and chair around my room that stands,
Was ship'd thro' dangerous seas from distant lands.'"

5. Act II, sc. ii.
6. See also *Modern Antiques, or, The Merry Mourners*, a farce by John O'Keeffe, produced at Covent Garden in 1791, which satirizes the classical antiquary. He is duped into accepting as genuine a hamper of pseudo-antiques, including, for example, Neptune's trident and one of Niobe's tears.
7. *Gentleman's Magazine*, 1790, pp. 217, 290; Nichols, *Illustrations*, V, 429–431.
8. Book V, ll. 91–106.
9. *Letters Written by the Late Right Honourable Lady Luxborough to William Shenstone, Esq.* (London, 1775), p. 233.
10. *World*, no. 15.
11. *Tatler*, no. 162; *Review*, no. 43.
12. *Connoisseur*, no. 139, 1756.
13. *Catalogue of Prints and Drawings in the British Museum*, no. 4175.
14. "L'usage s'est introduit depuis quelques années de revêtir la façade des boutiques, particulierement de celles des marchands d'étoffes de soie, de quelqu'Ordre d'architecture. Les colonnes, les pilastres, la frise, la corniche, tout y garde sa proportion, et ressemble presque autant à la porte d'un petit temple, qu'à celle d'un magasin." N. Rouquet, *L'Etat des Arts en Angleterre* (Paris, 1755), pp. 185–186.
15. Letter LVI.
16. *A Complete Body of Architecture*, 2nd ed. (1768), p. 20; cf. pp. 292, 445, 473.
17. *Essays, Moral and Literary* (London, 1778), Essay XXXVII, *On Architecture.*
18. *Ibid.*, Essay XIV, *On the Fluctuation of Taste.*

Chapter XVI

1. *A Sketch of the Spring-Gardens, Vaux-Hall, in a Letter to a Noble Lord* (London, n.d.).
2. Reproduced in Warwick Wroth, *The London Pleasure Gardens of the Eighteenth Century* (London, 1896), p. 291.
3. Illustrated in H. Avray Tipping's invaluable work, *English Homes, Period V, Early Georgian (1714–1760)* (London, 1921), Vol. I.
4. The fluctuations of English taste were reflected in the American colonies. According to an advertisement in the *South Carolina Gazette*, April 1, 1757, the James Reid house was "new built . . . after the Chinese taste." The Miles Brewton house (1769), Charlestown, is "full of Chippendale motives in which rococo, Gothic, and Chinese are mingled." Fiske Kimball, *Domestic Architecture of the American Colonies and of the Early Republic* (New York, 1922), p. 138.
5. Pp. 135–136. To save space, I group here all references in the following pages to this work: pp. 468, 521, 447, 522, 448, 521. References are to the edition of 1768.

Chapter XVII

1. *Spectator*, ed. Aitken, VI, 104.
2. Sir Reginald Blomfield and F. Inigo Thomas, *The Formal Garden in England* (London, 1892), p. 88.
3. *Quarterly Review*, XXXVII (1828), p. 306.
4. Basil Williams, *Life of William Pitt* (London, 1913), I, 191.
5. *Letters*, ed. Toynbee, IX, 413.
6. *Essay on the Genius and Writings of Pope*, 5th ed. (London, 1806), II, 178–179.
7. Vol. II, figures II and III.
8. Those editions of Grotius' *Adamus Exul* and Vondel's *Lucifer* which I have examined are unillustrated.
9. Ceramic exhibit in the Wallace Collection, London.
10. "Of Greatness," in *Essays, Plays and Sundry Verses*, ed. Waller (Cambridge, England, 1906), p. 432.
11. *Flora: seu, De Florum Cultura*, 2nd ed. (London, 1676), p. 2.
12. *Systema Horti-culturae: or, The Art of Gardening*, 3rd ed. (London, 1688).
13. Pp. 199–200, 205 (Part III, secs. I and II).
14. *Theory of the Earth.* See particularly Book I, chap. VI.
15. *Tatler*, nos. 161, 218; *Spectator*, nos. 414, 477 (cf. no. 412 on the pleasures of the imagination).
16. *Ichnographica Rustica; or, The Nobleman, Gentleman, and Gardener's Recreation* (London, 1742), III, 7–8.
17. *Ibid.*, Preface.
18. *Essay on Modern Gardening . . .*, ed. Alice Morse Earle (Canton, Penn., 1904), p. 55.
19. Mr. Christopher Hussey would take away the distinction of being the first landscape gardener from Kent and give it to Vanbrugh. I wish that I could agree with the writer of such an interesting book as *The Picturesque* (London, 1927). It is remarkable that if Vanbrugh was responsible for such a revolution in taste, his achievement was not recognized by his contemporaries and is not mentioned by a single eighteeenth-century writer, even though gardening was continually a subject of discussion. Mr. Hussey's theory seems to postulate, rather improbably, I think, that the new style of gardening was not a slow growth, but a conception for which Vanbrugh deserves the entire credit. Moreover, Mr. Hussey says that "Vanbrugh's experiments" were "echoed" by Addison in 1712 and Shaftesbury in 1711. As the designs for Eastbury and Claremont upon which Mr. Hussey lays such stress were not prepared by Vanbrugh until 1718 and 1719 respectively, they could not have influenced the opinion of Shaftesbury, Addison, Pope, or Switzer. See *The Picturesque*, p. 128, and H. Avray Tipping and Christopher Hussey, *English Homes, Period IV*, Vol. II.
20. *Ichnographica Rustica*, II, 201; III, 6, 37, 107.
21. Pp. 16–17, 24–29, 48 (chaps. II, V, VIII).
22. See as one instance pp. 33–35.
23. The following advertisement in Batty Langley's *The City and Country Builder's and Workman's Treasury of Designs* (London, 1740) is interesting evidence of how an eighteenth-century gardener might exploit his talents:

"Designs for Buildings, Gardens, Parks, etc. in the most grand Taste, and just Computations of their Expense, made by Mr. Langley, in Mead's Court, Dean Street, Soho. By whom Correct Plans of Estates, in Lands or Buildings, as also of Gardens, Parks, etc. are most beautifully made: And Grotto's, Cascades, Caves, Temples, Pavillions, and other Rural Buildings of Pleasure, designed and built. Also Engines made for raising Water in any Quantity, to any Height required, for the Service of Noblemen's Seats, Cities, Towns, etc. Young Gentlemen taught Architecture and Drawing by Thomas Langley."

24. Joseph Spence, *Anecdotes*, ed. Singer, p. 260.

25. *Ibid.*, pp. 12, 208–209.

26. *Works*, ed. Elwin and Courthope, IX, 300–303.

27. It is commonly asserted that the mount, characteristic of medieval and Elizabethan gardens, disappeared in the seventeenth century. This impression seems to be erroneous. The large mount (6) in Pope's garden was sufficiently extensive to warrant the representation of its spiral path in the plan. Pope himself told Spence that at Ryskins Lord Bathurst should have given elevation to his flat terrain by the erection of "two or three mounts" (*Anecdotes*, ed. Singer, p. 12). Rocque's plan (1737) of Weybridge, Surrey, shows an elaborate mount with artificial classic ruins. In a satire upon gardening in the *Universal Spectator* (no. 190) the mount is enumerated in a list of garden features. In an edition of Defoe's *Tour* (1778, I, 214) a garden at Reigate is mentioned as containing a mount.

28. See *A Plan of Mr. Pope's Garden* . . . (London, 1745).

29. *Works*, ed. Elwin and Courthope, VI, 383–384. Searle's list of the contents of the grotto appears in the *Plan* published in 1745.

30. Published in *Verses on the Grotto at Twickenham* (London, 1743).

31. *Works* (London, 1803), V, 189.

32. *London* (London, 1809), VI, 496. A tradition that Pope was responsible for the introduction of the weeping willow (*Salix babylonica*) into England apparently has no foundation. The story that he planted a willow-twig which he found in Lady Suffolk's basket of imported figs is no longer accepted. Probably in 1748, four years after Pope's death, the weeping willow was brought to England from the Euphrates by a Mr. Vernon and planted on his estate at Twickenham. Obviously Desdemona's song and the circumstances of Ophelia's death are not to be associated with the weeping willow, for the tree was unknown to Shakespeare. See G. S. Boulger, *Familiar Trees* (London, 1907), p. 151. It would be interesting to know when the term "weeping" was first applied to this type of willow. Was it the inspiration of some eighteenth-century sentimentalist?

33. *Letters*, ed. Toynbee, IV, 397.

34. [Pugh], *London*, VI, 496.

35. Warwick Wroth, *The London Pleasure Gardens of the Eighteenth Century* (London, 1896), p. 54.

36. Compare a similar mechanical contrivance for catching the public fancy: "This is to acquaint the Curious, That at the North Isle of the Royal-Exchange, this Evening, is to be seen, The so fam'd Piece of Machinery, consisting of large, Artificial Wax Figures, five Foot high, which have all the just Motions and Gestures of human Life, and has been shewn at Bath and Tunbridge Wells; and by them will be presented *The Beggar's Opera*" (*London Daily Post*, March 10, 1740–41).

37. Nicoll (*A History of Early Eighteenth Century Drama, 1700–1750*, pp. 332, 349) assigns the revised *Merlin* to William Gifford, and *The Royal Chace* to Edward Phillips. He has not noted the revival of these two operatic works in the spring of 1740–41.

38. John, Lord Hervey, *Memoirs of the Reign of George the Second* (London, 1884), II, 204.

39. *Essay on Modern Gardening*, ed. Earle, pp. 53–55.

40. *A General Plan of the House and Gardens at Stow, together with Sixteen Perspective Views . . ., Engraved by George Bickham* (London, 1753).

41. *Works*, 4th ed. (London, 1773), II, 115.

42. *Recollections of Some Particulars in the Life of the late William Shenstone, Esq.* (London, 1788), p. 9.

43. Vol. I, pp. v–vi. The author was Thomas Martyn.

44. On this whole subject see Elizabeth Manwaring, *Italian Landscape in Eighteenth-Century England* (New York, 1925).

45. *Works*, 4th ed. (London, 1773), II, 281, 115.

46. *Ibid.*, I, 25.

47. C. A. Moore, "Shaftesbury and the Ethical Poets in England, 1700–1760," in *Publications* of the Modern Language Association of America, XXXI (1916), 264–325.

Chapter XVIII

1. *Journal*, Feb. 11, 1772.
2. Book IX, ll. 76–80.
3. Chap. XIV, pp. 49–50; chap. V, pp. 24–29.
4. No. 76.
5. Shenstone, *Works*, 4th ed. (London, 1773), II, 333.
6. Letter LVII.
7. Part II, sec. XIV.
8. *Works*, 4th ed. (London, 1773), II, 111, 121, 113.
9. Book I, ll. 1–2, 216–278; II, 259 ff.; IV, 95–96, 644.
10. Vol. I, pp. 152–153; II, 39, 96–102.
11. *Johnsonian Miscellanies*, ed. G. B. Hill (Oxford, 1897), I 323

Chapter XIX

1. *Letters on the Beauties of Hagley, Envil, and the Leasowes*, II, 136–137.
2. *Observations upon Modern Gardening*, pp. 173–174.
3. *Select Letters*, I, 91–92; *Letters written by . . . Lady Luxborough to William Shenstone* (London, 1775), p. 189.
4. *Correspondence of Jonathan Swift*, ed. Ball, III, 93–94.
5. Nichols, *Literary Anecdotes*, IX, 266–267.
6. Nichols, *Illustrations*, II, 666.
7. *Observations upon Modern Gardening*, p. 206.
8. *Letters written by . . . Lady Luxborough to William Shenstone*, pp. 164–277.
9. *Works*, 4th ed., II, 113–114.
10. *Copper Plate Magazine*, 1778.
11. Nichols, *Literary Anecdotes*, VI, 311–313.
12. *Pharos*, no. 37 (London, 1787); *Anti-Jacobin*, no. 36, "The New Morality"; William Beckford, *Azemia*, 2nd ed. (London, 1798), II, 46.
13. *Observations upon Modern Gardening*, pp. 134–139.
14. Nichols, *Illustrations*, I, 639.
15. 2nd ed., III, 335–336, 347 (chap. XXIV).
16. *English Garden*, Book IV, ll. 79–93, 99–109.
17. *Observations upon Modern Gardening*, p. 131.
18. *Autobiography and Correspondence of Mrs. Delany*, ed. Sarah C. Woolsey (Boston, 1880), I, 357–358.
19. *Sentimental Magazine*, Oct., 1773.
20. No. 3788. The adjective *grotesque* as here applied to Chatterton's monument means that the tomb was made of rough-hewn, unshapely rocks, that is, it was grotto-like.
21. Climenson, *Elizabeth Montagu*, I, 189–190. Moralist though he was, John Wesley was not impressed by all that he saw when he visited Stowe in its decline. His comment in his *Journal* (Oct. 13, 1779) is as follows: "The large pieces of water interspersed, give a fresh beauty to the whole; yet there are several things which must give disgust to any person of common sense. 1. The buildings called Temples are most miserable, many of them both within and without. Sir John Vanbrugh's is an ugly, clumsy lump, hardly fit for a gentleman's stable. 2. The temples of Venus and Bacchus, though large, have nothing elegant in the structure, and the paintings in the former, representing a lewd story, are neither well designed nor executed. Those in the latter are quite faded, and most of the inscriptions vanished away. 3. The statues are full as coarse as the paintings, particularly those of Apollo and the Muses whom a person not otherwise informed might take to be nine cookmaids. 4. Most of the water in the ponds is dirty and thick as a puddle. 5. It is childish affectation to call things here by Greek or Latin names, as Styx and the Elysian Fields. 6. It was ominous for my Lord to entertain himself and his noble company in a grotto built on the bank of Styx, that is, on the

brink of hell. 7. The river on which it stands is a black, filthy puddle, exactly resembling a common sewer."

22. Nichols, *Illustrations*, II, 665.
23. *Lady Julia Mandeville*, ed. E. Phillips Poole (London, 1930), p. 57.
24. Act II, sc. i.
25. Climenson, *Elizabeth Montagu*, I, 150; *Mrs. Montagu: her Letters . . . from 1762 to 1800*, ed. Reginald Blunt (London, 1923), II, 104.
26. Ed. Charles Whibley (London, 1926), I, 215–216 (Book VI, chap. II).
27. *Letters*, ed. Toynbee, III, 179.
28. Climenson, *Elizabeth Montagu*, II, 106.
29. Nichols, *Illustrations*, IV, 479.
30. Defoe, *Tour* (London, 1748), I, 251.
31. Lord Rosebery, *Chatham: His Early Life and Connections* (London, 1910), p. 307; Basil Williams, *Life of William Pitt* (London, 1913), I, 191, 192, 196, 201.
32. *Johnsonian Miscellanies*, ed. Hill, II, 3.
33. *Journal*, July 13, 1782.
34. Boswell, *Life*, ed. Hill, V, 521.
35. Schreiber Collection, Victoria and Albert Museum.
36. *Letters*, ed. Tovey, II, 234 (Sept. 24, 1761).
37. *World*, no. 38.
38. Pp. 366–367.
39. *Gentleman's Magazine*, XXXV (1765), 95.
40. *Letters*, ed. Toynbee, VI, 188.

Chapter XX

1. *Letters on the Beauties of Hagley, Envil, and the Leasowes*, I, 32–33.
2. *Elements of Criticism*, 2nd ed., III, 344.
3. Samuel Derrick, *Letters* . . . (Dublin, 1767), Vol. II, Letter XXXIX (from Ockenden, 1760).
4. *Evelina*, Letter XLVI.
5. "Upon Taste," in *Works*, ed. J. W. M. Gibbs (London, 1885), I, 329.
6. Boswell, *Life*, ed. Hill, IV, 19; *Johnsonian Miscellanies*, ed. Hill, I, 187.
7. *Works of William Cowper*, ed. Southey (London, 1836), II, 183.
8. *Love of Order*, Canto II.
9. *Works*, ed. Southey, VI, 179–180 (Letter to Lady Hesketh, July 28, 1788).
10. *George Barnwell* (Boston, 1800), pp. 10–11.
11. Act II, sc. v.
12. Act II, sc. i.
13. See *A Collection of Prints, from Pictures Painted for the Purpose of Illustrating the Dramatic Works of Shakspeare, by the Artists of Great Britain* (London, 1803), 2 vols.; *A Catalogue of the Pictures in the Shakspeare Gallery, Pall-Mall* (London, 1789).

Chapter XXI

1. Myra Reynolds, *The Treatment of Nature in English Poetry between Pope and Wordsworth*, 2nd ed. (Chicago, 1909); Christopher Hussey, *The Picturesque: Studies in a Point of View* (London, 1927).
2. I, 236, 9.
3. Act I, sc. iii.
4. *Works of James Hervey* (Edinburgh, 1792), I, 84.
5. *Tour*, ed. Cole, II, 452, 562, 581, 679.
6. *Works*, 3rd ed. (London, 1776), III, 341 (Letter I).
7. *Autobiography and Correspondence*, ed. Woolsey, I, 382.
8. See Letters XXXVII–XXXIX, in Samuel Derrick, *Letters* . . . (Dublin, 1767).
9. *Ibid.*, Letters XIII–XVIII. The full title is *Letters written from Leverpoole*,

Chester, Corke, the Lake of Killarney, Dublin, Tunbridge-Wells, and Bath. There was a second edition in 1769.

10. *The Intimate Letters of Hester Piozzi and Penelope Pennington, 1788–1821*, ed. Oswald G. Knapp (London, 1914), pp. 201, 253.

11. Vol. II, p. 210.

12. 2nd ed. (London, 1808), I, 349–351.

Chapter XXII

1. *Letters on the Beauties of Hagley, Envil, and the Leasowes*, I, 62.
2. Letter XLVI.
3. Book VII, l. 125 of the first draft.
4. Defoe, *Tour* (1742), III, 290.
5. Boswell, *Life*, ed. Hill, V, 504, 489–490.
6. "The Cascade," in *Euphrosyne* (London, 1776), p. 263.
7. *Columella* (London, 1779), II, 130–131.
8. Ed. Whibley, II, 119 (Book IX, chap. VIII).
9. *Lounger*, no. 31.
10. "The Hermitage," in *Euphrosyne*, p. 262.
11. Ed. Whibley, I, 134 (Book IV, chap. V).
12. *Love and Freindship and Other Early Works* (London, 1922), p. 89.
13. *Of Taste: An Essay Spoken at the Anniversary Visitation of Tunbridge School, 1756.*
14. Thomas Amory, *Life of John Buncle* (London, 1766), I, 43–54, 214–215.
15. *Johnsonian Miscellanies*, ed. Hill, II, 427–428; Boswell, *Life*, ed. Hill, V, 433, 516, IV, 486.
16. No. VII, in *Works* (London, 1803), III, 204–205.
17. *Connoisseur*, no. 135. In 1767 the satire was republished at London in *A Collection of . . . Pieces of Poetry with Variety of Originals by Moses Mendez.*
18. Act II, sc. ii.
19. Department of Prints, British Museum.
20. Morris is here using the word *eye-trap* thirty-four years before the date of its earliest occurrence as given in the *New English Dictionary*. *Eye-trap* seems to be modeled after *clap-trap*, a theatrical term for describing a trick to catch applause.
21. *World*, no. 51.
22. *Idler*, no. 93.
23. *The Spiritual Quixote*, ed. Whibley, II, 114 (Book IX, chap. VI).
24. Letter XIV, p. 37.
25. *Love and Freindship*, p. 138.
26. Vol. II, pp. 230–233.
27. Dr. Syntax as the name of a pedant occurs in the *Lounger*, no. 86.
28. Cantos I, XIII, XIV, XIII.

Chapter XXIII

1. *Letters*, ed. Toynbee, I, 71–72.
2. *Memorials, Personal and Historical, of Admiral Lord Gambier*, ed. Lady Chatterton (London, 1861), I, 16, 43–50.
3. Lionel Cust, *History of the Society of Dilettanti*, ed. Sidney Colvin (London, 1898).
4. Climenson, *Elizabeth Montagu*, II, 52.
5. *A Register of the Premiums and Bounties given by the Society . . . 1754–1776* (London, 1778).
6. *The Architecture of Robert & James Adam*, I, 108–109.
7. *Letters*, ed. Toynbee, X, 93; XIII, 321.
8. A. F. Tytler, *Memoirs of the Life and Writings of the Honourable Henry Home of Kames*, 2nd ed. (Edinburgh, 1814), II, 63–64.
9. *Select Views of London* (London, 1816), pp. 13–14.
10. P. 393.

INDEX

INDEX

References are to volumes and pages, Roman numerals indicating the former, Arabic, the latter. In a compound item, each volume reference carries until it is superseded by another.

The abbreviations 'f.' and 'ff.' indicate that the reference is to the page designated and to that next following or to the two next following.

Architecture (*continued*)
zation of ancient houses, 47–54; the building mania of the eighteenth century, 55–77; the reflection of architectural ideas in letters, 78–96; satiric criticism of classical architecture, 97–113; town planning in the age of discipline, 163–179; the challenge of the Middle Ages, ii, 43–86; classical criticism of "Gothic taste," 87–99; the challenge of the rococo, 100–114; the resurgence of the classic, 231–241.
Architrave, i, 4.
Argens, Jean Baptiste de Boyer (1704–71), Marquis d', ii, 23.
Argyle, Duke of, *see* Campbell.
Aristotle, i, 19, 69; ii, 24, 38.
Aristotle's Well, ii, 55.
Arita, i, 199.
Armstrong, John (1709–79), i, 20; *Of Benevolence*, 89.
Arthur (1486–1502), eldest son of Henry VII, ii, 75.
Arundel, Earl of, i, 25.
Arundel marbles, the, ii, 236.
Ashridge, ii, 85f., 231.
Asia Minor, ii, 234, 236.
Asiatick Miscellany, The (1785), ii, 15.
Asiatic Researches, ii, 15f.
Astley, Thomas (fl. 1745), i, 182.
Aston Hall, Birmingham, i, 10, 12.
Asymmetry, i, 36, 136, 259; ii, 145.
"Athenian" Stuart, *see* Stuart, James.
Athens, ii, 235, 236.
Atterbury, Francis (1662–1732), i, 243.
Auchinleck, ii, 217.
Audley End, i, 12.
Augusta of Saxe-Gotha, bride of Frederick Louis of England, i, 253.
Austen, Jane (1775–1817), *History of England*, ii, 214; *Love and Freindship*, 226f.; *Northanger Abbey*, 227; *Pride and Prejudice*, i, 76; *Sense and Sensibility*, ii, 197f.; *Tour through Wales*, 227.
Axial arrangement, i, 115f., 263; ii, 100.
Bacon, Francis (1561–1626), i, 51, 129, 133, 192, 264; ii, 116, 196; *Of Building*, i, 14ff.
Badeslade, Thomas (fl. 1720), i, 73, 139, 150.
Badminton, i, 150, 213.
Bagley Wood, ii, 50.
Baker, Thomas (fl. 1703), *An Act at Oxford*, i, 223; *The Fine Lady's Airs*, 190, 251f.; *Tunbridge Walks*, 101.
Balbec (Baalbec), ii, 235.
Ballet, the, ii, 21.
Balustrade, i, 28.
Barnwell, George, i, 255; ii, 196 ff.
Baroccio, Federigo (1528–1612), ii, 149.
Baroque, the, i, 60; ii, 149 ff.
Barry, Sir Charles (1795–1860), ii, 231.
Bartolommeo, Fra (1475–1517), painter of the Florentine school, ii, 149.
Baskerville, John (1706–75), i, 204f.
Bassenthwaite Lake, ii, 207.
Bates, Ely (fl. 1786), *A Chinese Fragment*, ii, 31.
Bath, i, 172–178, 205; ii, 178, 206, 224.
Bath, Lord, i, 76.
Bathurst, Allen (1684–1775), Baron, later Earl Bathurst, i, 151; ii, 69, 70, 135.
Battersea enamel, ii, 183.
Bavaria, i, 60.
Baynard's Castle, i, 83.
Beauchamps, Pierre (fl. 1675), dancing master and musical director, i, 96.
Beaufort, Henry, i, 83.
Beaufort House, Chelsea, i, 63.
Beaumont, John (d. 1731), i, 264.
Beckford, William (1759–1844), i, 57; ii, 84f.; *Modern Novel Writing*, 215f.
Beckle (Beccles), Suffolk, i, 53.
Bedford, Duke of, ii, 177.
Bedford, Stephen (fl. 1763), i, 205.
Bedford House, i, 50.
Bedlam, i, 95.
Beers, Henry Augustin (1847–1926), ii, 44, 58, 67.

Lomazzo, Giovanni Paolo (1538–1600), i, 4.
Lombardy, i, 161.
London, i, 35–39, 152, 164–172, 225ff.; ii, 52, 81, 222ff.; Great Fire (1666), i, 52, 53, 100, 165–168; ii, 224.
London, George, gardener, i, 135; ii, 126.
London Gazette, i, 43, 46, 47.
London Prodigal, The (1605), ii, 10.
London Society of Antiquaries, *see* Society of Antiquaries of London.
Longinus, i, 20.
Longleat, Wiltshire, i, 15, 150; ii, 72f.
L'Orme, Philibert de (1515–70), i, 124.
Lorraine, *see* Claude Lorraine.
Lothar Franz von Schönborn (1655–1729), archbishop and elector of Mainz, i, 177.
Loudon, John Claudius (1783–1843), *Encyclopaedia of Gardening*, ii, 118f.
Louis XIV, king of France (1643–1715), i, 96, 135, 177, 218, 232; ii, 100, 101, 186.
Louis XV, king of France (1715–74), ii, 100, 101.
Loum Kiqua, Chinaman in England, ii, 18.
Lovejoy, Arthur Oncken (1873–), "On the Discrimination of Romanticisms," ii, 43.
Lucas, Martha, ii, 57.
Ludlow, i, 53.
Lumley, Richard (1688?–1740), second Earl of Scarborough, i, 152; ii, 66f.
Lumley Castle, ii, 73.
Luneville, ii, 223.
Luxborough, Lady, *see* Knight, Henrietta.
Luxury, distrust of, i, 99, 103.
Lyly, John (1554?–1606), *Euphues*, i, 18.
Lyons silk, i, 98, 252.
Lyttelton, Charles (1714–68), i, 74f.; ii, 73.
Lyttelton, Elizabeth (Rich), Lady, second wife of George Lyttelton, i, 74; ii, 103f.
Lyttelton, George (1709–73), first Baron Lyttelton, i, 74f., 161; ii, 28, 103f., 163f., 181, 187, 202, 204.

Mackenzie, Henry (1745–1831), ii, 6f.; *The Man of Feeling*, 6, 195.
Macky, John (d. 1726), *Journey through England* (2nd ed., 1722), i, 53, 54, 208; ii, 60.
Magda, by Sudermann, ii, 11.
Mahogany Castle, in *Modern Novel Writing*, ii, 215f.
Maintenon, Madame de (1635–1719), i, 232.
Mainz, i, 177.
Maison Carrée, Nîmes, i, 31, 56.
Malmesbury, abbey, ii, 51.
Mandarin, i, 189.
Mandeville, Bernard (1670?–1733), *Fable of the Bees*, i, 99, 268.
Manilla Hall, ii, 165.
Mann, Sir Horace (1701–86), ii, 58, 74, 79.
Mantegna, Andrea (1431–1506), i, 117; ii, 149.
Mantua, Castello at, i, 6.
Manwaring, Robert, cabinet maker, ii, 109, 179.
Marana, Giovanni Paolo (1642–93), *L'Espion Turc*, ii, 26f., 28.
Marcellus, theater of, i, 241.
Marie Antoinette (1755–93), wife of Louis XVI of France, ii, 237.
Markham, Gervase (1568?–1637), i, 124, 127f., 129, 144.
Marlowe, Christopher (1564–93), *Dr. Faustus*, i, 22, 265; *Tamburlaine*, 18.
Marly, i, 135, 177, 190.
Marmion, Shackerley (1603–39), *The Antiquary*, ii, 89.
Marriott, Sir James (1730?–1803), i, 240.
Martin, John (1789–1854), ii, 119, 121.
Martins, the, French workers in lacquer, i, 205.

Walpole, Horace (1717–97), fourth Earl of Orford, i, 63, 75, 76, 77, 106, 196f., 206, 210, 214, 219, 227, 231, 233; ii, 28f., 33, 44f., 58, 59, 65, 71f., 74–81, 85, 86, 94, 96, 99, 117, 118, 126, 127, 134, 135, 143, 177, 178, 183f., 207, 208f., 218, 233, 239.
Walpole, Sir Robert (1676–1745), first Earl of Orford, i, 65, 73; ii, 35, 136, 137.
Wanstead, i, 208; ii, 70.
Warburton, William (1698–1779), ii, 165.
Ward, Edward (1667–1731), *The London Spy*, ii, 52f., 54f., 56, 65, 67.
Ward, Robert Plumer (1765–1846), *Tremaine*, ii, 195f.
Ware, Isaac (d. 1766), ii, 103; *A Complete Body of Architecture*, i, 34f., 69, 70, 71f., 105, 106, 209f.; ii, 97, 112ff., 238.
Warren, Erasmus (fl. 1690), i, 264.
Warren, Thomas (d. 1767), i, 186.
Warton, Joseph (1722–1800), i, 146, 241, 246f.; ii, 86, 95, 117, 118f., 148; *The Enthusiast*, 123, 186, 196.
Warton, Thomas (1728–90), ii, 45, 86; *The Pleasures of Melancholy*, 57, 151.
Warwick, ii, 164.
Watson, Richard (1737–1816), ii, 16.
Watteau, Jean Antoine (1684–1721), ii, 101, 105.
Watts, Susannah, *Chinese Maxims* (1784), ii, 37.
Waverley Abbey, ii, 67.
Waving line, the, ii, 154.
Webb, John (1611–72), i, 32, 58, 60, 83, 180.
Wedgwood, Josiah (1730–95), i, 77; ii, 240.
Wentworth, Thomas (1672–1739), Earl of Strafford, i, 151.
Wentworth, William (1722–91), Earl of Strafford, i, 175.
Wentworth House, Yorkshire, ii, 177, 183.
Wentworth Woodhouse, i, 64.
Wesley, John (1703–91), *Journal*, i, 95, 161f., 187f.; ii, 27, 31, 42, 149, 182, 183, 212, 252f.
West, Gilbert (1703–56), ii, 181; *Education*, 187f., 196, 199.
West, Richard (1716–42), ii, 233.
Westall, Richard (1765–1836), ii, 121.
Westminster, i, 225.
Westminster Abbey, ii, 52.
Westminster Hall, i, 6; ii, 183.
Westminster School, i, 102.
Westmorland, ii, 200, 201, 206.
Weston Underwood, ii, 194.
Weymouth, Viscount, *see* Thynne, Thomas.
Wharton, Thomas (1717–94), i, 210.
Whately, Thomas (d. 1772), ii, 143, 158, 161, 164, 169, 172, 181.
Whitehead, William (1715–85), i, 240f., 243; ii, 25, 94.
Wickins, friend of Dr. Johnson, ii, 217.
Wigs, ii, 184f.
Wildgoose, in *The Spiritual Quixote*, ii, 30, 211f.
Wilkins, Sir Charles (1749–1836), translator, ii, 15.
William III, king of England (1689–1702), i, 42, 46, 135, 142, 143, 213, 234.
Williams, Robert Folkestone (1805–72), *Strawberry Hill*, ii, 78.
Willis, Browne (1682–1760), ii, 60.
Willoughby, friend of Derrick, ii, 203.
Wilton, Wiltshire, i, 252.
Wilton House, i, 129, 134, 138.
Wimbledon, i, 129.
Wimpole, ii, 71.
Winchester, i, 52, 53.
Winchester Cathedral, ii, 60.
Winchilsea, Earl of, *see* Finch.
Winckelmann, Johann Joachim (1717–68), ii, 237; *History of Ancient Art*, 232.
Windermere, ii, 229.
Windsor Castle, i, 41f.; ii, 76.
Winged block, the, i, 64ff.
Wisbeach, ii, 53.
Wise, Francis (1695–1767), ii, 178.
Wise, Henry (1653–1738), gardener, ii, 126.